be brave

BroadStreet
PUBLISHING

BroadStreet Publishing Group LLC
Savage, Minnesota, USA
Broadstreetpublishing.com

be brave

© 2020 BroadStreet Publishing

978-1-4245-5962-6
978-1-4245-5963-3 (ebook)

Devotions composed by Janelle Breckell, Cari Dugan, Rachel Flores, Laura Krause, Brenda Scott, Carole Smith, and Christina Asmus.

Design by Chris Garborg | garborgdesign.com
Compiled and edited by Michelle Winger | literallyprecise.com

Printed in China.

19 20 21 22 23 24 25   7 6 5 4 3 2 1

resolution to abide

I am sure of this, that he who began a good work in you
will bring it to completion at the day of Christ Jesus.
PHILIPPIANS 1:6 ESV

The start of a new year can bring about a lot of emotions. Culturally we are told to quickly come up with a resolution. Often, we look back at our previous year and reflect on what we want to change. This has the potential to cause regret for a lost year or shame for what we did or didn't do.

With God, however, all things can be made new, regardless of if it is January first or mid-October. He is our good shepherd who promises to be our steady leader. It takes courage to trust him and not grow anxious as we abide in him. The thing that pleases his heart most is our trust in him. As we trust, our courage and bravery will increase.

Jesus, thank you that you will be my ever-faithful guide throughout this year. Thank you that I can rest assured you are always working on me, and because of that, I can simply abide in you and trust you to complete your work.

Are you sure, like Paul says, that God will complete that which he began in you?

rod and staff

Your rod and your staff,
they comfort me.
PSALM 23:4 ESV

It takes courage to follow God where we sense him leading. Sometimes the path is clearly obvious—a well-worn trail blazed by the saints that have gone before us. However, there are other times that we sense him leading in a new direction, on a new path. In some ways, it's not even a path; it's an uncharted trail that has yet to be traversed.

In these times, we need the assurance from God that this is the direction we are to walk in. When we are told he is our shepherd, it means that he knows how to usher us in the right direction for our lives. While we might be afraid that our bravery may cause us to take the wrong path, his staff will keep us from doing so. The hook of the staff will curl around us and pull us back. As the Psalmist says, that staff will be a comfort to us. We never have to worry because our good shepherd is always on the watch.

Jesus, thank you that you are good at using your staff of comfort. Thank you that you're quick to pull me back if I am wandering. I trust you to guide me.

Do you doubt God's skill as a shepherd?

the shepherd's role

*"I am the good shepherd.
The good shepherd lays his life down for the sheep."*

JOHN 10:11 ESV

For first century readers, a comparison to sheep was not lost on them. They knew sheep were vulnerable animals with no way to protect themselves. They knew that sheep responded well to leadership. And they knew that if sheep were to accomplish anything noteworthy, it was to the credit of their shepherd.

When Jesus announced that he was a good shepherd, it brought an incredible sense of security to his followers. It meant that they had a protector, defender, and leader. Shepherds care for their sheep and they are equipped to do what it takes to carry this out. The instinct to lead and protect sheep is so strong that they are willing to take on a predator, even unto death, so their sheep won't die. The benefit of following our shepherd is that we don't have to be brave and fight for ourselves—that is his job, and one he does quite well.

Father, thank you that you are my shepherd. When I am afraid, remind me that you fight my battles for me.

Are you comforted by the protection of your shepherd?

owner's manual

*To each is given the manifestation of the Spirit
for the common good.*
1 CORINTHIANS 12:7 ESV

All new phones come with an owner's manual. The manufacturer produces one specific to each phone they make. One phone might have GPS tracking installed while another has a great camera. If owners want to enjoy the phone to the fullest extent, they will read the manual. Our maker designed us even more intricately than a complex phone; we were fearfully and wonderfully made.

Without using our manual, the Bible, we will miss many of the unique features God put in us. Through his Spirit, he apportions each of us with giftings. May we take the time to draw near to him and inquire of him what special features he has put in us, for it will not only benefit us but also those around us.

Lord, thank you for gifting me with special abilities. Remind me to walk in my giftings so others can see you and your love.

Do you believe that God knows you better than you know yourself?

the right fuel

It is good to proclaim your unfailing love in the morning.
PSALM 92:2 NLT

There are many different fuel options at the pump. A driver can choose from regular, premium, and at some stations, an ethanol-based fuel. All three options will work in most cars, but some vehicles were designed to run best with premium gasoline. The engine will not operate at its optimum on regular gas, and long term it has the propensity to break down sooner.

God designed us not to simply trudge through our days but to thrive. In Psalm 92, he admonishes us to begin our days reflecting on his unfailing love. His intent is that we would be strengthened in our spirits to know that no matter what comes our way, we have been loved with a love that is incapable of failure. Can we function without knowing this? Sure, just like a car on regular gasoline. But we were designed to run on premium, each day remembering that we are loved so we dwell in grace and peace instead of anxiety and fear.

God, thank you that your love will never fail me. Please write that truth on my heart that I might never forget it.

Do you refuel with God's love every day or trust in something cheaper?

all things new

You know how full of love and kindness our Lord Jesus was: though he was so very rich, yet to help you he became so very poor, so that by being poor he could make you rich.

2 CORINTHIANS 8:9 TPT

We can't imagine a king in all of his splendor and richness, full of wealth and abounding in power as Christ was in heaven. We can try our best to picture the most majestic earthly kingdom, and then assume we would multiply that by one million. This is what Christ left when he came to dwell among us. He was born to parents on the move, not owning a home. When he ended his life, he didn't even have any financial means to take care of his mother; he had to entrust her to John. He was the epitome of poor.

He did this to abide with you. Not to hand you a variety of earthly riches, that will rust and fade away, but to pick you up out of your low estate, wash you clean, and hand you a robe of righteousness. You are wealthy in every sense of the word. All that the King has is yours. His promises for provision are abundant.

God, thank you for all the ways you have blessed me richly!

How do you see the richness of Christ in your life today?

still praying

*He is able to save to the uttermost those who draw near to God
through him, since he always lives to make intercession for them.*
HEBREWS 7:25 ESV

Some people have the benefit of being prayed for their
entire lives. From birth, they have had a steady stream of
prayers by faithful family members. That isn't the case for
everyone. Some didn't grow up in Christian homes or, even
if they did, they weren't necessarily praying homes. Do not
dismay if you fall into the latter category.

There is one who has prayed for you from the beginning.
His name is Jesus. It is his delight, and a sign of his inheritance
for you, that he prays. He sits right beside his Dad, with
scarred hands, asking for the reality of the completed work on
the cross to become your daily victory.

**Father, please strengthen me as I receive the availing
prayers of your Son.**

Do you believe Jesus hears you when you pray?

glorious design

"You are worthy, our Lord and God, to receive glory and honor and power, for you created all things, and by your will they were created and have their being."

REVELATION 4:11 NIV

You only need to pause and take a look outside to see God's glory reflected in every part of nature. Whether a delicate rosebud or full array of stars at night, his beauty and magnificence are evident. Not only do we see his creativity, but his intellect in the design of the interrelationships of the natural world. The way the wind creates the waves, the moon affects the tides, and a bird gathers sticks for its nest, are just a few examples of his remarkable design.

You are a part of this amazing nature as well. He created you as an image bearer, someone who reflects his glory. Be proud of the way he created you! You may not feel perfect, but he designed you with the same beauty as the rest of his creation; you are his handiwork.

Worthy Lord, thank you for all the amazing things you have created around me. Help me to stop and notice your creative design in nature. May I accept that I am beautiful because you have made me according to your will, and your will is perfect.

What can you appreciate about God's creation today?

my enemies

You prepare a table before me in the presence of my enemies.
You anoint my head with oil; my cup overflows.
PSALM 23:5 NIV

This psalm wasn't a cute thought to David. He had tapped into the truth that even when enemies were lurking around every corner, God himself could be found preparing a table. David felt served, cared for, and covered even when the enemy was upon him.

This is an incredible picture of God. He delights in serving us not just when things are calm but also when trials are upon us. In the moments we want to explode into frantic activity to protect ourselves from our enemies, God says, "Have a seat, child. Look, I have prepared a table for you, and I will serve you. Even though you are in a trial, your cup will overflow."

Father, thank you that you fight my enemies and serve me at the same time.

Have you experienced a time that you felt served by God in the middle of a trial?

fertile soil

"Go, and sin no more."
JOHN 8:11 NIV

A woman was caught in the act of adultery. Unlike the Pharisees who wanted her to die, Jesus gave mercy. Minutes before, she was covered in shame and humiliation—standing at death's door. She knew the Pharisees were right. She deserved death. Jesus saw this moment as an incredible opportunity to reach someone at their lowest point. The woman's heart was fertile ground for a Savior.

In God's gracious way, he uses sin as an opportunity to draw us close to himself. He knows that in the moments after we choose sin we are most vulnerable to the outpouring his love and forgiveness. When we sin, we should run to the arms of our forgiving God. It is one of the most courageous acts we can do.

Jesus, thank you that you delight to give mercy and forgiveness. Help me run to you and not away from you after I have sinned.

After you sin, do you run to God or away from him?

accused

Jesus stood up again and said to the woman,
"Where are your accusers?"

JOHN 8:10 NLT

God silences the enemy by speaking truth in the presence of their accusations. Sometimes we are so beaten down by discouragement or fear that we lack the strength to run to the Lord—especially when we feel like the enemy's camp is surrounding us.

The women caught in adultery knew she was powerless to escape her enemies and accusers, so God chose that to be the very place to save her. It wasn't in a private cave or at the temple. In their presence he stood and delivered her.

Jesus, give me the humility not to be self-absorbed. Help me to look to you in the moments when I am being accused.

Do you run to Jesus when your accusers surround you or do you listen to their lies?

heart truth

O Lord, who shall sojourn in your tent?
He who speaks the truth in His heart.
PSALM 15:1-2 ESV

Our thoughts need coaching because most of the time they will derail. It is natural to become self-focused throughout the day. In doing so, insecurities and fears can subconsciously be strengthened. It's important to pause throughout the day and take stock in what we have given our minds to.

There is great value in actively controlling your mind. It is critical to speak the truth to our hearts. Don't be discouraged when you see that you aren't walking closely with God. View it as a revelation from God to help you correct your course. He will give you the strength you need to align your mind with his truth.

Holy Spirit, I invite you to remind me to speak the truth in my heart today. Please show me when I am not and give me the grace to change my course.

Are you speaking truth in and to your heart?

your spot

"The place where you are standing is holy ground."
EXODUS 3:5 ESV

When God called Moses into ministry it was a sacred, holy moment. The Creator and the created came alarmingly close. Moses was only allowed to stand at a distance. But make no mistake, the encounter happened because the Creator wanted the connection.

You are invited to come close—very close—to your Creator. When you make time to draw near, a holy moment transpires. You are being invited to draw near to the one who can satisfy all your desires and heal your pain. Never feel guilty about carving out time for God—it is the best expense of energy there is.

Jesus, thank you for inviting me into a relationship where I am allowed to come close to you. Your blood has made a way, and I am forever grateful.

Do you have a place that you draw near to God?

a new song

He put a new song in my mouth,
a song of praise to our God.
PSALM 40:3 ESV

Since the beginning of time, songs have been written. One could assume that every topic has been covered: sorrow, heartache, hope, joy, healing—the list goes on. Yet, repeatedly we hear in Scripture that God has given us a "new song." It would seem as though something entirely fresh has come from the songwriter. With the millions of songs written, could it truly be a new song?

God's knowledge and wisdom are unmeasurable, and no created being will ever fully grasp the depth of God's persona. Even if they have walked with God their entire life, they will never arrive at a full knowledge of him. Therefore, not only has everything not been written about him in song, it never will be.

Jesus, thank you that there are still songs to be sung. And thank you that as I sing them, you receive worship and I receive joy.

Do you believe that God wants a new song from you?

great leadership

"The LORD will fight for you,
you have only to be still."

EXODUS 14:14 NIV

Moses led the Israelites when their fear was high. They had left Egypt but were now stuck between a sea and Pharaoh's army. They were certain death was coming. Moses knew he was powerless to save the people. But, it seems he also knew their salvation wasn't on him. It wasn't his job to save them; it was his job to point them to the one that could.

As a brave leader, Moses rallied the people around God's strength and not his own. He assured them they would be okay because God would fight for them. This was the reminder they needed. Great leaders don't encourage people to lean on them; instead, they speak courage to your heart to look to the God.

Father, help me remember that you love to fight for your children.

Do you choose courage and trust during adversity or fear and anxiety?

remembering

Those who are wise will take all this to heart;
they will see in our history the faithful love of the Lord.
PSALM 107:43 NLT

A struggling church called a prayer meeting so that the congregation would seek the Lord. During this meeting, a 93-year-old reminded everyone that God would be faithful. When questioned, he went on to list the countless times God had been faithful. In fact, in all his 73 years of attending the church, he never knew a time when God wasn't faithful. That simple reminder was all that many in the meeting needed. Instead of remaining a desperate prayer meeting, it turned into a worship service of gratitude.

In Psalm 107, the Psalmist spends 43 verses recounting the deeds of the Lord to those who needed that same reminder. When the way forward looks scary, sometimes it's wise to look back and see that there was never a time we weren't cared for or carried. Because of that, we know we can have peace now.

God, remind me of all the times you have been faithful to your church at large but also to me.

How has God been faithful to you?

not a waste

"The kingdom of heaven is like treasure hidden in a field, which a man found and covered up. Then in his joy he goes and sells all that he has and buys that field."

MATTHEW 13:44 ESV

In this parable, Jesus says the value of heaven is so large that it is worth selling everything you have for it. The price of the field in this story must have been high—so high that the man couldn't just use his savings to get it. He had to cash in everything he had to purchase it. But it was worth everything he had.

The parable applies to us as well. The kingdom of heaven is of incalculable worth. We won't be left in want if we choose to give up everything for it. Whatever we lose will pale in comparison to what we gain. It is not wasteful to give all our life's energy to pursuing God. When all is said and done, the wisdom of our decision will be glaringly obvious.

Father, when I get weary, remind me of the value of pursuing you.

Are you hesitant to give God everything in exchange for his kingdom?

a good student

*He guides the humble in what is right
and teaches them his way.*
PSALM 25:9 NIV

A seasoned teacher was sharing some highlights over her years of teaching. Regardless of personality type, there was one trait she enjoyed teaching the most—the humble learner. When she had a humble student—even if the student was fiercely behind—she was able to do great things with them in just one year. This, she reasoned, was because they did not resist her correction or direction.

In Psalm 25, David reminds us of this timeless truth. It is the humble who are able to be led. The humble don't insist they know the right path, the right answer, or the right opinion. Because of this, God can easily move them where he wants them. They don't resist his leadership. They enjoy it.

Father, help me to remain teachable and humble. I want your path for my life more than I want my own.

Do you resist God's leadership in your life or submit to it?

routines

It is good to give thanks to the LORD,
to sing praises to the Most High.
It is good to proclaim your unfailing love in the morning,
your faithfulness in the evening.

PSALM 92:1-2 NLT

Psalm 92 gives direction for celebrating the Sabbath. Because God is not only our maker but also our designer, we can trust that if he gives us perspective on how to rest, it must be precisely what our created frames need.

We are told to declare his steadfast love in the morning—to meditate on the fact that he has unfailing, steadfast love for us before we even begin our day. Additionally, we declare his faithfulness at night. Recounting the ways God has been faithful to us will be the best expenditure of our mental energy. Instead of mindlessly looking at other things, or anxiously worrying about tomorrow, reflecting on how God has never failed us will equip us for what is to come.

Father, thank you that you offer unfailing love and faithfulness to me.

Do you lean on God's love and faithfulness to refresh you?

gazing

You, O LORD, have made me glad by your work;
at the works of your hands I sing for joy.
PSALM 92:4 ESV

A gaze is different than a look. It is slower and more observatory in nature. A quick look might reveal some leafless trees, dirty snow, and ice in the driveway. But a gaze might show you some buds on that brown tree, some small animal tracks in the snow, and intricate ice crystals frozen in time.

The Psalmist declared that when we pause to enjoy God's handiwork around us, it will do something to our emotions—it will invoke gladness. As we recognize God's work we are met with great joy.

God, as I look at the work of your hands, I marvel that it was all by design and not accident. Surely you have given me joy.

Have you taken the time to gaze outside today?

*All you who
put your hope in
the LORD
be strong
and brave.*

PSALM 31:24 NCV

introduction

Courage isn't something that comes naturally to most. The only way to truly be brave is to walk in the confidence that comes from knowing God and relying on him to be your strength. When you spend time with him, he will fill you with peace and hope for the future. When you finally see yourself as God sees you, you will recognize the talents and abilities you have been blessed with and start operating in the fullness of those gifts.

Be encouraged with truth as you spend time with God, reflecting on these devotions, Scriptures, and prayers. Let him show you that you are radiant, you are strong, and you were created with a purpose. Take courage in God's love for you and be ready to conquer each day!

january

"Be strong and courageous! Do not be afraid and do not panic before them. For the LORD your God will personally go ahead of you. He will neither fail you nor abandon you."

DEUTERONOMY 31:6 NLT

thrive during winter

*To everything there is a season,
and a time to every purpose under heaven.*
ECCLESIASTES 3:1 KJV

Winter can be a time of inactivity. For farmers, winter is their slow season. For others, just the snow, rain, and chill make it difficult to be outside. But stillness and slowness do not mean nothing is happening. In nature, things are always happening below the surface. Birds are still eating, animals are still sleeping, and trout are still swimming under frozen ice.

Sometimes slowing down can be one of the most powerful acts in the life of a believer. It is a declaration of trust that the one who made us is still working and fighting for us. We allow the work and the seeds he has planted in us to grow and take even greater root in our hearts. Sometimes in our stillness, we have the greatest victories over our giants because we exhibit trust that God is still moving mightily.

God, teach us to not resist the slowness of winter. Give us the faith to see that you are still moving and working even if our physical eyes don't perceive it.

Can you believe God is working, even in winter, or have you become a complainer?

germinating in winter

"Abide in me, and I in you. As the branch cannot bear fruit by itself, unless it abides in the vine, neither can you, unless you abide in me."
JOHN 15:4 ESV

When winter comes, although things look quiet on the outside, there is much life and growth brewing under the surface. Just because we don't see life budding up from the ground, it does not mean that no growth is happening. It is hidden from our eyes. Many trees and plants that pop up in the spring were able to do so because the seeds were germinating in the winter months. And scientists have found that some seeds do better with a layer of snow on top of the soil.

This is true of us as well. There are seasons we feel like we are dripping with the evidence of God's activity in our lives. And other seasons where the work of God feels deeply internal—shifting our preferences and loyalties. Rest assured that any beautiful work you see externally in a child of God was first cultivated internally. God knows when to plant, water, and prune. The work is in his hands; we have only to abide.

God, give me the courage to believe you are at work even when I can't see it. Help me to trust in your love. You will complete that which you began.

Are you resisting God's blessings in winter by only looking toward spring?

let not

"Let not your hearts be troubled,
neither let them be afraid."
JOHN 14:27 ESV

In John 14, Jesus told his disciples not to let their hearts be troubled or afraid. The one who has the power to calm every storm—past, present, or future—knew that there was no need for fear in the heart of his children. God alone can silence every tormenting thought and plaguing anxiety.

As the omnipotent Prince of Peace, it is crystal clear to him that our hearts should never be troubled. But he knows that he can't force his peace on us. When dwelling on fear, we are allowing our hearts to be troubled. Let us heed his call today. We have the power, because of Jesus, to rebuke fear and receive peace.

Jesus, remind me, when I give way to fear, to turn and look at you. Thank you that you have all the peace I will ever need.

Do you let your heart become troubled or do you take captive thoughts of fear and anxiety?

brave belief

"Truly, truly, I say to you, whoever believes in me will also do the works that I do; and greater works than these will he do, because I am going to the Father. Whatever you ask in my name, this I will do, that the Father may be glorified in the Son. If you ask me anything in my name, I will do it."

JOHN 14: 12-14 ESV

One of the bravest, most courageous things we can do as children of God, is simply to believe him at his word. He takes great delight when his children trust that all his promises are good and true.

Beloved, today may you refuse cynicism, skepticism, and arrogance and instead courageously say to the Father, "I will trust you and, by faith, ask great things in your name."

Jesus, help me truly believe you today.

Have you resisted through doubt something God has asked you to believe him for?

unquenchable

Many waters cannot quench love;
rivers cannot wash it away.
If one were to give all the wealth of his house for love,
it would be utterly scorned.

SONG OF SONGS 8:7 NIV

Love is everywhere. When you stop to consider what love looks like, you begin to recognize it all around you. Love is in the mother kissing her child goodbye at the school drop off, love is in the coffee you share with a friend. Love is in the offer of help to move to a new house, it is in the playground when a child helps their friend get up after a fall. Love is such a precious and powerful gift that there is no price on it.

That's why you would laugh at someone for selling all their possessions to acquire love—it simply can't be bought. God is love and there is no limit or end to his love. If you are feeling a little discouraged today, lift yourself up with the reminder that his love for you will remain no matter what.

God, I need to feel your love in this moment. Thank you that your love is so strong that nothing can take it away. Help me to treasure your love, for it is priceless. Help me to share your love with the world.

In what ways can you pass on the unquenchable love of Christ to others?

a helper

"The Helper, the Holy Spirit, whom the Father will send in my name, he will teach you all things and bring to your remembrance all that I have said to you."
JOHN 14:26 ESV

When Jesus prepared his disciples for his departure from this earth, he told them they would be given a helper in his place. The first title Jesus gives the Holy Spirit in this teaching is The Helper. This helper came alongside the disciples and helped them preach the gospel in the face of adversity, find joy in their trials, remember all the things Jesus had taught, and remain steadfast in their testimony that Jesus was worth living for.

The Holy Spirit is your helper. He's willing to help you. He's competent. And he is always attentive. Ask him for what you need today.

Thank you, God, for sending the Holy Spirit to by my helper.

Is there a problem in your life that you have been trying to fix on your own instead of asking the Helper?

clean

"You are already clean because of the word I have spoken to you."
JOHN 15:3 NIV

In John 15, Jesus teaches what it means for his children to remain in his love. The entire chapter is directed to those who call him their Lord. Before he gets too far into his word picture, he makes sure his followers know something critical. He reminds them that they are already clean. It's as if he knew they needed this reassurance before he went any further in his lesson that day.

Sin separates us from God. It is not uncommon that even after confession, we still feel dirty. But we aren't. When we turn to him in humility and repentance, he makes us clean. He no longer sees the dirt, and neither should we. We are already clean.

Father, thank you for making me clean the moment I humble myself before you.

Have you unwittingly been listening to the lie that you are still dirty because of your confessed sin?

all truth

"When the Spirit of truth comes,
he will guide you into all truth."
JOHN 16:13 NLT

In John 16, Jesus prepares his disciples for his departure. He knows that they will be well cared for after he goes because he is sending the Holy Spirit. This is a strange concept for his followers who have clung to his every word and left everything to be near him. He takes time to still their fears by making sure they know that the Holy Spirit will be there to guide them into all truth.

We are also on the receiving end of this gift. The Holy Spirit is active today, and he leads God's children into all truth. He is good at his job. He is there to lead you as you lean on him. Ask him today; he will not fail to lead you to truth.

Father, thank you for reminding me to lean into the Holy Spirit for guidance and direction.

Do you look to Jesus as a source of all truth or do you lean on something, or someone, else?

exact representation

"The Father himself loves you."
JOHN 16:27 NIV

We know that God is fully represented in three persons: Father, Son, and Holy Spirit. All three perfectly represent God. It is quite easy to picture how Jesus walks and speaks because we have a number of firsthand accounts. However, sometimes when we are trying to picture God the Father, things can get fuzzy. This can be particularly true for those who have a poor picture of their human father.

That is why this declaration from Jesus is so precious. He makes sure his followers know that he is not representing only himself but also the one who sent him—the Father. The love they receive is not just from Jesus but also from their heavenly Father. If you want to know what God the Father is like, simply look at his Son, for they are the same.

Father, thank you that Jesus' love is an exact representation of yours.

When you think about God the Father, do you envision the character of Christ or a stern taskmaster?

Look up

Let us run with endurance the race God has set before us.
HEBREWS 12:1 NLT

The writer of Hebrews compares our Christian journey to that of running a race. When we run a race, particularly a long one, we need perseverance to not quit when it gets hard. Races often start out feeling quite manageable, but inevitably there comes a point when completing the race seems not only daunting but perhaps impossible.

When this happens, it seems like the runner's eyes lower to the ground and rest on the monotony of watching one foot after the other slowly propel them forward. When you watch the ground while running, your distance gained is almost imperceptible. However, when you look up, toward your goal, you become reinvigorated to endure and persist. Your call as a runner is to fix your eyes on God. If you watch the ground or look behind you, you'll grow weary. But eyes staid on him will give you all the strength you need.

Father, help me keep my eyes on you and not on myself today.

Do you stare at your discouraging circumstances more than at Jesus?

trustworthy

Your royal laws cannot be changed.
PSALM 93:5 NLT

The Psalmist proclaims that all of God's laws can be trusted. This means anything he asks of us or calls us to do is the best thing in that moment. He doesn't just give pleasant ideas or suggestions. His decrees aren't to be equally compared to our ideas. His are the best. The best solution and the best direction in any situation is whatever God is asking us to do.

We need not fear that his directives will lead us astray. You must know that you can entirely trust God. Whatever he is asking you to do is the most trustworthy path in your situation.

Father, thank you that with you I will find the most trustworthy path for my life.

Do you doubt that God will be faithful to lead you on the path that he called you to?

february

You have armed me
with strength for the battle;
you have subdued my enemies
under my feet.

PSALM 18:39 NLT

many cares

When anxiety was great within me,
your consolation brought me joy.

Psalm 94:19 NIV

Life can be wearing. Children of God are not exempt from trials. In fact, we are told we should expect them. We suffer alongside those who don't know God. The difference to our suffering, however, is in how we cope.

We can turn to God, the lifter of our heads, and allow him to take burdens off our shoulders. We can see him sitting with us in our pain and suffering. Mary and Martha actually saw the Lord weep with them. We have the privilege of receiving his consolation. When God consoles us in pain, it is not with empty words of wishful thinking; it is with authority and hope that anchors our soul and ultimately brings cheer.

God, remind me to turn to you when I am in pain, for your consolation brings joy to my soul.

Do you draw near to God or away from him when you are hurting?

to seek

I sought the LORD,
and he answered me.
PSALM 34:4 NIV

In this simple verse, there are two characters: God and man. For each character, there is a simple task. These tasks appear to work beautifully together—in harmony. We seek, and he answers.

Though we are children of God, we still live in a fallen world. Thus, our trials in this age will be innumerable. However, we are given a constant communication line with our Creator. We are told to seek him, to actively engage in prayer, contemplation, and worship. We forsake other things so that we can draw near to God. We needn't worry that this is wasted energy. God's delight is to answer his children. He loves when we pursue him, and he is happy to answer.

Father, please remind me to seek you above all else. Thank you that you will answer me.

Is there an area of need that you have been seeking from everyone but God?

to taste

Oh, taste and see that the Lord is good!
PSALM 34:8 ESV

Cookbooks and food magazines are filled with photos of food. There is an art to capturing food that makes the reader salivate when viewing the photo. However, you can never really know what something tastes like until you make it yourself and take a bite. You might buy the cookbook and even recommend it to others, but until you taste it, you don't truly know it.

In Psalm 34, David invites us to not be mere spectators of God but to jump in and experience his goodness for ourselves. He knows he can talk about how good God is but until we choose to engage God ourselves, we will never know his goodness firsthand. It's possible to talk about God, tell others about God, and even read about him, but never actually taste his goodness ourselves. The invitation remains today: taste and see! He is good.

Father, thank you that as I draw near to you, there is nothing but goodness to behold.

Do you have any accusations in your heart against God that challenge his goodness?

his eyes

The eyes of the Lord are toward the righteous
And His ears are open to their cry.

PSALM 34:15 NASB

You have God's attention. Do you remember when you were a child and you wanted your parent to watch you perform a new trick on the playground or at the pool? It was a precious moment when their conversation ceased, and you knew you had their full attention. You knew they were watching you. It gave you courage and emboldened you to show them something new.

Beloved, God the Father has his eyes on you as well. He is watching you because he loves you. In the same way that a parent is delighted by seeing their child try something new, God's eyes of kindness are drawn to you. This is particularly true when you need him. Rest assured you have his attention.

Father, thank you that I am loved and that you hear my every cry.

Are you crying out today for the Father's attention?

greater will

"I can do nothing on my own. As I hear, I judge, and my judgment is just, because I seek not my own will but the will of him who sent me."
JOHN 5:30 ESV

Jesus was divine, and yet in his humanity, he acknowledged his utter dependence on his heavenly Father to guide his every step. Jesus did what the Father wanted him to do, and because he was so sure of God's will he was able to confidently carry out his purpose on earth. We are not Jesus, but we are like Jesus! When he went back to the Father, Jesus promised to leave us a helper that would guide us in the same way that he was guided by the Father.

We have the Holy Spirit within us, and we, too, can be confident that God is able to achieve his purpose in and through us. As you head into the day, or the week, ahead, make it your intention to hear what God might be saying to you. Let him show you his will in the conversations that you have, in the decisions that you make, in the work that you do. You don't have to do it alone!

Father, thank you for sending the Holy Spirit who can help me see that I don't have to make decisions on my own. I know that you have good things for my life and I want to make sure that I am being guided into your will.

What do you need to seek Jesus about right now? Rely on the helper that Jesus promised you.

numbering

Teach us to number our days,
that we may gain a heart of wisdom.
PSALM 90:12 NIV

To number our days means to give thoughtful consideration to where we are headed. If you know where you want to be and the type of person you strive to be like, then you have your goal. Once you have your goal, it's important to take stock of your life and see if the way you spend your time is lining up with where you ultimately want to be.

While this might sound simple, it is something that we can't do on our own. We need the Spirit to help guide, inspire, and convict us. The Psalmist prays, "Lord, teach me." It's a cry that says we want to learn. We don't know how to do this well without God. We want to get it right. And that is precisely where God wants us to be. As we humble ourselves and ask for help, we gain a heart of wisdom.

Lord, please teach me by your Spirit how I should number my days.

Is there a time in the next few days that you can pause and re-evaluate how you are spending your days?

old age

The righteous will flourish like a palm tree.
They will still bear fruit in old age.
PSALM 92:12, 14 NIV

Children of God are often compared with trees in Scripture. Trees have a root system, branches, and often bear fruit. In addition, trees don't necessarily weaken with age. In fact, many trees become stronger as they age.

While our human body ages, there comes a point when it is no longer growing stronger. However, that is only our flesh. Our inner man can actually grow in strength even though our frame does not. As we are growing in strength in God, we are still able to bear much fruit later into life. Good, tasty, ripe fruit doesn't come to the young, baby Christians. It comes to those seasoned wise souls whose roots are as thick and strong as their branches.

Father, thank you that as I age, I need not fear becoming weaker in you. Help me bear fruit until my last breath.

Have you bought into the mindset of our culture that dreads aging? Are you trying to avoid aging? Will you accomplish anything by attempting this?

dust

He knows our frame;
He remembers that we are dust.
PSALM 103:14 NKJV

Praise God that he, the one who has requirements of us, is also our Maker. That means he knows precisely what we are capable of and what we aren't. He will never ask something of us that we can't do. For, as our designer, he has intimate knowledge of our inner workings.

We need not fear that our outer frame is wasting away. We need not be ashamed that we aren't as physically strong as we once were. That is nothing to be ashamed of. It is by design. Are you feeling frail today? Have no fear; you were not asked to have superpowers. With God as your supplier of strength, you will be able to accomplish all that he is asking of you.

Jesus, thank you that you know my frame. You know where I am weak, and you will give me the strength that I need.

Is there a way that you can embrace your weakness instead of resisting it?

payment

He does not deal with us according to our sins,
nor repay us according to our iniquities.

PSALM 103:10 ESV

Oh, what good news for today and every day! We have all sinned. Everything you have ever done, or thought has been seen by God. Nothing has snuck past him. That isn't the marvelous news. While awe-inspiring that there is a God who can see everything, it's what he does with that knowledge that makes him remarkable.

He doesn't make us pay for what we have done. He doesn't hold guilt and condemnation over our heads. He isn't waiting for us to soar so that he can then remind us what we have done and watch us fall. He will not repay us for anything we have done. All atonement is done by Jesus, so we can be set free to stand before him blameless.

Thank you, Father, that you have paid for my sins. I never could have done that, and I'm grateful to be set free.

Do you deal with others with the same grace God has dealt with you?

steadfast

As high as the heavens are above the earth,
so great is his steadfast love toward those who fear him.
PSALM 103:11 ESV

We cannot measure the distance between the heavens and the earth. God can. The distance is utterly immeasurable. The extent of its greatness is so large, we just have to say it is unknown.

That is the picture we have of God's steadfast love toward us. A steadfast love is incapable of failure. Because it is steadfast, it will not waiver or wain. It cannot weaken because nothing is strong enough to damage it. Let this love support you and all your failures today. God delights to provide a love that will never fail.

Father, thank you that your love will never fail me. Though I fail, you do not.

Can you humbly lean into God's steadfast love, or do you proudly trust in your own righteousness?

remember

Remember the wondrous works that he has done,
his miracles, and the judgements he uttered.
PSALM 105:5 ESV

We are called to pause and remember the works of God. A Hebrew was trained to look back and recount the works God had done in Israel, for themselves but also for their children. This was foundational in their lifestyle of worship.

This word isn't just for them. We are called to remember the works and miracles that have been recorded. Why should we take time to remember them? Because by nature, we will forget. When we remember what God has done over time, it removes anxiety and fear of what he will do in the future. It also reveals his characteristics of love and provision. It tells us that the same God who miraculously split the Red Sea and raised the dead is still moving today in my life and the Church. Because of that, I need not fear.

Father, I remember what you have done. I worship you because there is none like you.

Can you take time to remember God's interventions in your life? If so, write them down.

power

"You will receive power when the Holy Spirit comes on you."
ACTS 1:8 NIV

After Jesus's ascension, he gave the promised gift of the Holy Spirit to the disciples. They were told to wait for this gift before they proceeded any further. Jesus knew it would be fruitless to attempt to carry out any exploits unless his followers were filled with his Spirit. As they waited, the Holy Spirit came and filled them with power. This was a power they lacked prior to this moment. It wasn't something they could conjure up on their own. Jesus wanted them to know that a new power would come.

That same power is there for all of us who ask. God hasn't given us a spirit of fear but one of power. You don't need your own power, God will give you his through the Holy Spirit.

Holy Spirit, please fill me anew with you power that I might love and serve well.

Have you asked the Lord for his power through the Holy Spirit or do you lean on your own strength?

perfectly patient

Jesus Christ might display his perfect patience as an example to those who were to believe in him for eternal life.
1 TIMOTHY 1:16 ESV

It takes a lot of courage to attempt something that is difficult. It takes even more courage to continue attempting it after failure. Perseverance and courage are only developed in us after coming face to face with failure and fear.

What is more praiseworthy: someone who tried something hard once and succeeded the first time, or the person who keeps trying after they have already failed? Surely it's the latter. When you look at Christ as you try something that you have already failed at, know that he is patient. Scripture says that not only is perfectly patient. He doesn't grow weary of your attempts. He is still there because he has all the patience in the world. Get up again; he is cheering you on.

Jesus, thank you that you are patient with me. Give me the courage to try again.

Is there an area of your life where you are too discouraged to try again? Would believing God is patient with you give you the courage to try once more?

self-promotion

In your relationships with one another, have the same mindset as Christ Jesus: Who, being in very nature God, did not consider equality with God something to be used to his own advantage and being found in appearance as a man, he humbled himself by becoming obedient to death—even death on a cross!

PHILIPPIANS 2:5-6, 8 NIV

Who is lifting you up? A life lived in humility before God is one that looks to him to fulfill all our needs. In this manner, we are not thinking ourselves better than others, always needing to be lifted up by them or pushing ourselves above them. This humble dependence on God removes the need to prove ourselves to those around us; it gives us freedom to serve. Our world is constantly asking us how much power do you have? How much fame? Rank yourself amongst those around you.

When we are humble, we wait for God to exalt us, we don't push for self-promotion. In this waiting, in letting him fulfill our needs and be our source, we will find what it means to lay down our lives. We are to be obedient to death as well—to die to our selfish promotions and become alive to Christ.

Jesus, give me your humble mindset. I ask for humility and wisdom today.

Look to God in humility today, and then look around and ask: instead of competing, how can I serve and lift up?

the whole world

The LORD is a great God, and a great King above all gods.
In his hand are the depths of the earth;
the heights of the mountains are his also.
The sea is his, for he made it, and his hands formed the dry land.

PSALM 95:3-5 ESV

Do you remember the old song, He's Got the Whole World in His Hands? As a child, that seemed entirely believable. However, adults get skeptical. Without realizing, they can walk away from childlike faith and become cynical.

Know today that it is true. God does hold the entire world. Every valley, sea, mountain, and desert are his. Marvel at that again today. You have a personal relationship with the one who made the earth. His work is displayed in grandeur, yet he also invites you to draw near—into the palm of his hand.

Father, thank you that you are not only holding the world but me as well.

Have you grown more cynical and skeptical as you age or more childlike?

my eyes see

I had heard of you by the hearing of the ear,
but now my eyes see you.
JOB 42:5 ESV

There is a difference between hearing about something and seeing it yourself. It is possible to be entirely familiar with Scriptures and yet not know God. When there is strain in your relationship with God or you are walking through a testing season, as Job was, it is easy for God's words and decrees to become a burden. Where you once yielded to him out of love, now you are doing it out of duty. Without hearing his tone and seeing the tenderness on his face, his decrees seem heavy—like they are coming from a taskmaster and not a kind Father.

As Job declared, look at God with your eyes today. Any directive that you hear from him with your ears needs to be seen through a kind, gentle face whose eyes hold tremendous compassion. His is the face of Jesus which was nothing but compelling to the lowly.

Father, help me not just hear you but also see you with the eyes of my heart.

Are you hungry for more of the Lord or simply satisfied by casually hearing his Word?

good deeds

Be careful to live properly among your unbelieving neighbors. Then even if they accuse you of doing wrong, they will see your honorable behavior, and they will give honor to God when he judges the world.

1 PETER 2:12 NLT

We are called to bear fruit in the form of good deeds. This isn't something to shy away from. The world will know we are Christians by how we love one another. Our radical acts of love will do two things: encourage the recipient and draw others to God.

Good deeds don't get enough credit. While we shouldn't advertise when we do them, we should be eager to pour them out all day long. Our aspirations should be to leave a trail of good deeds in our wake. Smiles readily given, forgiveness displayed, and acts of kindness should be ear markers of Christians. Let us love not just in word but in good deeds today.

Father, help me boldly show who you are by kind, generous, selfless good deeds.

What can you do today that will encourage someone and show non-believers the radical love of God?

unjust suffering

This is a gracious thing, when, mindful of God, one endures sorrows while suffering unjustly.

1 PETER 2:19 ESV

There aren't many things more beautiful than a child of God suffering because of his name. If you have an opportunity to be treated unjustly because of God, by grace don't refuse it. It is esteemed to suffer for the name of Christ. While we should not seek this out, it is inevitable at times.

Find comfort in the fact that Christ too suffered unjustly. He was falsely accused and suffered as a result of it. However, he knew not to get discouraged because he entrusted himself to God's ultimate ruling on the issue. While you may not get justice in this age, rest assured it will come. Persevere; the Lord sees you. He has actually given you a place of honor to share with him in suffering.

Jesus, please sustain me through this trial. Give me courage to endure.

How can you draw strength from the suffering of Jesus?

walk in victory

"I have told you these things, so that in me you may have peace.
In this world you will have trouble. But take heart!
I have overcome the world."

JOHN 16:33 NIV

Take heart. In many other translations, this verse says, "take courage!" A rally cry from Jesus to every one of us. What is it that is supposed to embolden us? The fact that Jesus has overcome this world. The Greek word for overcome here is "nenikeka" which means to "be victorious over." This word is used in perfect tense, which means it is a completed action in the past that continues to impact the present. The completed action of Christ's death on the cross continues to bring us victory into the present day.

You are not told to overcome on your own, and there is no way you could! But take courage, because you are on the winning team. Have you ever been on a sports team or watched your favorite team on TV win? The confidence and elation is nothing compared to what we have as Christians. Living a life of courage is walking out the fact of victory in your life. The celebration of Christ's victory did not stop 2,000 years ago. Let it ripple into your life today.

Jesus, thank you for overcoming the world! Thank you for the peace that this brings me.

How can you walk in victory today?

be with him

Let my passion for life be restored,
tasting joy in every breakthrough you bring to me.
Give me more of your Holy Spirit-Wind
so that I may stand strong and true to you!

PSALM 51:12 TPT

Pain comes from holding on to the old when something new is being born. This is a new season. There aren't answers or decisions in this segment. There is renewal. There is redemption. God does not leave things broken; he heals and makes them better than they ever were. He doesn't merely improve, he gives something entirely new. You don't need to worry about what's next. Don't think too far ahead. Just be with God. That's all you need right now. Be with him.

Don't make any rash decisions. Don't give up. Wait and see where God brings you. Wait on him. Don't be afraid. You have your own gifts, your own anointing. He has given you everything, and he has been teaching you how to use it. It will be different this time. Everything he has promised will come to pass. This is only the beginning. Use this season of time to be with him. It's a new season of hope, beauty, and breakthrough.

Lord, I embrace this new season of life you are pouring out over me. Fill my eyes with the glorious vision and plans you have for me.

What do you need to experience breakthrough in? How is God calling you forward into his new season?

love my children

If possible, so far as it depends on you, live peaceably with all.
ROMANS 12:18 ESV

Continue doing the right things and you will see opportunities overwhelm your path. You don't have to seek the things you desire. God brings them to you when you follow closely behind him. Now is not the time to settle; now is not the time to cave. Now, is when you rise. God has you exactly where he wants you.

It may be tempting to look to the earth for healing because that's what you've been taught. Look to God when your heart breaks and ask him to show you healing. Allow your heart to experience his ways. He wants to heal you, so you can be a healer of his people. He has called you to be his voice of compassion. He has called you to not judge but to love. Connect with him at the heart level.

Lord, give me strength to make the choice to look to you for love and healing. Allow me to be intentional with your people as you have been intentional with me.

Loving people can be a challenge, but it is our calling. Ask God who he is calling you to love today and list ways to act.

walk boldly

The Lord is always good and ready to receive you.
He's so loving that it will amaze you—
so kind that it will astound you!
And he is famous for his faithfulness toward all.
Everyone knows our God can be trusted,
for he keeps his promises to every generation!

PSALM 100:5 TPT

God's best is yet to come. Don't give up. Trust him. Your past, your worries, your fears can be done away with. He is releasing you into a new phase. He has released joy, peace, and prosperity of your soul over you. Keep stepping out into courage. Keep living in boldness. Keep saying "Why can't I?" He has created you to be a person of power and a person of influence. He trusts you to live out his love. You are a storehouse of peace.

When God speaks something over you, he creates something new in you. He can create new things at any time.

Lord, create new levels of courage and boldness within me. Help me to demonstrate your heart on earth even when it feels scary.

How can you step out in courage today? List the ways God is revealing in this moment.

rest your heart

God, hear my cry; listen to my prayer.
I call to you from the ends of the earth when I am afraid.
Carry me away to a high mountain.
You have been my protection,
like a strong tower against my enemies.

PSALM 61:1 NCV

What are your burdens? What are your pains? Do you trust God with them? Do you trust him to answer them in his time? Do you know that God only has good in store for you? That his ways are higher than yours? Remember every minute of every day that he is your confidant, advocate, warrior; he sees you. He sees your needs. He sees your heart. Trust that he will come through for you.

God will be with you through it all. He will cover your pain with his love. He will lift you up; you will not be defeated or destroyed. He is fighting for you; he has never stopped and never will. You are precious to him, you are special and made for specific purposes. You were made to love, to give, and to serve. Never tire. Trust in him and remember that darkness is only temporary.

Lord, remind me of your relentless love toward me. Lift my head up in times of despair and help me to fix my eyes on your great mercy.

What do you do in times of need? How can you rest your heart with Jesus in times of pain?

the only plan

People can make all kinds of plans,
but only the LORD's plan will happen.
PROVERBS 19:21 NCV

Pay attention to the road signs. Pursue what God gives you. Pay close attention. There is gold in his words and treasure in his dreams. He wants you to focus on him and seek the direction he is asking you to go. He is your guide. God is teaching you his voice, visions, and the way he sees people.

He gives you a new book in life. There was not another chapter in the one you were living. Keep pressing into him. He will make you a leader of the very people who intimidate you if you speak the words he gives without fear. His Spirit rests heavily upon you with great power and conviction. He is holding you and will never leave your side.

God, help me to let go of the comfort I cling to and surrender my will to yours as I step into the new plans you have created for me.

Which of your plans do you need to let go of? Can you trust that God's plans are better?

preserved

You have granted me life and steadfast love,
and your care has preserved my spirit.

JOB 10:12 ESV

When there is adversity in our lives we often feel weak and vulnerable. Fear can arise that we might be losing ground: losing our courage, endurance, or even hope. According to this passage, God actually takes the time to preserve our spirit. If something is preserved, it means it is kept so it won't spoil; the goodness of it is protected.

In the kingdom of God every ounce of suffering in our lives is used for his glory. In addition, his unfailing love strengthens us so our own spirits are preserved.

Father, thank you that your steadfast love will carry me when I am hurting. Thank you that you are a caring nurturer and you take the time to preserve my very spirit.

Do you question God's care in seasons of suffering?

thought chamber

*"The gatekeeper opens the gate for him, and the sheep listen
to his voice. He calls his own sheep by name and leads them out.
When he has brought out all his own, he goes on ahead of them, and
his sheep follow him because they know his voice."*

JOHN 10:3-4 NIV

Singularity of voice is the skill a child of God must acquire.
In our minds there are many voices: the accusing voice of the
enemy, our own doubting self-talk, reverberating echoes of
memories, past accusations, culture, family, friends, the list
goes on. Our thought chamber is a crowded room with a lot
of noise!

There is one voice that is like rushing waters. One voice
that stills us. One voice that roars like a lion, speaks familiarity
like a good shepherd, and whispers with the intimacy of a
friend. We need to let Jesus take center stage and perform
a solo. It takes practice to quiet the crowd and focus on his
eyes. Find a quiet place and hide in his Word. When life gets
noisy, listen for the voice that calls you his own.

Still my heart and mind, Lord. Speak. I am listening.

Can you recognize God's voice today?

blessed to give

I have been a constant example of how you can help those in need by working hard. You should remember the words of the Lord Jesus: "It is more blessed to give than to receive."

ACTS 20:35 NLT

Jesus' teaching seems backwards. We might want to argue that clearly the way to gain is to hold onto what you have—it's basic math. Here Paul quotes another principle that seems backwards to us but is the forward thinking of the kingdom of God. We can't break this down into a math equation. We can't say if we give money away we will be blessed with more money. (Although this happens so often!)

The point is that greed often hinders the Gospel. It causes us to ball up our fists and never let go. It's not only the rich who struggle with greed. How can we access our level of greed? Do we only pursue ventures that will pay? If God asks us to give freely of our resources, do we become afraid? Greed is rooted in the fear of not having enough. But God has promised to provide. We need to share our talents, position, and influence, serving with our gifts no matter the gain.

Thank you for equipping me, Jesus. Help me to find areas to give and serve no matter what.

Is Jesus calling you to give?

sleeping mask

Patient endurance is what you need now, so that you will continue to do God's will. Then you will receive all that he has promised.

HEBREWS 10:36 NLT

What emboldened the early church to act how they are described in this chapter of Hebrews? They put up with beatings, public shame, loss of possessions, and saw their friends treated the same. Is it inside all of us as well, that ferocious courage that does not back down?

Have we been lured to sleep by our possessions and popularity? The early Christians came to know Christ and that light illuminated their lives in such a radical manner that they began to reflect it. People didn't like being awoken from their dark state, so they reacted. But the early church had their eyes set on the hope of eternity, the promise of Christ, so the negative response of the world didn't matter. They grasped onto the view that earthly troubles are small compared to the weight of eternal glory. If we want to be full of courage, we need to shake off the sleeping mask and begin to reflect the glory of God.

Father, make me a reflector of your light today. Keep my eyes focused on the age to come.

Have you become too comfortable in this world that you have lost sight of the hope of the age to come?

consistent hope

May the God of hope fill you with all joy and peace in believing, so that by the power of the Holy Spirit you may abound in hope.

ROMANS 15:13 NRSV

Hope. It is whispered in the budding on bare branches after a long winter. It races through the droplets set free from the ice, melted down and moving once again. Experience it in the shifting of the wind across your face from a painful slap of cold to a gentle caress of warmth. The brilliant colors of the tulips shout it out as our monochromatic world has the saturation turned up. The chorus of birds sing in harmony: hope. The season of spring brings us a reminder of what we can be filled with daily.

In Christ, there is no such thing as false hope. There is only unshakeable, unmovable, constant, abundant, hope. All the temporary things will rust, rot, and be lost in the age to come. Our anchor lies in the fact that Christ is coming back, he has prepared a place for us, he will wipe away every tear, and he will make all things new once more. If hope seems lost, readjust to an eternal mindset and watch it bloom again.

God, you are my hope, and you display hope in the creation around me. Thank you for true, everlasting hope. Anchor me in it today.

In what way has your hope been set on the wrong thing, and how can you adjust it?

march

"I told you these things so that you can have peace in me. In this world you will have trouble, but be brave! I have defeated the world."

JOHN 16:33 NCV

inside out

Love is patient and kind. Love is not jealous,
it does not brag, and it is not proud.
1 CORINTHIANS 13:4 NCV

It's a Scripture known to so many and we certainly would agree that love displays itself in patience, kindness, and humility. But what about those times when patience and kindness are not present in our words and actions? What about those days when we feel so overwhelmed that our immediate response to a difficult person is impatience or an unkind word?

In those times, remember this: God is love. He is patient, he is kind, and he is merciful. Let that thought wash over you so you absorb some of the grace your Creator has for you. It's God within you that helps you conquer your feelings of jealousy and pride. It is that God who enables you to love bravely.

God, I know that love is the best quality I could have and could ever give. I choose to accept your grace for areas that I have not shown love, and I allow your love to change me as I head into this day and the week ahead.

What has been the hardest quality of love for you to display? Is it patience, kindness, or humility? Let God's love work on you from the inside out.

the other shoe

Love is not rude, is not selfish, and does not get upset with others. Love does not count up wrongs that have been done.

1 CORINTHIANS 13:5 NCV

Sometimes the world seems like everything that love is not. People are rude and selfish, and we seem to get upset an awful lot. How do we not get upset when we feel wronged? It seems an impossible ask. It is often said that a child behaves badly when they are hurt, tired, afraid, or hungry. The same can probably be said for us. Sometimes when we are feeling particularly hurt by someone, it is helpful to ask what they might be going through. Perhaps they are afraid, hurt, tired, or simply hungry!

God loves us, in spite of the way we behave, and while we shouldn't let others walk all over us, it's always better to step into their shoes for a moment and ask God to give us perspective. Forgiveness helps to get rid of the scores of wrongs that we might be tempted to add up.

Lord, in those times when I am feeling upset with someone who has wronged me, give me the ability to see over the fence and into what they are experiencing. Help me to protect my heart, but to also forgive and move on.

Is there someone, or a few people, who you feel have wronged you lately? Take a moment to forgive and wipe that score against them clean.

belonging

This is how we know that we belong to the truth
and how we set our hearts at rest in his presence.
1 JOHN 3:19 NIV

In a world competing for truths, and voices telling you to own your truth, what can be left to say of knowing anything for certain? Truth has the assumption that there is a right belief, beyond all personal subjectivity and experience. While everything that we experience is a level of truth, there is a greater truth about our lives and existence that can only be found in Jesus.

The truth is this: you belong. In a world where we desperately try to find our place, fit in with certain groups, and share common ground, we can often feel isolated. God's truth is that you are a part of his family, and nothing is going to change that. As you dwell in the reality of your belonging, let your heart find the divine presence of the living God, and let yourself rest in it.

Loving Lord, thank you that I belong to the truth. Thank you that I belong in your family, as a child, sibling, parent, or friend to those who are on this journey with me. Allow me to rest today in this assurance.

How do you know you belong to the truth? What truths of this world are competing against the knowledge of your belonging to the family of God?

giver of life

This is how God showed his love to us: He sent his one and only Son into the world so that we could have life through him.

1 JOHN 4:9 NCV

As a follower of Jesus, you will have experienced his grace, strength, compassion, and joy in the middle of your circumstances. But not only did Jesus do something that was life changing, the Scripture says it was life giving when Jesus came into the world.

We were given a new life, a new reality, when Jesus became flesh, lived amongst us, died, and rose again. Experiencing humanity and the evil of the world was a sacrifice for both our heavenly Father and Son. God loved us so much that he was willing to walk through it to give us a completely transformed life, not just for this time, but for eternity.

God, thank you for a love that was undeniably life changing for me. Allow me to experience the changes that your love brings to my life each day. I also thank you for the hope that this life is the beginning of my eternity with you. As I reflect on this new life, let my heart be stirred with joy.

What does it mean to you to have been given life through Jesus?

rhetorical or not

"LORD, the God of our ancestors, are you not the God who is in heaven? You rule over all the kingdoms of the nations. Power and might are in your hand, and no one can withstand you."

2 CHRONICLES 20:6 NIV

There are times for rhetorical questions, and times for real questions. We don't know what the writer of the Scripture was expressing, but it might be freeing to know that you can express doubts and certainty to God, and that all forms of your expression can actually grow your faith.

Perhaps you are in the middle of some personal turmoil right now. It's okay for you to ask if God is really sovereign. On the other hand, you may be experiencing a particular blessing that allows you to state, "Yes, God you are powerful and in control!" Whatever you might be experiencing, know that God can withstand your doubts and will delight in your praise.

God, give me the courage to face you with my doubts in troubled times. As I share my doubt, give me faith to trust that you are still with me, every step of the way. Transform my faith to be able to praise you for your everlasting presence.

Where is your heart right now in terms of being confident of God's sovereignty? Express that to a God who loves you.

caterpillars

We all, who with unveiled faces contemplate the Lord's glory, are being transformed into his image with ever-increasing glory, which comes from the Lord, who is the Spirit.

2 CORINTHIANS 3:18 NIV

Transformation can be a beautiful thing, but that doesn't mean it doesn't require challenge and hard work. Consider the caterpillar that spends much of its life preparing for the transformation. It stops eating, hangs itself upside down, and spins a cocoon which dissolves its former matter and begins to create new matter. It goes from crawling on the ground to soaring in the sky.

It's remarkable, mysterious, weird, and wonderful. What a striking analogy of our transformation with Christ. The whole process from beginning to end is incredibly important. We can't skip out certain stages, we can't go backwards, we really just have to go with it! Jesus is already working within you, and day by day, you are increasing in glory. Believe it, and let his Spirit guide you into freedom.

Jesus, lover of my life, I allow your Spirit to work in and through me, so I may graciously accept the often difficult process of transformation. Thank you that at the end of this, my life will be a reflection of your radiance.

What part of the transformation process do you feel like you are in?

light and momentary

We do not lose heart. Though outwardly we are wasting away, yet inwardly we are being renewed day by day. For our light and momentary troubles are achieving for us an eternal glory that far outweighs them all. So we fix our eyes not on what is seen, but on what is unseen, since what is seen is temporary, but what is unseen is eternal.

2 CORINTHIANS 4:16-18 NIV

It can be hard to be in the middle of turmoil and see your situation as light and momentary. Paul had persecution, imprisonment, church conflict, false teaching, and a myriad of other troubles to deal with; yet, he was able to find his perspective in fixing his eyes on the eternal hope in Christ. Your situation and particular difficulty is important to Jesus; never undermine your emotional stress. But don't lose heart because Jesus is doing something deeper, better, and eternal in your life.

These Scriptures encourage us to look beyond and above our circumstances to find hope. If we stare too hard at where our feet are going, we may miss the joy of looking at the end destination.

Jesus, I choose today to lift my eyes beyond my own discouragement, struggles, and pain, so I can be encouraged that it will all be worth it in the end. Help me to not lose heart, but to find it.

How might your circumstances be achieving an eternal glory for you that outweighs how they are currently making you feel?

heart decision

Each of you should give as you have decided in your heart to give. You should not be sad when you give, and you should not give because you feel forced to give. God loves the person who gives happily.

2 CORINTHIANS 9:7 NCV

Ugh. Money. It's hard to talk about. We'd like to think of ourselves as generous people, but let's face it: money is really hard to let go of. For most of us, budgets are tight; we may have enough to live on, but rarely does it feel like there is a lot of extra floating around. Relax.

The Scripture tells us to listen to our heart when it comes to giving. If your heart is generous toward a person, project, or organization, then free your heart, and unclench your hands! When you give out of a heart that wants to give and doesn't feel obligated or forced, you will be blessed with joy. This is the delight of a cheerful giver. Give when your heart tells you to—and when it does, give bravely, give generously, and give with joy.

Provider God, you are always caring for me and I acknowledge that I have many needs that have been met through your provision. Give me a generous heart—one that is willing to joyfully give when it feels like the right thing to do.

What is your heart guiding you to give toward right now?

divine expectation

His divine power has given us everything we need for a godly life through our knowledge of him who called us by his own glory and goodness.

2 PETER 1:3 NIV

Many define Christianity by standards of godliness from earthly expectations. We are taught about doing the right thing and being an upstanding person within society and among our peers. How hard it can be, then, when we fail to meet these standards. We can be overly critical and hard on ourselves for not being the person we ought to be.

It might take a moment, but consider where your standards come from. Does your desire to do the right thing come from either your own expectation or others'? The Scripture says that our godly life comes through our knowledge of Jesus, through divine power, and through Christ's goodness. Trying to live a good life through our own striving is always going to leave us wanting. Lean into the glory and goodness of Jesus and let him give you what you need to be the person he created you to be.

Thank you, Jesus, for the reminder that I do not need to strive to attain godliness, rather that I need to be eager to know you and rest in your glory and goodness. Help me to become more like you through receiving your divine power within.

What earthly standards and expectations might the divine be encouraging you to let go of?

just cause

"Be courageous! Let us fight bravely for our people and the cities of our God. May the LORD's will be done."
2 SAMUEL 10:12 NLT

Reading or watching the news can leave us feeling pretty hopeless about the state of our world. We see stories of people whose lives have been ruined by injustice, discrimination, war, and natural disasters. The lives of those who are vulnerable to personal destruction need protection, and it needs to come from those of us who are strong enough to help.

This is the time to be courageous, to stand up for those who are weak and hurting. We need to allow the pain of others to affect us enough to do something about it. Fight bravely for these people. Pray, offer practical and financial help, stand in solidarity with the marginalized, and watch the love of our compassionate God change lives, cities, and nations.

Great and loving God, thank you for giving me the strength to fight for the cause of those less fortunate than me. Give me courage to act bravely on the behalf of others who are hurting and in need of help. Let me be a part of accomplishing your will to love unconditionally.

Who do you need to stand by and be courageous for? How can you help?

icebergs

May the Lord lead your hearts into a full understanding and expression of the love of God and the patient endurance that comes from Christ.

2 THESSALONIANS 3:5 NLT

The common expression "the tip of the iceberg" makes reference to what we fail to see lying underneath the surface. In fact, science tells us that an iceberg has the majority of its mass lying below the water, unseen.

When we experience the love of God for the first time, it really is just the tip of the iceberg. Our lives are a journey of exploring what God's love really means, and just when you think you've grasped it, you dive a little deeper and find out it's that much bigger again. God's loved is expressed in so many ways, and it's our privilege to see, hear, and feel that expression throughout all of our various happenings. This week take time to notice the way that God is expressing his love toward you, and allow that to transform the way you extend love to others.

God of immeasurable love, give me the endurance to dive deeper into this journey with you. Grant me the clarity of vision to notice the unexpected places in which I am experiencing your love.

In what way has a recent experience revealed the depth of God's love that you perhaps hadn't recognized before?

futile arguments

Remind everyone about these things, and command them in God's presence to stop fighting over words. Such arguments are useless, and they can ruin those who hear them.

2 TIMOTHY 2:14 NLT

Arguments rarely result in getting what you want. We will often use our words to try to persuade, defend, or get a certain reaction. Rarely do we stop to consider the personal bias that sits beneath our arguments, and rarely do we admit that we are doing more harm than good.

It's not to say that we can't have differences in opinions and beliefs; it is to say that arguments over these differences are useless. Instead of showing tolerance, graciousness, and peace, we too often display intolerance, judgement, and division. This is why the Scriptures appeal to us to stop fighting—it simply doesn't reveal Christ to those around us. So, take a deep breath, or a lot of deep breaths, and let Christ win.

Christ, my Savior, at times I have been so frustrated with other believers. I don't understand where they are coming from and sometimes I feel desperate to convince them that they need to change! Help me to see the futility of arguments and give me the willpower to let go.

What struggles and arguments are you having with others in your life? Take a moment to consider if Christ can be seen in these, and if not, let it go.

living words

All Scripture is God-breathed and is useful for teaching, rebuking, correcting and training in righteousness, so that the servant of God may be thoroughly equipped for every good work.

2 TIMOTHY 3:16-17 NIV

You may have heard that the Bible is our instruction book for life. Perhaps that is too simple or maybe a little too mechanical of an explanation. It's true that we can follow the rules of the Bible and live good lives, but the reality is that when life gets complicated, simply following some rules may leave us feeling discouraged or empty. Scripture is more than that.

The words in this collection of writings are God-breathed—meaning that they can bring a dynamic and interactive relationship with our Creator. Sometimes those words teach us a truth about life, occasionally they change our feelings toward a person, often they give us the courage to do the noble thing. The promise is that these living words equip us to display the goodness of God. They allow us to become the image bearers that he created us to be. Let Scripture guide and grow you little by little each day.

Holy Spirit, thank you for breathing life throughout your timeless Word. Help me wrestle, question, grow, and transform as I relate to your Word. Give me fresh understanding of things that I have read over and over. Reveal a different part of yourself to me as I engage wholeheartedly in this journey.

What is God equipping you for right now, and what Scriptures have you found useful for this time in your life?

devoted disciple

They were continually devoting themselves to the apostles' teaching and to fellowship, to the breaking of bread and to prayer.
ACTS 2:42 NASB

If there's one verse to make a church group feel guilty, it's this one. It's hard to imagine how any of us could live like this in our day and age. Imagine a constant stream of teaching, eating, and praying with your Christian friends. To some that might sound pleasant, but for many, it sounds impossible. Read between the lines. Of course, these people had homes, families, and the routines of life, just like we do.

The idea of continual devotion is simply the positive routines and habits that the believers dedicated themselves to—much like the habits we try to form in our Christian faith. We read devotionals, we pray, we go to church, we serve or gather with church groups. If this isn't part of your life, be encouraged to make a habit of it. Believers need each other, and they are encouraged by the devotion of others.

Jesus, I admit that I sometimes feel disconnected from the church or other believers. I can get so absorbed in my job, my duties, and tasks of life. Give me the boldness to get involved with other believers this week.

How can you become more engaged with believers this week?

spiritual wisdom

We continually ask God to fill you with the knowledge of his will through all the wisdom and understanding that the Spirit gives, so that you may live a life worthy of the Lord and please him in every way: bearing fruit in every good work, growing in the knowledge of God.

COLOSSIANS 1:9-10 NIV

We are wired to look at education as a means to an end; once we receive our qualification we can head into our careers and earn a decent living. God's knowledge, however, isn't about what we can gain in life but about what we can gain in relationship with him. Knowing God doesn't require a PhD, it requires following Jesus through the guidance of his Holy Spirit.

You won't please God by meeting the right requirements, but he will be pleased with a heart that acknowledges his way above your own. Rely on the Holy Spirit, today, and notice how you are able to continually seek wisdom in all that you do. Let growth take place, one day at a time.

Holy Spirit, guide my thoughts and decisions today. When I find myself confused about my life, purpose, or relationships, please assure me that you will fill me with wisdom and understanding so that I can still live a life of joy, love, and peace.

What are you finding difficult to understand right now? Ask the Holy Spirit to fill you with the knowledge of his will.

forgive them

Bear with each other and forgive each other. If someone does wrong to you, forgive that person because the Lord forgave you.

COLOSSIANS 3:13 NCV

Forgiveness is a lot easier said than done. The hardest part of forgiveness just might be that we may never really feel better about the wrongs that have been committed against us. Our hurt can run pretty deep, and being ready to forgive seems too formidable. Remember that there is one who can identify with your pain. Jesus experienced betrayal, scorn, mockery, and physical pain, and while he was suffering on the cross, he offered up a prayer of forgiveness for those who had wronged him.

If you are having trouble forgiving someone who has hurt you, remember Christ's words on the cross, "Father, forgive them." Allow God's forgiveness to go before you and then prepare your heart to forgive. Letting go of pain is always better than holding on to bitterness.

Jesus, thank you for the forgiveness that I have experienced from you, and for the forgiveness I have experienced from others. When I am facing difficult relationships and interactions, prepare my heart to forgive. Allow me to be patient and compassionate with those who have done wrong.

Is there someone in your life who needs your forgiveness? Remember the forgiveness of Christ, and bravely offer the same grace to others.

representative

Whatever you do, whether in word or deed, do it all in the name of the Lord Jesus, giving thanks to God the Father through him.
COLOSSIANS 3:17 NIV

When you work for a company or organization, you are expected to represent that particular brand or identity. Organizations who have a good reputation typically have a culture that their people are committed to being a part of. When you think of that company or brand, you can identify a certain value.

When you become a follower of Jesus, you also become his representative. Your personal relationship with Christ will inspire you to express something of his love, goodness, and grace to the world around you. You don't always need to shout that you are doing things in his name, you just need to simply be aware that your words and actions are influenced by his grace. Be encouraged today that you will represent him wherever you go.

Thank you, heavenly Father, for the expression of Christ that I am able to share with the world. Let my words and deeds be a good and loving representation of the love and goodness of Jesus.

What part of Christ do you know you are representing well, and what might you need to let shine a little brighter this week?

one way

"You shall follow the LORD your God and fear Him; and you shall keep
His commandments, listen to His voice, serve Him, and cling to Him."
DEUTERONOMY 13:4 NASB

The Israelites lived in a time where different people groups would follow many gods and carry out a lot of traditions associated with idol worship. It was really important for the Israelites to know who their God was and what his guidelines were for their lives. Israel was a nation that God wanted to bless, but they needed to stay on the path he had set before them.

These Scriptures hold true for us today. Our culture puts its mind, heart, and hands to serving itself, so we need to remind ourselves regularly that God has promised us something greater in a life lived for him. As you head into your day, do your best to follow his ways, listen to him, serve him, and cling to him.

Lord, I know that you have good plans for my life and that a life of honoring you is the best thing I could aim for. I choose to cling to you today because I know that you are more important than anything I desire in this world. I choose to follow you.

Where is God guiding you at the moment? Take some time to listen to his voice and surrender your journey to him.

soak it in

Let my teaching fall on you like rain;
let my speech settle like dew.
Let my words fall like rain on tender grass,
like gentle showers on young plants.

DEUTERONOMY 32:2 NLT

If you think back to your lessons at school, can you recall teachers who were especially good? Perhaps they were so good because they showed care for the students, maybe they were humorous, or maybe they just seemed to know how to explain things so you could understand them. We typically learn the best from teachers or things that don't scare us away, confuse us, or cause us to become frustrated. We learn when we can clearly understand what is being taught, even if the concept might be complex.

This is how God longs for his words to teach you. He wants his ways to be understood like a gentle rain; like dew drops that settle on your heart to nourish your soul. He knows that your heart is tender, and he won't give you what you are not ready for. Let yourself grow in his knowledge, allowing the best teacher to cultivate something deep and beautiful in your life.

Loving Teacher, continue to guide me in your ways. Help me to learn lessons about this faith and my journey with you. I don't want to be stubborn or difficult, so I surrender my heart to lifelong learning and growth.

What is God trying to teach you right now? Accept his teaching like rain and let it soak deep into your heart.

the maker

As you do not know the path of the wind,
or how the body is formed in a mother's womb,
so you cannot understand the work of God,
the Maker of all things.

ECCLESIASTES 11:5 NIV

As a human race, we have made many scientific and technological advances to better understand things like the anatomy and weather patterns. As advanced as we are, however, there are still so many things that bewilder, amaze, and amuse us—including the human body and the weather! If we can be amazed by the things that we do know, imagine all of the things we do not.

The way the world and every complex thing within it interacts simply cannot be known—except by the maker of all things. Aren't you glad that your life is in his hands? You might be facing some very confusing times, some things seem ordered and others chaotic. Whatever life is throwing at you, remember that God is at work and that he knows his work very well.

Maker of all things, I submit my vague understanding of how life works to your boundless wisdom. Help me to trust in your sovereign hand that will guide me and keep me at peace, no matter what is going on around and within me.

What questions and confusion do you have right now that would be better placed in the hands of your Creator?

a high price

He is so rich in kindness and grace that he purchased our freedom with the blood of his Son and forgave our sins.

EPHESIANS 1:7 NLT

The Bible speaks of us being slaves to sin. This picture expresses that there was no way to free ourselves from the consequence of sin: death. When God gave up his Son, Jesus, to die on the cross, he was paying the highest price possible to gain us our freedom.

It was this kind of "richness" that bought us out of death into life. It's worth considering how much God paid for us, but we don't need to feel guilty, because our heavenly Father knew that we were worth it. He loved us so much, he wanted us back at all costs. Consider his love, and let it give you an extra boost to get through today.

God, thank you that you lavished your kindness on me, so I could be free. May I express that same kindness and grace to the people around me, so they will also experience the freedom that comes from believing in the truth.

What have you experienced freedom from since believing in the grace of Jesus?

approach bravely

In him and through faith in him we may approach God with freedom and confidence.

EPHESIANS 3:12 NIV

You have probably seen, or even experienced, times when children hide behind their parent's legs when they are concerned or afraid of the situation or person they are approaching. We all need reassurance, and we are usually quick to draw near to the people we trust and know will keep us safe.

Jesus is that person for us. He came to rescue humanity from the fear of separation from God; he came to present a God who is approachable. Let him take your hand today, and guide you into the presence of your compassionate and merciful God. Let the closeness of Christ give you the freedom and confidence of knowing that this is exactly where you belong.

Dear Jesus, I take your hand right now and ask you to guide me into the presence of the King. Thank you that I belong in this kingdom and that I have the freedom to be near to God.

What barriers do you have in approaching God with freedom and confidence?

resistance

Submit to one another out of reverence for Christ.
EPHESIANS 5:21 NIV

In a world of equal opportunity and pursuit for equality, submission can be a tough pill to swallow. Perhaps there are just too many hang-ups with that word in English. If submission seems like a stumbling block to you, try thinking about the word acceptance.

The way the Scripture wants us to understand submission is perhaps best when thinking about its antonym. The opposite of submission is resistance, and this is where all sorts of trouble can brew. If you think of some recent arguments you may have had, you were probably resisting the idea, emotions, or actions of someone else. While you have equally valid ideas, emotions, and actions, lean into the love of Christ and learn to accept or relent once in a while, so his grace can be experienced through you.

Jesus, I know that you have been gracious to me, time and time again. I know that you accept me as I am and have never resisted me. Let me be someone who puts aside myself for the sake of others.

In what ways have you been resisting something because of your own desires, and how might Christ be asking you to change?

let grace win

If you bite and devour each other,
watch out or you will be destroyed by each other.
GALATIANS 5:15 NIV

Watching animals in the wild hunt, defend, and fight for territory can be brutal. We are not wild animals, but it might pay to stop and think about whether we are acting like them. When we start to assume or say unkind things about people, it can be the start of an attack on character or a judgement of the way things are being done.

God doesn't call us to be the judge of what others say or do, he wants us to have control of ourselves. Instead of being ready to attack or defend our territory, we should be quick to forgive, to try and understand others' perspectives, and stay out of the danger of judgement. Always let grace win.

God, thank you that you created us all equal. I pray that I would have enough self-control to keep myself from making judgements about what other people do and say. Keep my heart full of grace so that it spills over into the way that I treat others.

Do you need to experience God's forgiveness for speaking unfairly about others? Do you need to receive healing for those who have hurt you?

the charitable church

Whenever we have the opportunity,
we should do good to everyone—
especially to those in the family of faith.
GALATIANS 6:10 NLT

Church squabbles happen everywhere. You may have been involved in them to varying degrees and perhaps you know how hurtful they can be. It's important to remember that God recognizes the Church as the body of Christ. This means that the enemy wants to destroy it; it also means that we need to do our utmost to protect it.

Whatever community of believers you belong to, be sure to do your best in contributing to its health. Avoid gossip, support those who are struggling, offer help where you can, speak well of people. If everyone is doing their part to do good to everyone, especially the community of faith, we will be equipping our church to show the world the love of Christ.

Jesus, I pray for the Church, worldwide. I thank you that you have chosen us to bond together so that your name can be glorified. Protect your Church, protect the unity of believers, and help me to do good to everyone.

How can you make a positive difference to your community of faith this week?

a gentle approach

*He is able to deal gently with those who are ignorant
and are going astray, since he himself is subject to weakness.*

HEBREWS 5:2 NIV

If you have ever seen a lost pet, you will know that they are not easy to approach. They are fearful and untrusting. Approaching a lost pet quickly will cause them to scamper and may contribute to them being further lost. Instead, caution and gentleness will help you get close.

This is the picture that Scripture gives us of Jesus' approach to the lost. He didn't come to scare the ignorant, he came to attract them with gentleness and grace. He knows, firsthand, our human experience and he knows what we need. Let the approach of Jesus be your approach as well. Be gentle with those who are yet to know him and trust that they will be drawn by your kindness.

Thank you, Father, for your kindness toward humanity. Thank you that you came as a humble servant who knows how to approach us with care and gentleness. I pray for those who are lost right now that need to find you. Let them experience your grace.

How could you soften your approach to others who are in need of Christ's love?

as long as life

Our great desire is that you will keep on loving others as long as life lasts, in order to make certain that what you hope for will come true.

HEBREWS 6:11 NLT

Lifelong love is harder than it sounds. There's a reason why many marriages and relationships don't last. Love requires vulnerability, and this invites the possibility of being hurt. You may have experienced hurt from having loved someone, but you have probably also experienced the unconditional love of others.

In times of hurt, remember those who have loved you their whole lives—perhaps a parent, a sibling, or a friend. Lifelong love does exist, and it is Christ's desire to see everyone being loved for their whole lives. When we experience this kind of love, we know a small measure of God's love for us. This is what will heal humanity, and we can have confidence that love will ultimately win.

Jesus, I bring all my hurts to you and ask you to heal my heart so I can love others fully and unconditionally. Help me to share your love with others, as long as life lasts, so that the light of your love can shine into a broken world.

What pain have you experienced from a love that didn't last? Can you open your heart to forgive? Allow the love of Jesus to transform you so you can keep on loving.

peace work

Strive for peace with all men, and for the holiness without which no one will see the Lord.

HEBREWS 12:14 RSV

Peace is a word used to describe a sense of feeling calm and relaxed. We may think of ourselves as lying back on a deck chair in the sun with no work to do and no one around to disturb us. Being relaxed is a wonderful thing, but it is more the result of the work of peace. True peace, the kind that the Scripture speaks of, takes a bit of effort on our part. That's why God's Word says we need to strive for it.

It's the responsibility of all people to live in harmony and reconciliation with one another—not just with the people we like, but especially with the people we don't. Harmony isn't about everybody being the same, it's about everybody being different and getting along. Think of those people, today, who you find difficult to walk alongside. Strive for reconciliation with those people and watch God display his holiness through you.

Holy God, I submit my feelings and insecurities to you, knowing that you love me and will help me to get along with others. I choose to follow peace, not fear, getting along with the people that you bring across my path whether I feel the same as them or not.

Who are the people in your life that are different from you? Are you striving to live in harmony with them?

Offer to others

Let us offer through Jesus a continual sacrifice of praise to God, proclaiming our allegiance to his name. And don't forget to do good and to share with those in need. These are the sacrifices that please God.
HEBREWS 13:15-16 NLT

In ancient culture, offering things to the gods was done in order to please the god and bring favor. Our God does not need our lavish gifts to be pleased; he is nothing like the idols of old. Our God is living and near. Instead of offering something to him, he wants us to offer something to others. This is why Scripture tells us to do good and share.

It's good to be reminded of the simplicity of faith in Jesus. As you go about your week, find a way to offer something to others. Remind yourself to pray for a person who is struggling, bring food to a family in need, or offer a sympathetic ear to someone who is grieving. There are so many ways we can reach out, and it pleases God's heart when we do.

God, I want to please you through my care and concern for others. Bring me opportunities to do good and share with those in need.

What is God reminding you to do for others today?

redeem the wrong

Seek the Lord while you can find him. Call on him now while he is near.
Let the wicked change their ways and banish the very thought of doing
wrong. Let them turn to the Lord that he may have mercy on them. Yes,
turn to our God, for he will forgive generously.

ISAIAH 55:6-7 NLT

Humanity has always struggled with good and evil. While it's important to focus on the good, we cannot forget that evil is still present. The Scriptures are full of expressions of people who are feeling bewildered, hurt, and afraid of evil. Can you hear the echo of your own heart in these expressions? It is good to desire that the wrongs of this world would be redeemed.

Pray for those who choose to live in selfishness, who choose harm over good. Ask God to intervene and have hope that they can turn from the very thought of doing wrong. God is able to be merciful to all people, and indeed he will forgive generously.

God, I pray for the hearts of those who do not know you yet. I ask you to prevent evil from forming in the hearts of those who lack love. Draw them to you, and when they find you, may they find the forgiveness that you promise to give them.

What evil are you fearing right now? Ask God to change the ways of the wicked, and then surrender your fear and let him fill you with peace.

your story

I will tell about the LORD's kindness and praise him for everything he has done. I will praise the LORD for the many good things he has given us and for his goodness to the people of Israel. He has shown great mercy to us and has been very kind to us.

ISAIAH 63:7 NCV

You have a story to tell. When you think back over the years, reflect on the things that revealed God's goodness, graciousness, and love. Perhaps it was an illness or healing, a relationship or a relationship breakdown, it might have been a joy or a disappointment in your career. God is right next to us in all the things that life throws at us.

You may not have recognized him at the time, but hopefully you can attest to his kindness as you remember how you got through those times. This is your story and just like the Israelites, it is worth telling and repeating. Your story is important, so be brave and speak it out!

Thank you, Jesus, for the unique life that you have given me. I don't always understand why I have been through the things I have been through. But I can see your kindness and mercy in all that I have experienced. I trust that you will continue to show me kindness in all that I'm yet to face.

Where can you see God's goodness, mercy, or kindness in your present circumstance?

april

Wait patiently for the LORD.

Be brave and courageous.

Yes, wait patiently for the LORD.

PSALM 27:14 NLT

step back

Understand this, my dear brothers and sisters: You must all be quick to listen, slow to speak, and slow to get angry.

JAMES 1:19 NLT

Self-control is not often the first virtue you associate with loving others. However, the ability to manage your emotions and reactions is fundamental to being kind and gracious. It may take some practice to not retaliate quickly when someone is blaming you unfairly. Just like in a physical boxing match, we naturally want to defend ourselves from the blows.

You may be in the middle of some tough disagreements or arguments. Give yourself a moment to step back, to listen to what is being communicated. If you can, allow some time for you to process what is being said, and how you feel about it. Let God guide your heart as you slow down and step into his graciousness for others.

God, it can be really hard in the heat of the moment for me to control my emotions and what I say. Please remind me in those times to take a step back and slow down so I can be a person who shows love through self-control.

What strategy can you put in place when you recognize the need to take a step back from a difficult conversation or situation?

the desire beneath

*Since we know he hears us when we make our requests,
we also know that he will give us what we ask for.*
1 JOHN 5:15 NLT

When birthdays or anniversaries are coming up, we often get asked about what we want as a gift. You may be someone that answers that easily, or you might take a while. Eventually you have an answer of what you would like or even need, but you never really know if you are going to get it, and you often have to wait until that significant day to find out!

We should be confident that God hears us when we tell him what we want or need. Perhaps we haven't had the confidence to voice it, but he knows our heart anyway. Could we consider that God knows the true desire behind our requests, and that this real desire is what we end up getting? It's a thought that might be worth pondering today.

Loving Father, thank you that you know my heart's true desire. Give me confidence to ask you for what I want, knowing that I don't need to feel guilty just for asking. I trust that you will give me what I truly desire.

What do you need or want from your heavenly Father? Ask him, knowing he will hear you.

yet to come

*He will yet fill your mouth with laughter
and your lips with shouts of joy.*
JOB 8:21 NIV

Joy is the most natural thing when you are experiencing something exciting, fun, humorous, or satisfying. But the Scripture today comes from the book of Job, and if you know anything about this guy you will know that he was possibly feeling the most miserable anyone could feel. Job went through incredible pain: physically, mentally, spiritually, and emotionally.

How is it that this book of the Bible assures us that God fills us with laughter and shouts of joy? The clue could be in the word "yet." We may not be in a situation that feels very joyful; yet, there is hope of a day coming when we will once again laugh and shout with joy. If your world feels like that right now, hold on to the "yet."

Lord, may I always hope for what is yet to come. During those days I feel apathetic, sad, or downright depressed, I choose to look ahead to a day where my mouth will laugh and shout with joy. Fill me today with your assurance that this joy is waiting for me.

What do you see that is yet to come for you? What hopes do you have for a brighter tomorrow? Dwell on these hopes and be assured that joy will be restored to you.

getting better

Those who do right will continue to do right, and those whose hands are not dirty with sin will grow stronger.

JOB 17:9 NCV

Do you remember what it was like to learn how to swing by yourself? At first you were pushed by someone; then you were taught to move your legs back and forth and shift your weight around. Soon you were able to soar as high as you could go. We always start out a little shaky when we learn things, but eventually we get better. This is like the journey of our faith.

We have to practice having a good heart toward people, we need to repetitively forgive and show grace. We also need to have integrity in our schools, homes, and workplaces. All of this isn't necessarily natural; it has to be learned and repeated so we can effortlessly soar in righteousness. Don't worry about being perfect, just start to put some good into practice.

Thank you, Jesus, that I don't have to start out perfect. May I continue to do right when I am confronted with challenging decisions so I will grow from strength to strength.

What are you doing right? Keep doing it and watch the righteousness of Jesus become stronger within you.

from the heart

"A time is coming and has now come when the true worshipers will worship the Father in the Spirit and in truth, for they are the kind of worshipers the Father seeks. God is spirit, and his worshipers must worship in the Spirit and in truth."

JOHN 4:23-24 NIV

When Jesus met the women at the well, she questioned him about the right place to worship. As a Samaritan woman, her people worshipped on a certain mountain whereas the Jews worshipped on another. Jesus' answer might have seemed perplexing, but he was getting to the heart of the matter.

Now that God had appeared to the world in the flesh, worship was not about the ritual, the culture, or the place. Jesus pushed beyond the boundaries to reveal that worship comes from within and is an experience of truth between the Creator and the created. You have the opportunity to worship God wherever you are today. Meet him with a genuine heart.

Holy Spirit, thank you for dwelling inside of me and filling me with your grace and mercy. I worship you now with all of my heart.

Where and how do you worship Jesus? Have you made room for him in your heart?

lost and found

"You too have grief now; but I will see you again, and your heart will rejoice, and no one will take your joy away from you."

JOHN 16:22 NASB

Grief is something that no one wants to experience, but while we live in a broken world, it will come to us. Perhaps you have experienced a broken relationship, loss of a loved one, or a move from one city to another. There are many experiences of loss and they are all followed by grief. We don't need to fear the experience of grief; it is a natural and common human experience and we are never alone in feeling this way.

Jesus acknowledged that we will experience grief, but it comes with a reassurance that there will be a day when our joy will be complete, and we will no longer experience loss. So be brave, child of God, that while you experience heartbreak on earth, Jesus will restore your joy to you. Cling to him in your anguish and rejoice in your blessings. He is with you in it all.

Jesus, thank you that you will never leave my heart. In my most distressing times, may I always know your presence. I look forward to the day when you return and our joy will be everlasting.

How have you experienced Jesus in the middle of your despair?

unto others

"Do not judge others, and you will not be judged.
Do not condemn others, or it will all come back against you.
Forgive others, and you will be forgiven."

LUKE 6:37 NLT

You might not consider yourself a judgmental person, but all it takes is a reflection on your thoughts about others' actions or decisions to realize that you take part in some form of judgment, probably on a frequent basis. This isn't to make you feel guilty; rather, to bring to light that we are, by nature, judgmental creatures.

We come with a sense of knowing the difference between right and wrong, and we feel free to state when we think others are wrong. The trouble is, the Bible says this isn't our job! Furthermore, it says that when we engage in pointing the finger at others, we will become the subject of judgment ourselves. So, how can we avoid judging and condemning? Forgive. This doesn't mean turning a blind eye to wrongdoing; it just means that we don't get to decide the verdict.

Jesus, thank you that I can leave judgment up to you. Help me to consider other people's actions and behaviors with grace so that I will also be treated with graciousness.

What or who have you been judging lately? Hand over your judgement, with humility, and rejoice in your own forgiveness.

pure practices

Pure and undefiled religion in the sight of our God and Father is this: to visit orphans and widows in their distress, and to keep oneself unstained by the world.

JAMES 1:27 NASB

What images come to mind when you think of the word religion? You might see church buildings, gatherings, rituals, and spiritual habits. Perhaps you think about wars between religious groups or the separation of church and state. Religion can be all of these things, but simply put, religion is worship that is observed by others.

This Scripture talks about the best kind of outward worship—to care for the vulnerable. Orphans and widows were some of most vulnerable people in Jesus' time, and he was very concerned about taking care of them. When you consider what you can do for the sake of religion, take a look at the practical wisdom Scripture can give you. The purest sign of our worship is to let our hearts become so compelled with compassion that we draw near to those in need.

Lord, I don't want to be a religious person just for the sake of keeping rituals and doing duties to please you. Cultivate a heart of compassion within me for the marginalized in our society, and give me opportunities to help those people in a practical way.

Who might God be leading you toward to extend a hand of help?

a safe arrival

"He returned home to his father. And while he was still a long way off, his father saw him coming. Filled with love and compassion, he ran to his son, embraced him, and kissed him."

LUKE 15:20 NKJV

The story of the prodigal son is always a beautiful picture of the undeniable and exuberant love of our heavenly Father. Unfortunately, many people cannot relate to this kind of father. Some of us have been extremely disappointed and hurt by our earthly dads and we can't quite grasp what true parental love looks like.

If that's you, read this Scripture over and over again until you understand how God feels about you. He waited for you to come home, and when he saw a glimpse of you approaching, he ran to you. Not holding anything of himself back, he approaches you with nothing but acceptance and joy. You are loved unconditionally by a safe and caring God.

Heavenly Father, I don't always have the right picture of you in my mind. Heal me from hurts from my own father so that I can see you beyond that. Give me a sense of knowing the truth of your love beyond my human experience.

What kind of Dad have you had? Whether good or not, ask God to reveal himself in a way that you find safe and loving.

poor posture

"Blessed are the poor in spirit, for theirs is the kingdom of heaven.
Blessed are those who mourn, for they will be comforted."
MATTHEW 5:3-4 NIV

The posture of being poor in spirit and grieving is one of humility. When we are literally poor, or lack financial advantages, small things become meaningful. A person who lacks money will know that eating three meals a day or having a car to travel around in is a blessing. In the same way, grief has a way of showing us what really matters.

A person who has experienced loss longs for the small things—the hand to hold, the conversation over coffee. If you have experienced either of these, be encouraged by the wonderful new perspective that you have on life. You know what truly matters, and because of this humility, you will experience the kingdom of heaven with great joy and relief. Be comforted, knowing that your joy will return.

King of my heart, thank you for allowing me to soak in humility: an absolute assurance that I am worthy of your kingdom along an assurance that I need your grace. Thank you for the lessons of life that have given me the right perspective.

What have you experienced or gone through that has given you a new perspective in your faith?

healing

"I say to you, love your enemies.
Pray for those who hurt you."
MATTHEW 5:44 NCV

Praying for those who hurt us feels like a very unnatural response. You may understand all too well the emotions that come when someone has caused some measure of grief in your life. Sometimes it is the people we love the most who hurt us, other times it is those who don't know us very well. Our natural response to hurt is to defend, accuse, or bring the other person to justice, or we run from the situation and shut down our emotions. These responses are not wrong, but God does want to bring healing to the pain.

Loving your enemy isn't about willingly allowing people to hurt you; it is about bringing healing to your heart. When we pray for those who have done wrong to us, we are giving voice to our pain, expressing our emotions to God, and handing over the burden for him to deal with. It might take some time to bring it before God, but be encouraged that when you do, your heart will feel lighter.

Jesus, I have some pain in my heart from others who I feel have betrayed me and not shown me love. Thank you that you understand my pain. I choose today to hand that pain over to you and ask that you work in the heart of those who have wronged me. Help me to let go.

What is your natural response to being hurt? Pray for those
who have hurt you, but give yourself grace and time to
do this.

sparrows and locks

"Are not two sparrows sold for a penny? Yet not one of them will fall to the ground outside your Father's care. And even the very hairs of your head are all numbered. So don't be afraid; you are worth more than many sparrows."

MATTHEW 10:29-31 NIV

Jesus liked to use vivid imagery to describe his love and care for people. There's nothing that special about sparrows; in fact, they were worth less than a cent. Yet Jesus says they are still cared for by God in heaven. An even more amusing and memorable picture might be of God counting how many hairs you have on your head and noticing every time you lose a strand.

This is how these parables work, we get a vivid picture in our heads, and it reminds us of how extravagant and careful the love of God is. You might be worried about provision right now or wondering if God cares at all. Well, read this Scripture again. If he cares for the meagre sparrow, he will certainly care for you. And if he knows the number of hairs on your head, he certainly knows you.

Jesus, thank you for reminding me of how well you know me and how much I matter to you. I give my current stress about needs over to you, trusting that you will take care of me.

What are your needs right now? Be bold and ask Jesus to meet those needs.

the dance

"He who receives you receives Me,
and he who receives Me receives Him who sent Me."
MATTHEW 10:40 NASB

When God came in human flesh, he restored unity between the Creator and the created. The divine being became one of us, lived, died and was resurrected to a new life. This was a display of the human process of being redeemed and restored. When we believe in Jesus, we acknowledge that we are part of this new creation.

This is what Jesus means when he says that whoever receives you, receives him. You are a part of Christ, and he is a part of the Divine. So, when you share the love of Christ, you are inviting people to participate in this union between humankind and divinity. As you approach the days ahead, remember that you represent Christ; try to see it as a privilege, not a burden. His Spirit is the enabling power within you.

Jesus, thank you that you have made a home within my heart. I want to represent you to the people around me, so they feel welcomed into this new life. Let them receive me, and in turn, receive you.

How can you best represent Christ this week?

building it up

*"Every kingdom divided against itself will be ruined,
and every city or household divided against itself will not stand."*
MATTHEW 12:25 NIV

Do you remember a moment when you realized you just couldn't do it on your own? Today's culture encourages us to be independent. We can drive where we want, choose our own education, and decide what communities to belong to. This freedom of choice is a gift, and yet it can also lead to us feeling as though we are the masters of our own destiny. As independent as the modern life may be, we are still part of many social structures.

This means that at some point, you will need to rely on others. It's better to learn how to live in harmony with others than to see your workplace, church, or home become divided. If you are in a situation now where you are starting to see division, don't become part of the problem. Taking sides will only cause more fractures. We are called to unity, because this is what makes us all stronger and better people.

Lord, thank you for an eternal kingdom that will never be divided and will never end. Help me to work with the imperfect organizations and groups of people that I am part of, so I am a part of building things up rather than tearing them down.

What kingdoms, cities, and households are you part of? How can you work toward building up these things?

calloused

"This people's heart has become calloused; they hardly hear with their ears, and they have closed their eyes. Otherwise they might see with their eyes, hear with their ears, understand with their hearts and turn, and I would heal them."

MATTHEW 13:15 NIV

Have you ever put on a pair of new shoes and formed a blister by the end of the day? It's a common problem. Once the blister is gone, it becomes a callous, and you stop feeling the pain. This is sometimes like the Christian faith. The story of Jesus and what he has done can cause people to feel all sorts of things—sometimes it can become downright uncomfortable. So, they let their hearts become calloused and then they no longer have to respond to the truth.

For those who remain open to Jesus' words, they are sure to see clearly, to understand what he has done for them, and they would be ready for the new life he has created. Be encouraged today to stay open to the truth, even if it gets uncomfortable. Jesus is always looking to restore you.

Jesus, thank you that I have seen the truth and light of your Word. I want to remain open to see you and to hear you. May I always be tuned in to your truth.

What are some things you have closed yourself off to that Jesus wants to open up?

blessing

"May the LORD bless you and protect you. May the LORD smile on you and be gracious to you. May the LORD show you his favor and give you his peace."
NUMBERS 6:24-26 NLT

When was the last time someone prayed a blessing over you? It is comforting to experience someone expressing their desire to see you blessed. You may have come from a praying family where you experienced your parents' prayers over you. Perhaps you never grew up with blessings.

Today is a different day. This is a blessing especially for you. These are ancient words and yet today the Holy Spirit is bringing the words freshly to you and for you. May you be blessed and protected, today. May you feel God's favor toward you and acceptance of you. May you experience his unexplainable peace in the middle of all your circumstances.

Holy Spirit, thank you for bringing this blessing to me right now. I ask that you remind me of these words throughout my day, and that your blessing would flow through me and I would in turn, pass on the blessing to others.

What blessings can you be thankful for today?

hopeful

*God is not man, that he should lie, or a son of man,
that he should change his mind. Has he said, and will he not do it?
Or has he spoken, and will he not fulfill it?*
NUMBERS 23:19 ESV

When people have disappointed us over and over again, we tend to become distrusting of others. This is understandable; it's easier to have doubts and skepticism than to hope and be disappointed. Today, God wants to remind you that he is not an imperfect human, and he doesn't lie or give you false hope.

God has promised to be near you in all things, and he has promised to love you through everything. The hope that you have in his promises is true, and you have every right to believe in them. Strengthen your heart and be brave in what he has promised to do for you. God will not let you down.

God, I'm sorry for losing hope in your promises. I know that you understand my brokenness and distrust but give me the strength to believe again in your unfailing love.

How can you restore your hope in God's goodness, today?

diamond in the rough

This I pray, that your love may abound still more and more in real knowledge and all discernment, so that you may approve the things that are excellent, in order to be sincere and blameless until the day of Christ.

PHILIPPIANS 1:9-10 NIV

When a diamond is found in nature, it does not look at all like what we see on a shiny ring. While valuable, a diamond from the ground is dirty and uneven, hence the saying "a diamond in the rough." This is like our process as followers of Christ.

We have always been incredibly valuable, and this is why Jesus endured the cross for us. But as we walk more in his presence, we find that our rough parts become smoother and shinier, and we get better at understanding and displaying the love of Christ. Instead of being discouraged by your rough edges, think about how you are being shaped into something excellent as you go through the process of refinement. You are becoming more exquisite by the day!

Jesus, sometimes I still feel pretty rough around the edges. Help me to know my own value and to believe that you see me as beautiful and priceless. Let me accept the process of refinement so I can display more of your beauty.

What areas of your life feel like they are rough and in need of polishing? Let Jesus do some refining work on those areas.

rejoice always

Rejoice in the Lord always. I will say it again: Rejoice!
PHILIPPIANS 4:4 NIV

Oh, to be ever the optimist! This verse feels like it belongs to those who are able to keep positive in the middle of the worst crises. For the rest of us, however, it might feel like we are capable of failing this always rejoice command on a daily basis. Life just isn't that nice all the time. You might not like your job, you may be in a difficult patch in your relationship, you may just be annoyed at your neighbor or someone at school.

There are endless situations in a mere day that leave us feeling like not rejoicing. So, what are we to do when things seem dull, frustrating, or depressing? Rejoice in the Lord! Yes, turn your focus off yourself, and let your eyes turn toward Jesus. If you start to think of his goodness, grace, and mercy, your heart will slowly but surely find its joy and hope again. Don't despair, rejoice!

Lord, in those times when I am feeling discouraged, remind me to turn my heart and my mind toward you. As I thank you for your love for me, renew a spirit of hope within me.

What can you rejoice in the Lord for right now?

perspective

I know what it is to be in need, and I know what it is to have plenty. I have learned the secret of being content in any and every situation, whether well fed or hungry, whether living in plenty or in want. I can do all this through him who gives me strength.

PHILIPPIANS 4:12-13 NIV

Life doesn't seem to want us to be content. Contentment isn't valued; it is seen as average. We are geared toward improvement, novelty, and getting ahead. This creates a feeling of unsettledness in our minds and hearts and it soon creeps into what we start to pursue. We think that if we had a better career path, more money, and a better lifestyle we would finally be happy. Yet this only leads to wanting more.

What Paul says, in this Scripture, is that he has learned the secret of being content. This means that he sees something others may not. It's a matter of perspective. When we are able to value relationship over circumstance, love over material things, and eternal over temporal, we have learned the secret of contentment.

Thank you, Jesus, for reminding me that relationship, love, and eternity are more important than anything else. Teach me contentment in all circumstances.

What have you been unsettled about lately? Bring some eternal perspective to it.

wiser

Wise people can also listen and learn;
even they can find good advice in these words.
PROVERBS 1:5 NCV

Ask any teacher who their best students are and they will say those who want to learn. It doesn't matter so much about an individual's intelligence or aptitude, it is almost always about attitude. This is the best way to think about wisdom.

We might associate wise with intelligent, but the Scripture here says that wise people are still listening and learning. The attitude of a wise person is that there is always something more to learn, and there is good advice yet to discover. Instead of wishing you were wise, or thinking you are wise enough, keep your heart open to listening and learning from Scripture. Find advice in the living Word of God.

Almighty God, I praise you as the Creator of this universe— the one who knows exactly how everything fits together. Help me to trust that I can find your wisdom in Scripture and in other followers of you. Give me opportunities to welcome good advice into my life.

What can you listen and learn about from the Scriptures this week?

generational wisdom

*Listen, my son, to your father's instruction
and do not forsake your mother's teaching.
They are a garland to grace your head
and a chain to adorn your neck.*
PROVERBS 1:8-9 NIV

Remember when you thought your parents knew nothing? They couldn't relate to your experience, they didn't know how tough it was to grow up in the environment that you had. And then you got older, and will likely get accused for the same thing. It's not that generations before us don't understand what we are going through, it's that they do understand, and they want to protect us from making the same mistakes and falling into the same difficulties they did.

Make an effort to listen to that older person who is giving you advice about your life. Perhaps there is some simple beauty to what they are saying; it might even be just the thing you need at the right moment. Accept wisdom, and beauty will follow.

Lord, thank you for my parents, and other older people, who have gone through life's experiences before me. Help me to graciously accept the advice they give with an understanding that it could help me. Thank you for the insight of the generation before me. Give them confidence to pass on their wisdom.

What teaching or instruction have you been receiving from the older people in your life?

good guidance

He who heeds discipline shows the way to life,
but whoever ignores correction leads others astray.

PROVERBS 10:17 NIV

Picture the sheep being guided by the shepherd. When it begins to wander, the shepherd will gently use his rod to steer it in the right direction. If the sheep still doesn't correct itself, the shepherd will have to use more force. Occasionally, the sheep might get completely off course, and this could distract other sheep who will easily follow the wrong path.

This is how the Bible likens our spiritual journey. Jesus will always gently guide us, but when we start to resist, the guiding might feel a bit more painful: not because Jesus is being forceful, but because we are resisting. No one likes correction. It can be painful, embarrassing, and humbling, but it is far better to heed the gentle correction than to wander down a path that God never intended you to go down. Be encouraged to listen to your loving shepherd today.

Good Shepherd, I sense your gentle guiding of my paths each day. Help me to go with your guidance and not to resist your gentle correction when I begin to walk astray. Let me always trust in your leading rather than my own understanding.

In what ways are you prone to go off course? How is Jesus getting your attention to get you back on track again?

patient understanding

Whoever is patient has great understanding,
but one who is quick-tempered displays folly.
PROVERBS 14:29 NIV

Have you ever found yourself being more patient with a stranger than with your friends or family? For some reason we seem to be able to let the stranger go in front of us at the supermarket or smile when a child pushes past us. But we don't seem to have the same courtesy or politeness for our family who get in the way! Nor do we seem to hold it together when our loved ones lose their temper or say something unkind. Remind yourself of this next time your temper threatens to take over your patience.

When you stay calm and choose to give others an opportunity to express themselves, you might also give yourself the opportunity to hear their heart and the reason behind their actions and words. Remember the grace that Christ has equipped you with and try to reflect this same grace to your nearest and dearest.

Lord, give me the ability to keep myself calm in those times when others are really pushing me to anger. Give me wisdom and insight as I choose to listen rather than react.

How have you shown grace to a loved one lately? How can you stop to consider what their heart is really expressing?

extinguish the fire

A gentle answer will calm a person's anger,
but an unkind answer will cause more anger.

PROVERBS 15:1 NCV

Have you mastered the art of making a fire? Even if you haven't done it yourself, you will know that fire needs kindling and a bit of oxygen before it starts to really take off. As you feed the fire, you cause it to grow and become stronger. This is how the Scriptures liken our response to anger.

If we response with anger or defensiveness and show no grace, it will add just the right elements to make that person even more upset. Think of the last time you had an argument and how hard it was to control things from getting worse. If we can take a moment to pause, keep calm, and respond with grace and gentleness, we will help to calm the other person. It's worth trying.

Jesus, I know that you respond to me with patience and grace when I am angry. When I am confronted with someone else's anger, give me self-control so I can respond in peace and be part of the solution in putting the fire out.

Can you think of ways to respond the next time you are confronted with someone's anger? Having a strategy before the scenario happens can help prepare you for a good response.

well timed

A person finds joy in giving an apt reply—
and how good is a timely word!
PROVERBS 15:23 NIV

There are situations in life where you feel lost for words. Often this is in moments of deep grief, sudden shock, or extreme surprise. Overwhelming emotions can be hard to express and when someone shares these emotions with us, we don't always know how to reply. The Bible speaks a lot about being slow to speak, so God doesn't expect us to know what to say immediately.

An appropriate response to someone doesn't have to be quick, it's just good if it's timely. The next time you find yourself lost for words, give yourself time to think and pray about a response. There's wisdom in letting the Holy Spirit guide you with encouraging words. Think of the joy you can bring to someone, perhaps not instantly, but in time, with the right words.

Holy Spirit, give me words to share with those who need to hear some encouragement or wisdom. Thank you that I don't need to come up with the right things to say, but that you give me time to ponder an appropriate response. May my words to others be filled with insight and hope.

When was the last time you felt like you weren't able to give an appropriate reply? Ask God to give you some encouraging words for that person—perhaps now is the right time for them to hear it!

the dam

Starting a quarrel is like breaching a dam;
so drop the matter before a dispute breaks out.
PROVERBS 17:14 NIV

The picture of breaching a dam is quite an impacting way to consider what happens when we start arguments with others. Often our small quarrels don't seem that offensive or harmful, but each small thing can contribute toward building layers of negative feelings that ultimately burst when you keep trying to argue or defend your point of view.

It's worth stopping to consider if it is really that important that you win the argument. The Scriptures seem to think that it's better to let it go than to let a full dispute take place. Being a peacemaker isn't always easy, but if you give it some long term perspective, you may be able to see that it is better to lose an argument than to lose a friend.

God of peace, give me the same spirit of serenity so that I have the strength of character to let go of an argument even though I think I am right. May peace and love come before my need to be justified.

Can you think of an argument or disagreement that you are trying to win right now? Are you willing to let go of it for the sake of peace and friendship?

being supportive

A friend is always loyal,
and a brother is born to help in time of need.
PROVERBS 17:17 NLT

God's design of community is worth reminding yourself of when you are feeling either exasperated by people or entirely alone. We were created to have relationships and ultimately this is why we have families and friends. We are naturally drawn to talk, share, laugh, play, and work with one another. As everyone has experienced, however, relationships are hard work. Sometimes friends are not loyal, and sometimes brothers do not help.

Perhaps you have been that friend or sibling who hasn't been able to provide the loyalty or help to the other. Our relationships need the healing work of Jesus Christ in order to relate well. Think of that friend, brother, or sister who needs you right now, and ask Jesus to give you the right attitude to offer them just what they need.

Jesus, I admit that I haven't always been there for my friend or family member. I get so caught up in my own life that I don't show the right love or support for them. Forgive me, and help me reach out to them today so I can be part of your restorative plan for all people.

What can you do to support a friend or person in your family today?

insults

A brother who has been insulted
is harder to win back than a walled city,
and arguments separate people
like the barred gates of a palace.
PROVERBS 18:19 NCV

Dealing with insult is one of the harder things to overcome. We are easily hurt by people's accusations and criticisms because they cut to the core of our self-worth. Perhaps you are currently experiencing the pain from someone's lack of charity and graciousness toward you. It's even harder when those insults come from someone that you have loved and trusted—a family member or close friend. Take some time to reflect on what you have done with that pain.

These Scriptures are God's words to you, and he knows that we tend to put up walls and create separations to avoid the pain again. What walls have you built around yourself, and how can you let the healing love of Christ into your heart? It's okay to create space from those who hurt you, but allow Jesus in. He is safe and will provide the care that you need in order to heal.

Jesus, I know that I have built walls so I don't get hurt by people. I ask that you gently guide me to break down the walls that don't need to be there and build pathways to let people in who truly love and care for me. Thank you for understanding my heartache. I invite you to come and heal the brokenness.

What insults and arguments have taken a toll on your heart?
Give yourself space to reflect on those and let Christ's love
guide you into the right steps toward healing.

loyal

One who has unreliable friends soon comes to ruin,
but there is a friend who sticks closer than a brother.
PROVERBS 18:24 NIV

When you read this verse, what person comes to mind? You may be thinking of someone who has been very unreliable or perhaps you are smiling at the thought of that one friend who feels even closer to you than your own family. Relationships are a blessing, and it's worth taking the time to consider what friends are encouraging you and what friends are not.

We can still be hospitable and charitable toward those friends and acquaintances who have not been loyal, we just need to be cautious when it comes to having expectations of them. As for those friends who have proven their loyalty and unconditional love for you, keep them close and find ways to be a blessing to them.

Faithful God, thank you that you have led the way and shown me what unconditional love really looks like. May I be a friend that is able to show that kind of loyalty to those who are really close to me. Bless my friends who show me this same kind of loyalty. Thank you so much for bringing them into my life.

What about your own loyalty? Are you loving your friends unconditionally?

may

"Lord, help us, your servants, to speak your word without fear. Show us your power to heal. Give proofs and make miracles happen by the power of Jesus, your holy servant."

ACTS 4:29-30 NCV

poverty

One who is gracious to a poor man lends to the LORD,
and He will repay him for his good deed.

PROVERBS 19:17 NASB

People can be poor in many ways. In our environment, we may not come across true poverty or see homeless people in our day-to-day lives. But there are those who suffer from poverty of joy, hope, and love. There are those around you, even today, who are hurting from their lack of being loved by someone or suffering from despair.

Ask the Holy Spirit to show you those who are poor in spirit and find a way to bring grace into their situation. It might be practical help, a kind word, or an invitation out for coffee. Let the grace that dwells in you be poured out on those around you and know that your heavenly Father will be overjoyed that you are sharing his love.

Holy Spirit, may I be aware of the people around me today who are suffering some form of emotional or spiritual poverty. Give me an opportunity to extend hope, joy, and love toward them.

In what ways and forms have you seen poverty in the people around you? Consider the ways that you can lend to the poor.

go get it!

Those who get wisdom do themselves a favor,
and those who love learning will succeed.
PROVERBS 19:8 NCV

We might think of wisdom as something that comes naturally to some people, or maybe it comes with cumulative experience over time. Both of those could be true, but this Scripture also says that wisdom is something that we can go and get. It's as if we have to know where to get it and have it ready for when we need it. When we ask God for a wisdom, he is ready to give it, but perhaps it's a good challenge for us to learn and actively pursue ways of knowing how to make good decisions.

What might you do when your child is rebelling, for example, or when money is tight? How do you make the decision between what job or course to take? The Bible has a lot to say about wisdom. Do yourself a favor and learn about it.

Wise and loving God, I know that you will always help me in times of need, but I also know that you are encouraging me to learn about your ways in those times when I am not feeling desperate. Remind me to search your Word for wisdom, so I am prepared for when those times come.

What situations are you facing, or might you face, that will require a lot of wisdom? How can you go and find wisdom?

good guarding

Above all else, guard your heart,
for everything you do flows from it.
PROVERBS 4:23 NIV

The pictures of guards outside the Queen's palace seems a little strong when it comes to matters of the heart. Yet consider the role of those guards. They are there to carefully watch who comes in and out of the gates and to make sure that nothing harmful can enter. Though they seem serious and tough, they are positioned to keep royalty safe. God created you from the inside out, and he knows how precious your heart is. You are royalty to him, and you need to be protected.

Be careful about what you let into your heart because what goes in will eventually come out. If you let light and love in, then your decisions, behaviors, and relationships will be influenced by this very same goodness. Be encouraged to read something positive and uplifting today, and let your heart be strengthened with the kindness of Jesus.

Precious Jesus, I know that you care deeply about my heart. May I continue to guard myself from any form of darkness that would seek to creep in. I ask your Holy Spirit to guide me into all things pure and right so that my heart overflows with goodness.

What can you do today to ensure that you let God's goodness into your heart? What can you do to better protect your heart?

gentle persuasion

*Use patience and kindness when you want to persuade leaders
and watch them change their minds right in front of you.
For your gentle wisdom will quell the strongest resistance.*
PROVERBS 25:15 TPT

Many of us find ourselves having to work for leaders, managers, or directors daily. It's not that easy to be the front person. Because of this, leaders will often build safety walls around them that are hard to break. Maybe you have a boss or person in leadership who you would love to see change a few things around your school, workplace, or church. This proverb is great in these situations. Don't go in with your complaints, grumbling and protesting. This will only make them resist you more.

Instead, ask God to give you patience and kindness. Speak to your leaders with respect and understanding. You might be surprised at how quickly they can change their minds when they feel you are on their side.

Jesus, thank you for the leaders that you have placed in my life. Help me to respect their position and how difficult it must be for them to lead people. Season my words with grace and care. Give me the courage to speak in a way that brings forth positive change.

What leaders are you struggling with right now? Bring them to God in prayer and ask for his grace and wisdom to speak with them.

pitfalls

The one whose walk is blameless is kept safe,
but the one whose ways are perverse will fall into the pit.
PROVERBS 28:18 NIV

Do you ever catch yourself analyzing and discussing what kind of mess people are going to end up in? When people are walking around in darkness, they are unable to see for themselves where it will lead them. We don't need to be the judge of the outcomes of poor decisions. Things that are not right will ultimately end up, as the Bible says, in the pit.

Our job is not to judge those in darkness but to ensure that we stay connected to the light source, so our path is lit well enough to be kept safe from falling into pits. It's better to avoid the fall rather than climb back out. Be encouraged that the Holy Spirit is ever present to guide you in the path of righteousness. Lean into the promptings of his Word.

Good Shepherd, I trust in you as my constant guide and companion, guiding me in the right paths so I do not make mistakes that lead me into a pit. May I always follow the light that leads me to you.

Where have you been tempted to go astray lately? How can you ensure you are able to stay on the right path?

settle down

Be angry, and do not sin;
ponder in your own hearts on your beds and be silent.

PSALM 4:4 ESV

When was the last time you said or did something in the heat of the moment that you later regretted? It happens in family life a lot and sometimes in our classrooms and workplaces. There are a lot of reasons why people can make us angry, and sometimes our anger is justifiable. Yet Scriptures tell us that we can't let that anger lead to sin.

The writer goes further to give us a good strategy: get away from the situation, go to a quiet space, sit still, be silent, and let your heart and mind settle. Express your heart to Jesus; he can handle everything you have to vent about the situation. Sometimes it's good to hear your own words and explanations without the rebuttals of the other person. Allow God into that situation so he can bring peace to your heart.

Jesus, I allow you into my heart right now so I can be ready for those situations that have been making me angry. Help me to remember the wisdom of walking away to somewhere peaceful when my emotions are getting the best of me.

Where is the safe and quiet place that you are able to get away to in the times you are most angry? Remember that place the next time you are caught up in an angry moment.

acceptable

Let the words of my mouth and the meditation of my heart
be acceptable to you, O LORD, my rock and my redeemer.

PSALM 19:14 ESV

You have probably had to submit an assignment for school at some time in your life. Often there is a lot of research and reading before putting things into your own words. It feels vulnerable when you submit your best work and have to wait to see if it's acceptable to a teacher. It might feel a little like that when you consider whether your words and heart are acceptable to God.

You might be inclined to think of the rotten things you have said and done and worry that he won't accept you. The writer of this Psalm would not have felt perfect either. It's simply an expression of the desire to do the right thing. The heart's intention is what matters to God; from a place of humility, he is given access to be your rock and redeemer.

O Lord, my rock and my redeemer, let the words of my mouth and the meditation of my heart be acceptable to you.

What words and feelings have you been expressing lately? Share them with God and let him redeem you.

restored confidence

Be my rock of refuge, to which I can always go;
give the command to save me,
for you are my rock and my fortress.
For you have been my hope, Sovereign LORD,
my confidence since my youth.

PSALM 71:3, 5 NIV

The people of Israel had been through a lot of hardship and although there was certainly some grumbling and doubts about it, they were also shown God's faithfulness throughout. This is why the psalmist is able to say that God is a rock and fortress, a safe place where we can always go. It might take a few tough experiences to recognize that God is always on your side.

You might be in the middle of some troubling times. Take a moment to think back through the years about other trials that you have come out of. Are you able to see God's faithfulness as he took your hand to guide you out? Be encouraged to regain that confidence in God's favor and love towards you. He longs to be your safe place, the one who will always stand firmly beside you.

God, I choose to take my refuge in you, today. I need help as I face these battles of life and I know you will never fail to stand before me, and alongside me. Fill me with hope and confidence for a better day.

What trials are you facing right now? Approach those difficulties with the confidence that the Lord is on your side.

undivided

Teach me your way, Lord, that I may rely on your faithfulness;
give me an undivided heart, that I may fear your name.

PSALM 86:11 NIV

Do you ever have those times when you are trying to make a decision with a big group of people and it seems to take forever to figure out a plan? Having a lot of differing opinions can be stressful and chaotic. Our hearts are divided like this when we fill them up with all kinds of distractions.

We aren't often careful enough to weed out the things that are competing for our affection and devotion. This can mean when it comes to making right decisions, we are pulled in many directions. Jesus, our Good Shepherd, has promised to guide us into paths of righteousness. We just need to be willing to devote our hearts to his words and teaching, and he will remain faithful in leading us into all of his promises.

Teach me your way, Lord, that I may rely on your faithfulness; give me an undivided heart, that I may fear your name.

What are some things that have come into your heart that are competing with your affection and devotion to Jesus?

even before that

Your eyes saw my unformed body;
all the days ordained for me were written in your book
before one of them came to be.

PSALM 139:16 NIV

We celebrate our birthdays as the day that our fully formed body came into the world and we breathed our first breath. Birthdays mark the beginning of our lives, but in this Scripture, God was celebrating you long before your birthday. He saw you before you were even formed; he knew that you were destined for life, even before that first breath. What an amazing God we have, who is not only all-knowing, but ever personal.

Take courage and strength from the truth that you were destined from the beginning and you have a wonderful purpose. Whatever you may be about to face in your day, hold your head high and remember the one who created you for such a time as this.

Heavenly Creator, thank you for affirming my existence. You are all knowing and awesome, and yet you cared about my little unformed body—my existence even before anyone on earth acknowledged it. Thank you for paying all that attention just to me.

How can the knowledge of God's total attention on you change the way you step into your day?

powerful virtues

Do you think lightly of the riches of His kindness and tolerance and patience, not knowing that the kindness of God leads you to repentance?

ROMANS 2:4 NASB

We tend to think of kindness, tolerance, and patience as some of the softer emotions. Consider however, the tolerance of a mother giving birth to a newborn, sacrificing her body and emotions for the love of a child. Think of the patience of a sister who sits alongside her sibling in the darkest days of her depression. Think of a daughter who cares diligently for her dying parent.

None of those actions are soft or meek. Kindness, tolerance, and patience can be fiercely, fervently, and powerfully loving. These Scriptures suggest that God's kindness, tolerance, and patience is exactly that—powerful enough to lead us to change our ways and never look back. This is nothing to think lightly of; it is life changing!

Almighty God, thank you so much for your kindness toward me. Make me stronger because of it. Thank you for your tolerance. May I be more accepting by experiencing it. Thank you for your patience. Help me to be compelled to change through understanding it. Help me to see the power in your gentleness.

In what ways are the attributes of God compelling you to change?

his strength

Look to the LORD and his strength;
seek his face always.
1 CHRONICLES 16:11 NIV

Our natural instinct is to cry out to God in a panic and desperately search for him when we find ourselves in crisis. However, we don't have to panic or feel distressed in the face of the unknown. We can just ask him for help and he will be faithful to meet us. His strength is readily available. We can know the joy of his presence and the comfort and stability of his faithfulness.

God calms our racing and anxious thoughts with truth. He offers us wisdom and direction in the middle of decision making. He pierces the darkness that preys on us with his light. He fills us with gratitude and thanksgiving and renews our faith. He breathes bravery into our weak and timid souls.

God, let my eyes be on you always so I can find joy in your presence and so I don't stumble and fall during difficult times. You keep me steady; you make me courageous.

Do you draw strength from God both in times of need and in times of peace?

everlasting peace

God is not a God of confusion but a God of peace.
1 CORINTHIANS 14:33 NCV

There are generally two types of decision makers. The first analyzes every angle and weighs every part of the decision carefully and slowly. They don't rush into anything. The second make decisions quickly and confidently. They depend on gut feelings rather than studying the situation. Neither decision maker is wrong in how they approach decisions because we are wired differently. But what happens after a decision is made?

When we make a decision that aligns with God's heart, peace is always present because he is peace. However, when we make a decision that may not be of God, confusion and uncertainly almost always remain. To have confidence in our choices, we need to know God and his peace that goes beyond our logical understanding.

Jesus, in every decision I make, may it be with you in the forefront of my mind and heart. May you bless it with peace and clarity, so I have assurance that you are present in the details.

What kind of decision maker are you? Do you measure a good decision by the sense of peace that does or does not follow?

restoration and grace

The God of all grace, who called you to his eternal glory in Christ, after you have suffered a little while, will himself restore you and make you strong, firm and steadfast.

1 Peter 5:10 NIV

In the middle of hardships and struggles, it is almost impossible to see how our hurt can be redeemed. Our focus is on our distress. We cry out for God to take away our suffering and pain, impatient for him to release us from feeling uncomfortable. We may even be angry that he didn't intervene when we desperately wanted him to.

He uses these times of pain to refine us. He takes what is broken and makes it new. He redeems and restores. Suffering is temporary; however, the work he does in us is eternal. It is his infinite grace that encourages us to be brave and persevere. We are thankful for hardships because in them we can find purpose and reward.

God, help me to surrender my struggles, knowing that in them you are doing great work in me. I can rejoice even in hard times knowing that you have a purpose for me.

Do you believe that God can meet you in your storms? And that when the rain dies down and the clouds clear that you will be stronger?

genuine servanthood

"Only fear the Lord and serve him faithfully with all your heart. For consider what great things he has done for you."

1 Samuel 12:24 esv

It's good to question where our servanthood comes from. Does it come out of a genuine desire to honor God, love him, and respect him? Because we want to truly please him? Do we serve wholeheartedly, joyously and willingly because we feel compelled to out of a thankful heart? Or does it come out of selfish ambition? A hope for reward or good favor?

No matter how we try, it is impossible to earn God's adoration. We should serve him because we are so thankful for the things he has already done. We should dedicate our lives to God out of adoration and reverence. Our heart response to his goodness is a genuine desire to serve the one who loves us so well.

Lord, may my motivation to serve you only come from knowing and experiencing all the wonderful ways you have already loved me. May my devotion to you be without selfish ambition.

Do you serve God out of a sense of duty or obligation? Or because you are overwhelmed with his love and desire to please him?

jars of clay

We have this treasure in jars of clay to show that this all-surpassing power is from God and not from us. We are hard pressed on every side, but not crushed; perplexed, but not in despair; persecuted, but not abandoned; struck down, but not destroyed.

2 CORINTHIANS 4:7-9 NIV

Jars of clay are delicate. They are made from the soil under our feet and molded with water. Clay is not an extravagant or costly material. It is dull and lacks luster. Clay jars break and crumble easily under the pressure of a strong hand. They are vulnerable to elements like heat and rain.

We are jars of clay. Sometimes we embark on situations feeling like we are inadequate, incapable, and weak. The truth is that without the power of God in our lives, we are fragile, easily broken, and destroyed. But still God chooses us. He chooses us in our weakness, in our fragility, and in our shortcomings. He chooses us despite our flaws and imperfections. We are more than dirt and dust, more than molded clay when we have God in our lives. It doesn't matter what comes our way to fracture or shatter us; he makes us unbreakable. We remain intact and he gets the glory.

Jesus, without you I am weak and easily broken. I am left vulnerable to those who want to hurt me. You are my treasure, the reason why no matter what happens against me, I am not destroyed. May my life be a testimony of your power.

Do you know how strong and valuable the treasure of Jesus Christ is in you?

spiritual hunger

Like newborn babies, crave pure spiritual milk,
so that by it you may grow up in your salvation.
2 PETER 3:18 NIV

If you have ever taken a minute to observe a hungry infant, you have seen just how desperate they can be. It doesn't matter if a bottle is delayed by one minute or ten, the reaction of hunger holds the same intensity. The need to eat is relentless and demanding. The cry for food is most often loud, angry, and repetitive. The craving so strong that their natural instinct is to fight for it.

As soon as they taste milk on their lips, though, they quiet and relax. Soon after their need to eat is satisfied, they surrender to a peaceful sleep. They are content, because in that moment they were fed. Milk is essential to every part of a baby's healthy development. Our need for the Lord's Word is akin to that of an infant's need for milk. We are dependent on it for survival, and yet we have become accustomed to pacifying that need with other distractions. How strong would our faith be if we took the spiritual food that our souls crave? God wants us to be strong, to be healthy, and to be fed.

Lord, grow in me a hunger for you that is only satisfied by you. Let me feed upon your Word, on your truths, on your presence, so I can be strong and healthy.

Do you crave God's Word? Or are you pacifying the need in other ways?

a new spirit

*God gave us a spirit not of fear
but of power and love and self-control.*
2 TIMOTHY 1:7 ESV

We experience a range of emotions every day, sometimes even hour by hour. Grief can be followed by immense joy, and love can be contrasted with unbridled anger. We grow accustomed to these varying feelings and accept them as a normal part of life. As we grow, we mature in our ability to control and understand emotions.

But what about fear? Fear is an emotion both difficult to control and understand. To what extent does fear have a place in our lives? There is a vast difference between feeling fear, and it being an intricate part of our being. When fear propels our steps, and weighs us down, we become ensnared by it. God gently reminds us that fear is not from him and it has no room to live in our spirits. Rather, he gave us a spirit of power, of love, and of self-control.

Jesus, thank you for giving me a spirit filled with power, love, and self-control. When I feel fear seizing my heart, and it threatens to control my steps, please remind me of who I am in you and the power you have given me.

Are you living filled with power, self-control, and love from God? Or are you living controlled by fear?

peace wins

You will keep him in perfect peace,
whose mind is stayed on You,
because he trusts in You.
ISAIAH 26:3 NKJV

Fear and peace cannot co-exist. It is impossible. One fills us with unease and anxiety. It feeds off difficult situations. The other allows us to rest and breathe deeply despite our situations. Perfect peace is a doorway to joy and true contentment. In order to experience perfect peace, it is crucial to trust God, to be obedient to his teachings, and to take hope in his promises. Without fully trusting him, true peace is impossible to grasp.

God is the King of peace. When fear, doubt, and worry rear their ugly heads, the only way to drive them away is with God's peace. It does not eliminate the hardships, but it gives us the courage to survive them. His peace sustains us through every difficult situation that is heavy laden with anxiety and fear. It even allows joy to grow where it seems impossible.

God, multiply my faith so that my trust is grounded in only you. Defeat any fear in my life with your perfect peace. May my eyes be on you and only you.

Are you constantly wavering between peace and fear? Do you trust in God completely to carry you through every trial you face?

his lamb

He tends his flock like a shepherd:
He gathers the lambs in his arms
and carries them close to his heart;
he gently leads those that have young.

ISAIAH 40:11 NIV

It can be difficult to fathom why the King of the universe wants to know and care for us. We are so small. But he is not a distant God. He doesn't keep his people at arm's length. He pulls us in close and carries us tightly in his arms. He keeps us safe and runs after us when we have wandered too far. He tends to our every need, ensuring we aren't hungry, cold, thirsty, or alone.

Unlike a domineering master, he wants to have a close and intimate relationship with us. One where he takes care of us and we trust him to. He doesn't watch over us because he has to but because he finds joy in spending time with us. Enjoy being with him today.

God, I find so much comfort in how much you love me— how you watch over me and take care of me. Thank you.

How do you view God? As a strict and controlling master, or as a friend who wants nothing more than to draw you close?

security

"For the mountains may depart and the hills be removed, but my steadfast love shall not depart from you, and my covenant of peace shall not be removed," says the Lord, who has compassion on you.
ISAIAH 54:10 ESV

Often we put our security in things we can see, feel, and trust. We depend on a consistent salary to feed our bodies and keep a roof over our heads. We watch our bank accounts grow and feel confident when we have healthy savings. We have an insurance policy for every possible tragedy and unforeseen loss. We count our friendships and are comforted with their relationships. It is easy to trust what is right in front of us, but none of these offer real security. We can lose positions, our bank accounts aren't immune to depletion, and friendships often fade over time.

The only secure thing we can trust and depend on is our relationship with God. He promises that his love and his peace will always be available to us. We can trust that in any hard circumstance, he sees us, and he will bring us through. He gives us the ability to remain standing when the floor is ripped out from underneath us because his hand is always steadying us.

God, help me to see that the security the world offers pales in comparison to the security you give me. Thank you for being the one I can trust and depend on throughout difficulties and hardships.

Who is your heart secure in? Is it in materials you can see, or the Father who sees you and loves you beyond your imagination?

soft clay

O Lord, you are our Father.
We are the clay, and you are the potter.
We all are formed by your hand.
ISAIAH 64:8 NLT

We are often our own worst critics. We look at the hidden places within and are ashamed. Our imperfections and shortcomings are both glaring and discouraging. We wonder how we can be used by God when we don't measure up? Guilt and shame can be consuming. We don't feel worthy, and we beat ourselves up over who we aren't. We want to be stronger, better.

God is not done with us. We are a work in progress. He is slowly and carefully crafting us in his image—molding us day by day, into who he wants us to be. We can surrender under his craftsmanship, trusting his hands, and leaning fully into the process of sanctification. We can position ourselves to be under his love and skill and be restored in his timing. He won't take his hands off the clay until he is finished.

Lord, it helps to remember that you are carefully crafting me in your image every day. Thank you for your careful and detailed work in my life. Help me to be patient under your hands and to love myself the way you do.

Do you become frustrated with the slow process of sanctification? Take hope. He is not done with you. You can trust the potter's hands.

faithfulness

"Whoever can be trusted with very little can also be trusted with much, and whoever is dishonest with very little will also be dishonest with much."
LUKE 16:10 NIV

We tend to rate the work of God. There are some things we don't naturally or eagerly jump at the chance to serve in. Maybe they are mundane and boring, or extra dirty and uncomfortable. Maybe we feel capable of more, so we scoff at less, and we gravitate to the things that seem more prestigious. It's not exciting to always work behind the scenes.

We need to prove that we are able and willing to be faithful in the seemingly insignificant, mundane, simple tasks. We need to take those things God asks of us and give them our full attention and effort. They need to hold just as much value to us as the bigger things. God cares more about the integrity and character that is shown in our work than the grandeur of the task. If we desire to be given more responsibility, it is vital for us to demonstrate that we can be dependable and trustworthy in everything we do.

Lord, help me to see your value in both the little and big things. I strive to be faithful in every task that you give me so I can be of good service to you in whatever you ask of me.

Are you frustrated that you don't serve in a bigger capacity? Are you faithful in every area of your work?

one master

"No one can serve two masters. Either you will hate the one and love the other, or you will be devoted to the one and despise the other. You cannot serve both God and money."

MATTHEW 6:24 NIV

A good reflection of our loyalty is a summary of how we spend our time. Are we focused on loving God and serving others well? Or is our time spent chasing down the riches of the world and satisfying our wants and needs? It is good to ask ourselves what consumes our time, our energy, and our focus? What consumes our heart and our time is ultimately who we are serving.

Our energy cannot be equally divided. Nor do we have the capacity to wholeheartedly serve the Lord and our own ambitions. One will surely win over the other. God battles for our loyalty. He wants all of our devotion, all of our time, all of our hearts. Too often he gets what is left over: a meager piece, if that. The appeals of this world are strong, but his appeal for our hearts is stronger.

God, you can have all of me. Consume my energy, my time, and my focus. My life is yours. I am completely devoted to you.

Where does your heart lie? Are you exhausting yourself trying to serve two masters?

surrender and rest

"Come to me, all you who are weary and burdened, and I will give you rest. Take my yoke upon you and learn from me, for I am gentle and humble in heart, and you will find rest for your souls. For my yoke is easy and my burden is light."

MATTHEW 11:28-30 NIV

When we are faced with a problem our first instinct is to grab it and not let it go. We have this belief that if we hold onto it tightly, we have some sense of control. Often that sense is false. It creates anxiety and lets fear flourish. The more we struggle to hold on, the harder the situation becomes, and the more exhausting the fight.

The attitude that God wants us to have toward our problems is one of bravery. He asks us to choose surrender over having control. A huge part of that brave choice is having faith in him. By surrendering our fears and letting go of worry, we are trusting God. We can relax our grip, lift our eyes and hands to the sky, and breathe. No problem is too big or too difficult for God to handle. When we trust him, we can finally rest.

God when I am faced with a crisis, help me turn my face to you. Help me to let go of my worries and surrender my fears to your power. I trust you enough to let go.

Do you trust God in every aspect of your life to surrender even those difficult parts to him?

a peaceful community

Does your life in Christ give you strength? Does his love comfort you?
Do we share together in the spirit? Do you have mercy and kindness?
PHILIPPIANS 2:1 NCV

Community is beautiful. To be welcomed into a family of believers, encouraged, and loved is a unique gift. But to love in close proximity to others can also be a great challenge. Differences in opinion have the potential to cause separation and divide any close relationship. It is possible to disagree with each other and still hold our friends in high regard. If we are truly experiencing God's love, we are able to mirror his heart.

Our attitudes toward others become shaped by his character. Because of his love, affection, and compassion toward us, we are able to reflect those actions. We are shown how to set aside our selfishness and be focused on loving those around us. We are taught how to give life to compassion and empathy. We're encouraged to choose kindness over arrogance. If we wear humility as a crown and chose to listen and understand rather than fight and argue, we will become closer to those around us.

God, may the compassion and kindness you show me overflow out of me onto others. Help me to treasure my community and to seek peace and unity in all my relationships, especially those that are more difficult.

Does your community embody kindness and compassion, and is that evident to everyone? How are you able to love your friends better?

abandoned masks

Let your gentleness be evident to all.
The Lord is near.
PHILIPPIANS 4:5 NIV

Generally, every strong emotion we have is a mask for another underlying emotion we have stirring within us. For example, anger can be a mask for fear, or irritability and impatience a mask for anxiety. These masks are often a way we try to protect ourselves from being vulnerable.

If we don't trust God, and allow him to fill us with his peace, these emotions will take control of us. They can damage relationships and push people away. No one wants to be around someone who is always angry, short tempered, or disagreeable. When we allow God to be close, when we allow him to invade our lives and sustain our hearts, our hardness is softened. Suddenly the masks are no longer needed. The gentleness of God that is within us becomes evident to all.

Lord, when I feel heavy with ugly emotions, help me to bring my cares to you. I trust you to fill me with peace and transform my hard heart into a soft one.

Are you wearing masks to protect yourself? What emotions can you give to God today?

joy thief

Do not be anxious about anything, but in every situation, by prayer and petition, with thanksgiving, present your requests to God. And the peace of God, which transcends all understanding, will guard your hearts and your minds in Christ Jesus.

PHILIPPIANS 4:6-7 NIV

Anxiety can make a person physically or mentally ill. It has a subtle way of overtaking rational thoughts. It eats away security and confidence. It can be debilitating and interfere with our ability to make wise decisions. It is also a joy thief. It interferes with the goodness in our life and replaces it with deep seeded fear. It is a liar. It wants us to feel like we have no control over our thoughts.

We are never at anxiety's mercy when we have our hearts and minds focused on Jesus. He encourages us to come to him and share our worries and fears with him. He gives us a peace that is more powerful than our fears. We can trust him and let his peace overcome every anxiety planted. He is our greatest confidant—our trusted and true friend.

Jesus, you encourage me to come to you when I am worried, so you can protect my mind from anxiety and fear. I am thankful that your peace fills me and allows me to breathe deeply, free from the anxiety that presses in.

Who do you turn to when you feel anxiety and worry? Do you know that you are not powerless to thoughts of worry and that God's intention for you is to be filled with deep peace?

deep contentment

I have learned to be content in whatever circumstances I am.
PHILIPPIANS 4:11 NASB

We can close our eyes and rest with ease when our worlds are in perfect harmony. It is easy to find peace in peaceful times. Happiness is at our fingertips and our steps are light and easy. In these seasons, it is effortless to raise our faces to the sky and say "Alleluia," and to declare his goodness. The struggle comes, though, when life isn't easy. When we are surrounded by heartbreak and disappointment. When grief feels suffocating, and hope seems so far away. When every day, even every moment seems impossible.

We forget in these times that true contentment, true joy, is still in our reach. We just have to open up our eyes and hearts to it. That seems easier said than done; however, when we learn to see joy in every circumstance, we are able to step bravely into each day set before us. Our circumstances do not define us; rather, joy becomes so rooted and engrained in who we are that finding peace becomes our second nature. True contentment, his genuine peace, cannot be easily shaken.

Jesus, you are my joy and my peace. And no matter what life throws at me, who you are, and what you promise is unchanging. I choose to look for you in every hard circumstance and be content. I am thankful that you sustain me through everything.

Is your contentment based on your present circumstances? Or is it rooted deeply in your faith in Christ?

a found love

I will show my love to those who passionately love me.
For they will search and search continually until they find me.
PROVERBS 8:17 TPT

God is mysterious and all encompassing. He is much bigger and more powerful than we can begin to understand. And yet, he doesn't hide himself from us. Not only is he present in our lives, he is patiently waiting for us to come to him. He is waiting to love on us. He wants us to know him in the same capacity that he knows us.

In order to search for him we need to slow down our busy bodies and minds, sit still in his presence, and listen carefully to him. When life is so busy, and full of so many things, it takes a great deal of discipline to carve time out in our day just to focus on our relationship with God. He is always there, always present, but sometimes we are too distracted to notice. It is in the quiet places that we are able to see him, feel him, and hear him. When we set our hearts out to search for him in these places, when we desire to know him intimately, and begin to look for him in everything, he reveals himself to us.

God, I want nothing more than to know who you are and the capacity of your great love for me. May my day be centered around seeking you, spending time with you, and listening to your voice. Be my quiet place.

Are you satisfied in your relationship with God? Do you desire to know him more intimately?

humble hearts

*When pride comes, then comes disgrace
but with humility comes wisdom.*

PROVERBS 11:2 NIV

Pride may present itself as a strength, but it is quite the opposite. Pride is isolating and limiting. It is also an easy characteristic to obtain, but such a hard one to let go of. In order to be humble and teachable, we are required to shed our pride, and that takes a great deal of courage. It is worth every growing pain and ache because the reward is so much greater.

Humility is an uncomfortable characteristic; it isn't something we obtain naturally. It asks us to be vulnerable—to share our weaknesses and be honest about our shortcomings. We have nothing to lose by choosing to sit still, quiet our hearts and minds, and remain teachable. When we are willing to keep ourselves open to be challenged and taught, we gain valuable insight and wisdom that we can then apply to our life, and our relationships. There is so much beauty and grace to be found in one's willingness to be humble.

Jesus, when I feel pride and arrogance toward others, please remind me to be humble and willing to learn. I desire my strengths to be in the ability to listen to others and admit when I may have made a mistake.

Do you desire wisdom in your life? Do you see how humility can be a strength?

june

"Be strong and do not lose courage,
for there is reward for your work."

2 CHRONICLES 15:7 NASB

a strong foundation

Those who fear the LORD are secure;
he will be a refuge for their children.
PROVERBS 14:26 NLT

Fearing God does not mean that grief, sadness or harm won't touch us, but it does ensure that we will remain secure in his love. When our hope is in him, nothing can defeat us. He is our refuge. He leads us through high waters and over crumbling rocks. We can trust him not to abandon us.

Fearing God doesn't mean that we should be afraid of him. He longs for us to honor him, respect him, and trust him. This type of fear keeps us close to him. Respecting God protects our steps. Honoring his Word helps us make wise decisions. Trusting him lays a foundation for a future that is strong and unbreakable.

God, may my days be spent honoring you and respecting your authority in my life. May my choices be layered with your wisdom.

Do you fear the Lord? What is your foundation made of? Is he your safe place?

destructive pride

*If you listen to constructive criticism,
you will be at home among the wise.
If you reject discipline, you only harm yourself;
but if you listen to correction, you grow in understanding.*
PROVERBS 15:31-32 NLT

A natural response to criticism is a swelling of our inner pride. Critical words can make our blood boil. We may want to reject the words immediately and turn our hearts away from the unpleasantness of the situation. It never feels good to be told that we are wrong, or that our approach could use some fine-tuning. We are quick to become defensive, so we avoid the insecurity all correction brings.

Criticism is a part of life and it can be used as a positive tool. If we can train ourselves to listen to the words of others, to let them encourage us to do better, to learn, to change, we are giving ourselves the gift of growth. If we constantly reject advice, we give pride the ability to harden our hearts, and we learn nothing. We don't grow. We don't obtain wisdom. We become stunted from our own inability and unwillingness to listen. Don't let pride become your stumbling block.

God, please help me to let others' correction be heard so I can grow in wisdom. Grow in me a humbleness that allows for stretching and maturing.

How do you react when you receive criticism? Are you slow to listen, or quick to reject correction?

the best medicine

A joyful heart is good medicine,
but a crushed spirit dries up the bones.
PROVERBS 17:22 ESV

Our emotions have a direct impact on our mental, physical, and spiritual health. When we choose to find joy even in pain and suffering, it has the capability of healing us. When joy infiltrates our hearts, the burden of suffering is lessened. Our pain takes on a different form and loses the ability to overtake every aspect of our life. We can breathe easier, laugh louder, and rest better.

Joy is closer to our reach than we think. It can be found when we mediate on God's goodness and provision in our lives. It can be found when we take the time to count our blessings and cultivate an attitude of thanksgiving. When we reach out our arms to those near us who are suffering, we can find joy in serving and loving others deeply. Joy is contagious, and its healing powers are endless.

God, you are joy. I invite you into every aspect of my life. Be the medicine my hurting heart desperately needs. I am grateful that you are the great physician.

Is your heart filled with overwhelming joy? Or is sorrow and misery crushing your spirit and making you sick?

blind faith

Trust in the LORD with all your heart
and do not lean on your own understanding.
In all your ways acknowledge Him,
and He will make your paths straight.
PROVERBS 3:5-6 NASB

When the whole trajectory of our lives suddenly changes, we may feel confused and like God has abandoned us. Everything that once made sense all of a sudden doesn't anymore. Sometimes it's difficult to see God in our suffering. He seems farthest away when we are hurting and confused.

We want someone to blame for our struggles and we want to make sense of the problems we are facing. So, we blame God. Where is he? Can't he see our suffering? Isn't he in control? Why didn't he prevent it? In our hurt we become angry with the one person who can comfort us. No matter what chaos and confusion is surrounding us, no matter how we make sense of what we are facing, we can trust that God is actively involved to help us, give us hope, and sustain us throughout it all.

Lord, when things just don't make sense, and I am struggling to find answers, please remind me of your kindness and your constant presence. Help me to trust you above all. Even when I don't have answers, my faith is in you.

Do you trust that God is in control even when he seems far away?

a strong weapon

A man without self-control
is like a city broken into and left without walls.

PROVERBS 25:28 ESV

Self-control is a powerful weapon. It keeps us from stepping into harm, from becoming entangled in sin. It helps us make wise decisions. It allows us to pause, to wait upon the Lord. It is a tool that God has graciously given to us, so we can be strong and protected in difficult in situations. Without self-control we open our hearts and minds to destruction and chaos. We will repeatedly stumble and fall. We become slaves to our fleshly desires. We are stripped of everything that makes us stand strong and protected.

We don't have to be enslaved to our impulses and chained to temptations and whims. We do not have to let our emotions and desires control us. We are given complete power and complete control. We are victorious against our impulses. When we seek self-control in our lives we become empowered to live a righteous and holy life for God. It is essential to living a life of freedom in him.

God, I want to serve you and only you. Thank you for giving me a spirit of self-control, and a way to defend myself.

Do you feel trapped by your impulses and emotions? Don't be discouraged or overwhelmed, you have been graciously given tools and the power to overcome.

true strength

Fools give full vent to their rage,
but the wise bring calm in the end.
PROVERBS 29:11 NIV

Strength is valuable and highly sought after. We admire strong people and aspire to be the strongest versions of ourselves. We invest in gym memberships and self-help courses. We look up to people who are outspoken and boisterous in the face of opposition. But what is the true definition of inner strength? It is much more than our muscle mass and confidence level. True strength can only be found in the character of God. He is mighty but he also gentle. He is kind and slow to anger.

Most often strength comes in the form of gentleness. It comes from the way we interact with people, especially those who are difficult to be around. Often gentleness requires a great deal of self-control and empathy. It asks us to hold our tongues and extend grace. It is often much harder to be gentle than it is to be the world's version strong. However, when we set our hearts to be like God, we are strong through our gentleness.

God, please help me to be gentle in all my interactions. Help me exercise self-control and to see every person the way you do. May my strength be in my ability to love others well.

Is responding to others with gentleness a struggle in your life?

tethered trust

The LORD defends those who suffer;
he defends them in times of trouble.
Those who know the LORD trust him,
because he will not leave those who come to him.

PSALM 9:9-10 NCV

When the weight of the world crushes our bones and dries up our souls, who or what do we look to for help? Sex, drugs, unwise spending, or unhealthy relationships? These end up being our undoing. They don't offer the same peace and healing that the Lord does. They promise to sustain us, but the relief is only temporary. And more often than not, they send us into a deeper spiral of destruction. These things increase our sense of hopelessness and hide us further into darkness.

God is our stronghold in times of need. If we ask him to sustain us when we are in trouble, he not only willingly opens his arms up, but he is also faithful to keep us unharmed. He grips onto us, promising never to let us go.

Lord, thank you for always being there when I need you. Thank you for being light and hope when darkness surrounds me. Cut off the strongholds that grip my soul, the addictions that overpower me, so I only look to you for help.

Who or what is your stronghold? Who is your trust
tethered to?

ability

God arms me with strength,
and he makes my way perfect.
He makes me as surefooted as a deer,
enabling me to stand on mountain heights.
He trains my hands for battle;
he strengthens my arm to draw a bronze bow.

PSALM 18:32-34 NLT

We aren't just children of God. We are his warriors, his conquers. That truth can be difficult to embrace. In the face of opposition we wonder, are we capable? Are we equipped? Are we able?

The God who calls us to the front lines, doesn't leave us vulnerable, he doesn't leave us to be bloodied and bruised. He goes before us. He puts weapons in our hands. In the middle of a battle, when we feel we aren't able, the one who battles for us all keeps us grounded. He breathes confidence in our souls. We can stand strong no matter what strength the enemy portrays because ultimately, we are stronger. He has trained us for these very moments.

Thank you, God, for being the one who fights ahead of me and behind me. I might quiver and shake, but you hold my hand steady.

What battles are you facing today? Do you know that you aren't fighting alone and that the battles have already been won?

loving shepherd

The Lord is my shepherd; I shall not want.
He makes me lie down in green pastures.
He leads me beside still waters. He restores my soul.
He leads me in paths of righteousness for his name's sake.

PSALM 23:1-3 ESV

Deep down inside of each of us is a desire to not only be seen, but to also be taken care of. When we feel broken down and bruised, there is nothing more inviting than a loving hand. Someone who sees our hurts and mends each one. The world is cold and sometimes heartless. There are times in life where we feel exhausted and unseen. We are desperate for someone to love us in the ways we were created to be loved.

We can depend on God to take care of every single need. He knows what we need even before we speak. He takes great care and delight in wiping our tears, speaking life and truth back into our souls, and calming the storms that rage within. He is our resting place. He is faithful to meet every one of our needs with his goodness. He does not leave us wanting, rather he fills us up, so we are overflowing with his peace and love. He did not create in us a need to be loved, to be left unloved. He loves each of us like no other ever can. Our need for him exceeds any other need or want we may have.

Lord, you are my calm, resting place. The only one that can satisfy my need to be seen and loved. Thank you for faithfully meeting my needs and for taking care of me.

Do you feel weary and tired? Let the Lord carry you to still waters, and rest in him.

a liar

The LORD is my light and the one who saves me.
So why should I fear anyone?
The LORD protects my life.
So why should I be afraid?
PSALM 27:1 NCV

Fear is a liar. It wants us to believe that we are subject to its power. It creeps slowly into the best part of our lives and crushes joy with its relentless fist. It often comes without invitation or warning, making its mark on our decisions and in our relationships.

The opposite of fear is courage. Our courage comes from the confidence that God will not forsake us. He goes to battle on our behalf. He does not leave us defenseless or weak. In him we no longer have anything to fear. This courage allows us to be brave, face oppressive powers, and be victorious. Courage breathes life into the hidden places within us that are stagnant. Courage defeats fear. When we trust the Lord with all our hearts and use courage as a weapon, fear has to flee.

God, in you I have nothing to be afraid of. Let your courage wash away any fear in my life. May I be brave and strong because of my confidence and security in you.

Is fear subtly invading your life and stealing your joy and peace?

loving counsel

I will instruct you and teach you in the way you should go;
I will counsel you with my loving eye on you.

PSALM 32:8 NIV

Making decisions for our futures can be overwhelming especially when the directions seem hazy. We don't want to make the wrong decision that will hurt us. Sometimes we just want someone to tell us what to do so we aren't weighted with the responsibility. It can be difficult to trust our own judgement and intuition.

Thankfully God is our faithful counselor and we can go to him with every decision we are wrestling with. He will give us wisdom when we ask for it and gently lead us in the best direction. He loves us so much that we can trust him to protect us from harmful choices. We don't have to face the unknown alone. God wants us to ask him for help; he even expects us to.

God, I don't want to make decisions alone. Give me wisdom and point me in the direction you want me to go. My trust in you gives me confidence to face my future.

What difficult decisions are weighing you down? Can you ask God for help?

be still

Be still and know that I am God.
I will be exalted among the nations,
I will be exalted in the earth!
PSALM 46:10 ESV

For some of us, being still, is very difficult, especially when we are facing crisis or uncertainty. We prefer to be in control, doing, moving. Our fears take over and propel us to keep going. In many ways we gain a sense of security by having a plan and seeing that plan carried out perfectly. But sometimes our refusal to pause is a reflection of our lack of faith. God wants us to be still, to surrender, to let go, and let him.

In our stillness we are able to hear God's voice and see him working clearly. We can release the tight grasp we have of our plans and surrender them to the one who has our best interests at heart. In our stillness he can quiet our anxieties and worries. In him we can be still when the world is crumbling, when uncertainty is present, and in our pain and hurt.

Lord, it is hard for me to be still because it is hard for me to surrender. But I know that you love me completely and have never let me down. I trust you.

Do you struggle to slow down and be still? Is your inability to surrender control a reflection of your lack of trust in God?

our rock

Truly he is my rock and my salvation;
he is my fortress, I will never be shaken.
PSALM 62:2 NIV

The enemy is relentless. He wants nothing more than to shake us deep in our core. He aims to steal our faith by attacking us where it hurts the most. He is sneaky and clever. He feeds into our insecurities, whispers lies into our ears, and breathes fear in our minds. He doesn't want to destroy every part of us. But God is our refuge—our fortress. He gives us the ability to live without fear even when the enemy is taunting us from every angle. He covers us with his love, armors us with his truth, and protects us with his power.

When we are centered in God, we are not easily moved. We can be stripped of our health, our finances, our loved ones, and yet we can rise up strong. We can be beaten, bloody, and bruised but still remain steadfast. We can stand boldly, face to face with our enemy. Unafraid. Untouched. Without our faith wavering. Because when God has a stronghold on our hearts, we are indestructible.

God, you are my safe place. You hold me up when the enemy attempts to tear me down. His ways are evil and threatening, but he will not be able to move me. I am strong in you.

Is your faith rooted deep in your Savior? Or do you find it wavering easily under the enemy's attacks? What keeps you from falling?

waiting patiently

Let all that I am wait quietly before God,
for my hope is in him.
PSALM 62:5 NLT

We are accustomed to fast and quick service. Waiting is hard and inconvenient, so we have built our world in ways that we don't have to wait for anything. Well, almost anything. There are still some things that we are forced to wait for: a doctor's diagnosis, the birth of a child, or that job offer or promotion we are really hoping for. We know that joy is just around the corner and it's only our impatience that makes waiting difficult or annoying. Other times, waiting is downright scary. It feels like we are standing on the edge of a cliff, grasping for someone to save us before we fall.

It helps to know that we are never alone in our waiting. God is present, and he is our saving grace. He knows the inner stirrings of our heart, the crippling fear that resides there, and he wants to replace it with his peace. When we know that he is in our difficult season, we can calm our minds and trust that we are not alone. No matter what the outcome or circumstance, God will see us through. We can cling to this promise as we wait and let go of our anxieties.

Thank you, God, for your promise to be with us through everything. I am grateful for you being with me in the waiting, seeing me through every circumstance and giving me joy.

Do you know that God is with you always so you can be brave in the face of the unknown? He has you, so embrace this time of uncertainty.

a new song

I shall sing of your strength;
Yes, I shall joyfully sing of your lovingkindness in the morning,
for you have been my stronghold
and a refuge in the day of my distress.

PSALM 59:16 NASB

There are stories woven throughout Scripture of God's great love for his people. We see him parting seas, crushing boulders, and quietening storms. He feeds the hungry and heals the sick. He cries with those who mourn, comforts the lonely, and stands with the forgotten. His character is consistent of a loving and faithful God who meets his people in their time of need.

Why do we so easily forget that the God we serve is the same God that has always been? If we look back through our own history, we can see how he has been faithful and present. How he picked us up from the darkness, breathed love and life into our aching hearts, and restored our souls. No matter what we face, we can be certain that he will not abandon us. By recognizing his great love for us, we can comfort and encourage those who are struggling around us. Our lives can be a great testimony of a God who makes us brave in hardship.

Thank you, God, that you have left me a detailed account of your goodness, not only in Scriptures, but in my own history. Thank you for being faithful and loving toward me. May my life be a testimony of your love.

In what ways have you seen God show up in your life and love you well? Who in your life can you encourage with your testimony of his goodness?

our home

His massive arms are wrapped around you, protecting you.
You can run under his covering of majesty and hide.
His arms of faithfulness are a shield keeping you from harm.
PSALM 91:4 TPT

Being in the Lord's presence is like being ushered into home—a warm, safe shelter. A place to ease our bodies and relax our hearts. A place where we feel protected. Where we can inhale and exhale. Where we are fed, clothed, and cared for.

Home is where we can let our guard down, close our eyes, and let go of all our worries. In a broken and harsh world, home is where we feel infinitely loved and wanted. A place where we are fully seen and welcomed despite our flaws and jagged edges. God invites us in to this place of refuge, to be with him. We can run to him with confidence that his arms are open to us and he is ready to embrace us tightly.

God, you are my home. The place where I feel so protected, wanted, and loved. When the world is cold and difficult and mean, you are my peace. You are the place I run and hide and know I will be safe.

Do you know that you can find belonging and safety in the arms of your Father? Is he your home?

unending kindness

From your kindness you send the rain to water the mountains
from the upper rooms of your palace.
Your goodness brings forth fruit for all to enjoy.
PSALM 104:13 TPT

Sometimes when we compare our lives to others, we begin to feel jealous. Why did God bless them, heal them, remember them, but not me? It's hard to understand why some people struggle and others don't. These questions often come from a place of insecurity or feeling inadequate. We want to know that we are as loved as the person next to us. Comparison can be so damaging. Taking score and measuring our lives against another is never helpful. Jealousy clouds our ability to see how much we are loved, and how much we have to be thankful for. It separates us from the goodness of God and allows bitterness to creep in.

God does not hold out on his children. He gives us his absolute best always. He cares about each of us equally. He ensures that not one of us is left wanting. We can be confident knowing he doesn't pick and choose who he is going to love and provide for. He chooses all of us every day. Not one of us is ever far from his mind.

Lord, when I am overwhelmed with struggles, it is easy to begin to believe that I am forgotten by you. Help me to focus on you and your great care and not on those around me. Replace my jealous thoughts with genuine appreciation of all you have blessed me with.

Do you have thoughts of jealously that are inhibiting you from knowing just how loved you are?

unbroken gratitude

What can I offer the LORD for all he has done for me?
I will lift up the cup of salvation
and praise the LORD's name for saving me.
I will keep my promises to the LORD
in the presence of all his people.
PSALM 116:12-14 NLT

When God saves us, what is our reaction? Are we overwhelmed with gratitude, or do we easily forget and move on without uttering thanks? We don't deserve his grace, yet he continues to give it to us. We've become so accustomed to him faithfully meeting our needs and coming to our aid, that we may take him for granted. Even worse, we voice our complaints toward the very one who gives without ceasing. We are spoiled in his love and we still demand more.

Our hearts are in desperate need of cultivation of humbleness so that gratitude can pour out often and freely. So our knees are bent toward him in worship. So we can easily see the blessings given to us. So our voices are in constant praise of the work he's done in our lives.

God, I am guilty of not giving praise where praise is due. You love me so well and, in my self-centeredness, I often forget to be thankful. Grow gratitude in me. Keep me humble and grounded—aware of all you do for me.

How may you have taken God and his blessings for granted?

love and laws

Great peace have those who love your law;
nothing can make them stumble.
PSALM 119:165 NRSV

Life is filled with rules, guidelines, and structure. Sometimes laws can feel restrictive. It can be tedious to constantly listen and obey. We rarely want to listen to other rules; we want to do things our way. We don't want our free will to be stifled. We want to be in control.

God's laws weren't created to take away our lives but to keep us safe. When a parent instructs a child not to run onto the road, it's not to spoil their fun but so they don't encounter tragedy. In the same way, God gives us his Word so we can prosper and live fully. His laws were given to us because he loves us. The exchange for obeying his laws is peace and assurance. It's in our human nature to reject rules that seem limiting, but if we were truly able to believe that God's intentions were good, and that boundaries keep us from suffering great harm, we would be in a place of feeling his absolute love.

God, I am grateful for your laws that keep me safe and bring me peace. Your laws are an assurance of your great love for me. They are a compass that keeps me from harm.

Do you view God's laws as his way of loving you?

overwhelming love

You created my inmost being;
you knit me together in my mother's womb.
PSALM 139:13 NIV

When a parent looks at their child, all they see is love. They are absolutely enamored with the child's entire being. They don't see imperfections, just beauty. This is how God sees us—perfect in every way. We are his creation, his artwork, his most prized possession. He knows us in ways no one else can. He sees us in a light that no one else will ever be able to.

It is a challenge for most of us to see what God sees in us, to love what he loves about us. We count our shortcomings while he calls us his beloved. We believe that we aren't capable while he whispers his strength. How would our images of ourselves change if we truly knew that we were significant, made with purpose and love? The insecurities we hold onto would surely fade and we would rise up with confidence, facing life with brevity. We would live the way he wants us to: free with the fullness that we are loved.

Lord, the way you see me is overwhelming, but it changes me from the inside out. May your love for me give me security and confidence in who I am. May my identity come from you only because you love me like no other.

Do you see yourself the way God sees you? Or are you burdened and limited with your own insecurities?

always was

*You are the Lord that reigns over your never-ending kingdom
through all the ages of time and eternity!
You are faithful to fulfill every promise you've made.
You manifest yourself as Kindness in all you do!*

PSALM 145:13 TPT

The world is constantly changing. It's hard to keep up. Culture shifts, and social structure evolves. Even relationships change over time. Nothing stays the same. When everything is constantly in motion, the one thing we can always trust to stay the same is God. He is consistently and infinitely kind. He rules with love, justice, and gentleness. Just like he always has. And always will.

When questions come about his faithfulness, and we are tempted to doubt him in our weakest moments, we can ultimately trust him because he has proven himself trustworthy. He is unchanging in a changing world. His promises remain the same. Our faith can be strengthened in the knowledge that we serve a God who is consistent in character and deed. We serve a God who has prevailed over all.

God, the way and speed of how things around me are always changing is unsettling. But I have peace and security in serving and being loved by a King who always stays the same.

Are you comfortable with change? Does serving a God who is unchanging bring you peace?

no more tears

I heard a loud shout from the throne, saying, "Look, God's home is now among his people! He will live with them, and they will be his people. God himself will be with them. He will wipe every tear from their eyes, and there will be no more death or sorrow or crying or pain. All these things are gone forever."

REVELATION 21:3-4 NLT

All of us have elements of pain, loss, hardship, and tragedy in our stories. Life can be brutal. It doesn't matter if we are rich or poor. Faithful of heart or weak in faith. Hardship does not discriminate, and grief knows no stranger. None of us are untouchable to loss. It's part of life.

But God sees, and it grieves him deeply when we hurt. He aches with us. Every tear is seen and counted. He doesn't leave us alone in our pain. He promises that even though today is difficult, a day is coming where pain and loss will no longer exist. A future free of the difficulties we face today is promised to us. Knowing what is coming can give us the courage to get through today—no matter how wrecked and broken it is.

God, I am so thankful that pain and suffering aren't everlasting. A life in you offers true everlasting hope and freedom.

Can you see God's promises and hope in the middle of pain? Do you believe that one day he will wipe the tears from your eyes for good?

a new life

We know that our old life died with Christ on the cross so that our sinful selves would have no power over us and we would not be slaves to sin.

ROMANS 6:6 NCV

Habits and patterns are easy to form but hard to break. Sin can feel the same way. Living a life free of sin seems unreachable. Temptations press in strategically. As believers, our intentions are good but our ability to refrain from old sin patterns can be difficult. But it's not impossible.

Satan wants us to feel enslaved and defeated by sin because he wants us to believe we are weak and powerless. He wants us to remain in the destructive pattern of failing and feeling discouraged. But the wonderful truth is, when Jesus died for us on the cross, our old lives died as well. We have been given the power against our sinful cycles. Even if we stumble and fall, he takes our hands, and helps us rise against it. His sacrifice on the cross, his Word, his hope, his constant presence in our lives, keeps us strong. We can take on our new identities with the assurance that our old lives no longer have a grip on us.

Thank you, God, that in you I am free from old habits and destructive ways. You have given me a new life and I am so thankful.

Do you feel constantly swept up in your old sinful patterns? Reject the lie that you will never be free from and embrace your newfound freedom in Christ.

act of faith

Faith comes from hearing, and hearing by the word of Christ.
ROMANS 10:17 NASB

There is a difference between hearing the Word of God and believing it. We need to hear in order to be given the opportunity to believe. But believing in the Word of God requires an element of trust that what has been written in Scripture is real and true. The very act of opening up our Bibles is an act of faith. We open it in expectation that God will meet us there. When we approach Scripture with an attitude of faith, we are never disappointed.

The Word of God is something tangible that we can feast our eyes on. It is given to us, so we can use it to build our faith. God's promises are weaved throughout the pages written just for us. Words of forgiveness, hope, grace, and infinite love are all in there. When we let Christ's teachings seep into our hearts, he becomes alive and real. Then we can truly step out bravely in obedience to his Word. We can experience him in ways that would be impossible if we were closed off to his voice.

God, I trust that your Word is real and true. My faith comes from hearing you and loving your Word. You give me confidence to step out in faith and completely trust that you will never let me down.

Is your faith built on hearing the Word of God or believing it?

genuine love

*Love each other with genuine affection
and take delight in honoring each other.*
ROMANS 12:10 NLT

One of the most difficult things to do is to love someone who doesn't want to be loved. To love those who push you away every time you try to help, those who are difficult, and those who are maybe even a little mean is discouraging, defeating, even costly.

Genuine love keeps showing up. It continues to extend a hand of grace. It serves in every capacity possible. It sees the whole person. Sometimes the hardness of a person is just a mask. Often those difficult people need to know deep down inside that they are worth the effort.

Lord, you love me so deeply and freely even when I push you away and act as if I don't need you. You continue to pursue me anyway, and I am so thankful. Help me to love others the way you love me.

Is there someone in your life that is difficult to love? Reach out to them today and let them know they are seen.

our gatekeeper

Don't copy the behavior and customs of this world, but let God transform you into a new person by changing the way you think. Then you will learn to know God's will for you, which is good and pleasing and perfect.

ROMANS 12:2 NLT

Every day we are surrounded by so much noise from the outside world. Messages are loud and relentless—how we should look, act, and think. Culture has its own set of rules and ideals, many of which differ from God's. Influences come at us in so many forms. Social pressure, media, politics, even close friendships. We process a high volume of information every day. Ideals can impact our characters and decisions. They can shape who we are and what we believe in. They can drown out God's voice.

It is so important to center ourselves in Christ and surround ourselves with positive influences. Our hearts need to be immersed in his Word, so he can transform our minds with truth. And we can learn how to decipher what is from him and what is not.

Lord, help me to hear you through the noise of the world. Help me to love your Word so it can transform who I am. I want to be more like you and less like the world.

Who is influencing your thoughts today? Is your mind protected from the influence of the outside world by being immersed in God's Word?

peaceful friendships

Let us try to do what makes peace and helps one another.
ROMANS 14:19 NCV

Relationships are hard work and sometimes very messy. It takes time and effort to keep them strong and healthy. In difficult relationships, we wonder if it's worth the effort especially if the conflict lies in differences of opinion and a clash of personalities. Our relationships with each other are a priority to God. He cares deeply about how we love and interact with each other, and it grieves him to see fighting and hurt between us. What is important to him should also be important to us.

Keeping peace can be difficult. We need to reach deep down inside to find forgiveness and grace. God knows and understands how complex and difficult relationships are. He asks us to work on them anyway. We have him to look to as an example. Our words are powerful. They can be used as a tool for peace and encouragement or as a weapon to cut down or cause turmoil and pain. If we are willing to use our words to build each other up, and focus on instilling love and value, we are glorifying God and pleasing him.

Lord, help me to love, build up, and encourage every relationship in my life, just as you love and encourage me.

Is there anyone in your life today that you could extend love, forgiveness, and peace to? Reach out to them today and let them know how valuable they are to you.

unity in friendships

May the God of endurance and encouragement grant you to live in such harmony with one another, in accord with Christ Jesus, that together you may with one voice glorify the God and Father of our Lord Jesus Christ.

ROMANS 15:5-6 ESV

God knows the true strength and power that lies in us being one body. It is why he asks us to come together at the same table and hold hands, despite our differences and varying opinions. He wants our voices not to drown each other out, but to be raised in unity. We are always stronger together. We can accomplish much more for his kingdom when peace binds us together.

Being unified takes work. We lay aside our pride and show humility. We love each other deeply. We are genuinely welcoming and inclusive. Sometimes fighting seems easier than working hard toward the same goal. It requires more effort, especially when we all come from vastly different places and experiences and don't see eye to eye. But fighting has no purpose, and nothing will be accomplished. Let peace win.

God, working with others doesn't always come easy to me. Give me a heart that is open and warm to those around me. Help me to cherish unity and peace so together we can better serve you.

Do you see division among believers? How can you encourage unity in your own circle?

words of integrity

In every way be an example of doing good deeds. When you teach, do it with honesty and seriousness. Speak the truth so that you cannot be criticized. Then those who are against you will be ashamed because there is nothing bad to say about us.

TITUS 2:7-8 NCV

Words are easy to come by. They flow out of our mouths effortlessly, giving description to our thoughts, teachings, and convictions. But if they aren't layered with integrity, do they carry any weight at all? Or do our words just make us look foolish and leave us open to criticism? When you live a life different than the rest of the world, it tends to draw attention. It is intriguing, and people are watching more than they are listening. Often Christians are given a platform without asking for one.

We need to be accountable to our teachings in action— even when we think we don't have an audience. This means extending grace, kindness, forgiveness, and love in every situation we encounter, and to each person we meet regardless of how difficult it may be.

God, may my convictions and teachings be clearly seen in my life in the way I serve, treat, and love others. May I live by my words and be seen as blameless in the eyes of others.

Are you more than the sum of your words? Or are you set on living out your own teachings? Do you speak truth when you interact with others?

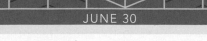

worth celebrating

God brought out his chosen ones with singing;
for with a joyful shout they were set free!
PSALM 105:43 TPT

The extent of God's affinity for us is overwhelming and difficult to comprehend. We are his precious children and he is so proud to be our Father, our protector, and the shepherd of our hearts. We are his chosen ones. The ones he has gone great lengths to fight for, to save, to call his own.

It's easy to think that we are small. That in the grand scheme of things our lives are insignificant. Who are we to matter so much to such a big God? But our freedom brings him great joy. He celebrates each one of us as we step into a life free of sin and bondage. He is elated when he sees us victorious because he our lives are valuable to him. He sings over us. He doesn't see us as worthless, but as a treasure worth celebrating.

God, you say that I matter. You celebrate me and love me in ways I cannot begin to understand. Help me to live, knowing I am loved by you.

Do you know your worth according to God? Are you able to see yourself as loved? As someone worthy of celebrating?

july

This is how love is made perfect in us: that we can be without fear on the day God judges us, because in this world we are like him.

1 JOHN 4:17 NCV

when temptation calls

*No temptation has overtaken you except what is common to mankind.
And God is faithful; he will not let you be tempted beyond what you
can bear. But when you are tempted,
he will also provide a way out so that you can endure it.*

1 CORINTHIANS 10:13 NIV

What a huge comfort it is knowing that God is watching out for us. When temptation is calling us by name it may seem impossible to resist, but know that God has already provided a way out or around your problems.

You can resist temptation and trials that come your way knowing that your heavenly Father sees you as a person of courage and great strength. He won't allow circumstances to break you. Often the best plan is to step back, take a breath, and pause. Ask God to help you see the obstacle from all sides. Consider all your options not just the first thing that jumps into your mind. The Lord delights in showing the way. Rest in the knowledge that he will protect you when trials and tests come your way.

God, help me build my courage by resisting when temptation calls. Let me ask for your help instead of relying on myself. I trust in you.

How has God helped you resist temptations in the past? How do you think you could plan ahead to avoid them in the future?

choosing to trust

Without faith living within us it would be impossible to please God. For we come to God in faith knowing that he is real and that he rewards the faith of those who give all their passion and strength into seeking him.

HEBREWS 11:6 TPT

The mere act of choosing to trust in God is courageous. It is often called a "leap of faith" because coming to God and believing in his ability to save and give us life requires trust. We trust him with our days and our futures. We have confidence that he will hear our thoughts and prayers, and he will comfort and encourage us.

When we are anxious and fearful, it is time to choose to trust those thoughts and emotions to God. Embracing his power and letting go of our own can be scary. The courageous and trusting can rest well in the knowledge that their heavenly Father will reward them with all riches of his glory.

Dear God, I want to be strong. I want to have the courage to trust in you at all times. Show me your ways and give me strength.

Are there areas of your life you haven't trusted God with? Can you name one problem you can give to him to handle?

the golden rule

"Do to others as you would like them to do to you."
LUKE 6:31 NLT

The Golden Rule may have been one of the first Bible verses you memorized. You may not have even known it was from the Bible. As children, when disagreements broke out on the playground our teachers would instruct us that we should treat others as we would like to be treated ourselves. When Merrydawn pushed Simion, she would be gently reminded to think of how she felt when someone pushed her. It's about respect. It's about kindness and caring.

Jesus instructed us about our relationships with others—not just the ones who love us, but everyone. A good way to remember how to respond to every situation is this acronym: THINK. Is it True? Is it Helpful? Is it Inspiring? Is it Necessary? Is it Kind? The truly brave child of God cares about how everyone is treated, not just friends and loved ones.

God, I don't always treat the people with respect and kindness. Help me to remember your Golden Rule as I speak. Help me to have pure intentions.

Can you pinpoint a conversation in which you failed to act kindly? Is this an area you need help in?

compassionate and gracious

"The Lord, the Lord, the compassionate and gracious God, slow to anger, abounding in love and faithfulness."
EXODUS 34:6 NIV

Each day we walk with the Lord, we hope to mature in him. The more we learn about his character, his goodness and compassion, his mercy and his love, the more we yearn to be like him. It makes no difference whether you are a relatively new Christian or have been serving him for a long life. The more you know of God and his lovingkindness the more convinced you become to better yourself. To soften your heart. To be like him.

What more could we want in our heart of hearts than to be compassionate and gracious? Slow to anger? Abounding in love and faithfulness? Looking into our own character is not always enjoyable. We tend to be selfish and prideful. We may be ashamed of things we have said or done. God is faithful to forgive us for yesterday and before. We can take a courageous stand and declare each morning, "Today is a new day. Today I will be compassionate and gracious to those I meet. I will be slow to anger. I will abound in love. I will be more like Jesus."

Dear Jesus, help me to be more like you. Help my actions to let others see you in me. Let me mature in my walk with you each day.

How did you show compassion this week? Can you identify a time when you succeeded in slowing your anger? Are you maturing as a Christian?

before and after

We are not saying that we can do this work ourselves.
It is God who makes us able to do all that we do.
2 CORINTHIANS 3:5 NCV

The doctor says, "I'm so very sorry, it's cancer." The world stops. Your heart stops. There is a whirring sound all around and whatever the doctor is now saying is lost in the noise. You will never forget the color of the room or what you were wearing but will evermore remember your life as BC (before Cancer) and AC (after Cancer). Perhaps it isn't a medical issue that seems insurmountable in your life. It may be a broken relationship, a job termination, a house fire, or car accident. Whatever it maybe it is a huge, traumatic point in your life that divides before and after.

We feel unable to cope, to function, or think. It may seem easier to crumple into a ball of quivering jelly, but the brave thing to do is to give it to God. He is strong. He is able. He is capable of handling it all. Trust him with your big, frightening problems. He may not fix it the way you hoped. Know that he knows you best and loves you more than you can imagine. He will help you through any circumstance that may come your way—even the very difficult ones.

God, I seem to hold onto the big problems in my life. Help me to hand them to you. I know you want the very best for me.

Have there been some defining moments in your life? How have you responded to them? Can you think how to prepare for the next one?

wise counsel

The way of fools seems right to them,
but the wise listen to advice.
PROVERBS 12:15 NIV

Social media has all the answers, or so it seems. Memes and inspirational posts on Facebook and Instagram can ring true. Is this where you get your affirmation? In this day of Fake News, it may seem hard to know what is really true. Be wary. Recently someone repeated something they were certain was true "because Abraham Lincoln posted it on Facebook." Of course, it was false because Abraham Lincoln died over a hundred years before Facebook existed! That's pretty silly.

So where do you go for advice? Do you have a trusted friend? Your mom or dad? Perhaps you go to a colleague or your pastor. When facing a question or dilemma a wise person will seek advice from a trusted source. God's Word can help if you know where to look. A concordance or Bible study book can help you find what you need. Being brave is putting in the effort to find wise counsel.

God, I need your wise counsel in my life. Please help me to find people and resources that can give me godly advice and information.

On what do you base your life decisions? Do you know someone who can help in time of need? Can you use resources to help you find the answers in the Bible?

fear

"Don't be afraid, because you will not be ashamed.
Don't be embarrassed, because you will not be disgraced.
You will forget the shame you felt earlier; you will not remember
the shame you felt when you lost your husband."

ISAIAH 54:4 NCV

"What is the capital of New Mexico?" In third grade, Madison's teacher had asked her to answer the question. Instead of answering Santa Fe, she quickly replied, "Santa Claus!" As she realized her mistake, the class erupted into laughter and Madison's face grew red. Oh, how that hurt. As the years went by, Madison was so embarrassed when someone would call out to her, "Hey, Santa Claus." That one small moment defined her. She became afraid to speak up.

Fast forward to Madison's ten-year high school reunion. She brought a little Santa Claus sticker and put it on her nametag. She embraced her past disgrace. No one laughed at her expense this time. They were enamored by the brave young woman who laughed along with them. Over the years, Madison had learned to let God dictate her worth. Like Madison, you can find strength to forgive and forget people or circumstances which caused you shame or embarrassment.

God, help me to not let the past dictate fear and shame. I want to be an overcomer. Please remind me of how much you love me and let me find my worth in you.

Did an event or person cause you embarrassment in your past? Can you forgive and move past it? Can you find the courage to trust God for a positive image of yourself?

comfort

*"He took them in His arms and began blessing them,
laying His hands on them."*
MARK 10:16 NASB

Life is full of disappointments. We find ourselves in difficult situations where we are afraid or grieving. Perhaps we've made a terrible mistake, or someone has wronged us. A stiff upper lip may suffice for a bit, but eventually we realize that our heavenly Father is waiting to comfort us. He wants to envelope us in his love. He wants to wrap us up in his arms. He wants to bless us with riches beyond our understanding.

Some of us have a hard time picturing God as our Father. Our own father let us down or wasn't around when we needed him. Was your earthly father a disappointment to you? Perhaps he was cold and uncaring, distant or absent for most or all of your life. He might have been abusive. Maybe you had a wonderful dad who loved and supported you, but you remember times when he wasn't there when you needed him. The important thing to know is that you do have a heavenly Father who is perfect. He will never disappoint you. He cares about you and loves you. He has your best interests at heart. His arms are always open and ready to comfort and bless you.

God, I find it hard sometimes to ask for your comfort because my dad let me down. Help me to see that you are my perfect Father, always ready to bless me.

Is it easy to see God as your heavenly Father? Does your relationship to your own dad get in the way? Can you ask the Lord for help in seeing him as a perfect Father?

good thoughts

One final thing. Fix your thoughts on what is true, and honorable, and right, and pure, and lovely, and admirable. Think about things that are excellent and worthy of praise.
PHILIPPIANS 4:8 NLT

Every day we are bombarded with bad news: climate change will cause the oceans to rise, dolphins and turtles are dying because we use plastic straws, the governments in faraway lands are killing children, this group hates that group, politicians jump to conclusions that seem to benefit only themselves and so on, ad nauseum. It can make even the most cheerful dispositioned among us depressed. A steady diet of bad company, deplorable movies, or depressing news feeds our souls in horrible ways.

The company you keep defines you. Surround yourself with people you admire. Listen to uplifting music. Watch movies that inspire you to be a better person. Read good books. Spend your time helping those in need. God wants only the best for you and his Word is full of advice that will make your life better. Do you desire a more abundant life? Seek what is true, honorable, and right, not the latest gossip. Look for what is pure, lovely, and admirable, don't rejoice in the dirt some reporter dug up. Fill your life with what is praiseworthy. Be courageous and willing to make yourself a better person.

Lord, help me to find the positive in my circumstances. I want to see the good in the people around me. Guide me in filling my life with praiseworthy thoughts and actions.

What are some ways you can weed out negativity in your life? Can you think of three basic changes you can make to cause your life to be more honorable?

seek advice

Without counsel plans fail,
but with many advisers they succeed.
PROVERBS 15:22 ESV

Life is made up of decisions. Some are big, life altering decisions, and some are small. Should we go to college, choose this or that as a profession, move to Milwaukie? Should we plant a garden, buy a house, live in an apartment, take that seminar, or go to coffee with a friend? What about becoming a vegetarian, putting money into savings, or adopting a pet? Some of our choices may not require much more than common sense. Eating sushi or meatballs is pretty much up to personal preference but big decisions require more.

Before you buy a car, you should research what you can afford to spend, new or used, is it reliable or can you fix most problems? You should find out what other owners think of the car. Is it a lemon? Does it get good gas mileage? What will it cost to insure? God has instructed us to research, to investigate, and to plan. A wise person will take this advice for the important decisions in life. God doesn't want you to fail. He wants to bless you and help you prosper.

God, help me to stop and think before making major decisions and ask for advice. Remind me to research the best way for me to go.

Do you have some big choices in your near future? Are there people you trust that you can ask to help you? Have you prayed about these decisions?

gratitude

Giving thanks always for all things to God the Father in the name of our Lord Jesus Christ.
EPHESIANS 5:20 NKJV

It is easy to live a life full of wants for the future. You may want tangible things: house, car, job, microwave, a 48" tv, or maybe you just want these things to be newer, fancier, and bigger. Perhaps you yearn for vacations to Ireland, a new relationship, a promotion at work, or just peace and quiet. Sometimes we act like children pouring over a Christmas Wish book wanting every fancy present they see. What happens when you don't get what you want? Do you become depressed and envious when you see what others have? Are all things desirable or necessary?

Aesop says, "Gratitude turns what we have into enough." When we thank God for everything we have, it brings contentment to our lives. Try counting your blessings. Make up a list. Thank God for your family and friends, your home, enough to eat, your hobbies, your job. You can be specific: my love of music, my siblings, my pastor, my green thumb. Thankfulness is a habit to cultivate. All these good things are from God!

Dear God, thank you for giving me such good gifts. Help me to be grateful for each one you have freely given to me. Help me be content and fill me with gratitude.

Are you content with what you have or envious of what you don't have? What can you do to cultivate gratitude in your life?

being trustworthy

A gossip betrays a confidence,
but a trustworthy person keeps a secret.
PROVERBS 11:13 NIV

Have you ever been told a secret? Perhaps it is really happy news. A friend is expecting or up for an award. They have shared the news with you but aren't ready to share it with the world. Can you keep that secret? Are you worthy of their trust? How disappointed will they be when they hear their own news passed around? Keeping confidence is surely a way to show someone how much you care and respect them.

Do you love a good rumor? Passing on the newest delicious tidbit seems to travel faster than the speed of light with no regard for truth or feelings of the people involved. Social media is full of innuendo and made up "facts." Gossip is a selfish act. It makes the teller feel important at the expense of others. When we care about someone, we want the best for them. We don't want to hurt them, their reputations, or their feelings. We want to respect their confidences and keep their trust. A wise person learns to control the tongue and keep trust.

God, I want to be trustworthy. Help me to be wise and trustworthy when I speak. Let me always speak well of others.

Do you tend to gossip? Can your friends count on you to keep a secret?

compassion

"If anyone gives even a cup of cold water to one of these little ones who is my disciple, truly I tell you, that person will certainly not lose their reward."
MATTHEW 10:42 NIV

Jessica was waiting in line at the grocery store impatiently counting the large number of items she had on her to-do list before she got home. There was an older woman in front of her at the check-out station who seemed a bit short on the money needed for her entire order. The clerk was telling her the prices of various items that could be put back to lessen the bill. Items came out of the bags and some were put back. People behind Jessica began to make jokes and loud comments about the length of time it was all taking. A slow tear began down the lady's cheek and she seemed unable to make her decisions.

Though money was always tight, Jessica stepped forward and quietly spoke to the clerk, "How much are we short?" "Twelve dollars and forty-seven cents," came the reply. Jessica leaned down to the elderly woman and asked "Ma'am, may I make up the difference for you?" The woman's face lit up and she smiled. "Thank you so very much. I am raising my grandchildren and sometimes there's more month than money." How excellent it is to have compassion and empathy.

God, help me to see the needs around me and act. Let me be a servant to those who can use my help.

Have you let opportunities to show compassion slip by? How can you be more aware of the needs of others?

choose joy

*A joyful heart makes a cheerful face,
but when the heart is sad, the spirit is broken.*
PROVERBS 15:13 NASB

Everyone experiences deep sadness and disappointment in life. Sometimes it may seem your life is full of them. You can't catch a break. Take heart when you experience trials and nothing goes your way. Broken promises, relationships, and disappointments can seem an unending theme. Our Father has promised us joy. He understands joy and sadness more than we know. God's Word says that when we are sad, our spirit is broken. Don't let it stop there. Find joy! Look for joy! Choose joy!

In the Bible, joy is mentioned over 250 times. When you feel broken, you can choose joy—the joy of the Lord—and it will be the strength you need. When all happiness is taken from you, choose the joy of the Lord! When you are hurting, look to the joy of the Lord and bravely move in another direction. Make a new friend. Help a neighbor. Pay for a stranger's coffee order. Choose joy—the strength you need to repair a broken spirit.

God, sometimes I feel so sad. Nothing seems to go right. Help me to seek your joy. Put a smile on my face and make me a blessing to others who need joy.

Can you see how helping others might bring you joy? Can you see past your own circumstances to be a blessing to someone with a broken spirit?

little white lies

Love does not delight in evil but rejoices with the truth.
1 CORINTHIANS 13:6 NIV

"Did you call the doctor back?" "Yes." (I'll do it tomorrow.)

"Can you teach Sunday School for me next week?" "Sorry, I have to help my aunt move." (I don't really want to teach fifth graders. They scare me.)

"You owe us $100." "The check is in the mail." (I will pay it next Friday when I get paid.)

How easy it is to tell those little white lies. Seemingly they hurt no one and we rationalize they may even help someone feel better. But a lie, is a lie, is a lie. They are the result of a selfish heart. These falsehoods are told to make our life easier and they don't reflect the truth as God shows us. White lies are a habit and not one of our most shining moments. Being brave enough to be honest with those you deal with is a way of showing respect to them. It may be uncomfortable, it may be inconvenient, but being truthful is the right thing to do.

Lord, help me to be honest in all things. Let me see how telling little white lies are wrong. Help me have the courage to be honest.

When was the last time you told a lie? How did you feel? Do you listen to your conscience at these times?

patience

The Lord is not slow in keeping his promise, as some understand slowness. Instead he is patient with you, not wanting anyone to perish, but everyone to come to repentance.

2 PETER 3:9 NIV

We have instant-everything. The internet is answering questions, giving us directions, and so much more. We can talk or FaceTime people on the other side of the globe in real time. An ATM will dispense cash from our bank at any time of day or night. There is an Instant Pot to cook in, a microwave and fast food for instant dinners. Amazon has opened up an instant shopping mall. And somehow, we wait for three minutes at the post office and we're agitated because of the delay.

We've all heard the line: "Well, I wished for patience and look what happened!" The inference is that lots of longsuffering problems ensued. God's timing is different than ours. In 2 Peter 2:8 we read, "But do not forget this one thing, dear friends: With the Lord a day is like a thousand years, and a thousand years are like a day." Take time with others, slow down, and look around you, meditate on God's Word. Your heart will listen better, your attitude will improve, and your problems will not deter you from happiness.

Lord, help me to slow down and listen for your still, small voice. Allow your patience with me to determine the way I treat others. Help me to hope in my circumstances.

Is your life hectic? Can you think of ways or times you can pause and slow your heart and soul? Do you think you could benefit from this?

potential

In all the work you are doing, work the best you can.
Work as if you were doing it for the Lord, not for people.
COLOSSIANS 3:23 NCV

At parent-teacher conferences every year, many parents hear that their child isn't working to their potential. What does this mean exactly? The student may have a C average or even regularly do A+ work and still not do the schoolwork they are capable of. Sometimes the jobs we have to do are just boring. It might be painting a bathroom, digging a garden, collecting data for your boss, but it seems like busy work. It can be easy to let it slide and just do a "good enough" job. But is that really what God has called us to do? He wants us to go the extra mile and do excellent work.

When we work hard, when we work well, we show others the light that is God living in us. It may be hard to imagine working for your boss as if he or she were the Lord, but imagine how pleased he or she will be with your work. What is good for God is good for your boss and good for you too. It's such a simple concept. Try to do everything you do as if you are doing it personally by invitation of the Lord. Do the very best you can.

God, help me to always do my best. Help me to see how the task I am presented with is a task to do with you in mind.

Have you ever performed a shoddy job just to get it over and done? How did you feel afterwards?

gentle breaking

You have also given me the shield of Your salvation;
Your gentleness has made me great.
2 SAMUEL 22:36 NKJV

Each year the US Bureau of Land Management gathers up wild horses and puts them up for adoption. To be able to ride these horses they must first be gentled and trained. Long ago it was thought that the best way to approach this was to be loud and rough. It was called "breaking" the horse. It is approached differently these days: now we "gentle" the horse. The trainer or whisperer gains the trust of the animal, always speaking quietly and going slowly. The result is an animal who cares for, rather than fears, his human owner. Theirs is a relationship of affection and trust.

Proverbs 15:1 says "A gentle answer turns away wrath, but a harsh word stirs up anger" and it is true with people too. God has shown us by his own gentleness how to act with our friends and acquaintances. Would you rather have a reputation of being a kind and gentle person or one who stirs up angst and anger wherever you go? Let's be slow to anger, abounding in love.

God, help me to be gentle to those around me. Show me opportunities to respond and not react in my daily situations. Help me to determine to think of others before myself.

Do people consider you gentle? Are there ways you can think of to change this?

forgiveness

Bear with each other and forgive each other. If someone does wrong to you, forgive that person because the Lord forgave you.

COLOSSIANS 3:13 NCV

Holding a grudge can actually make you sick. Extensive research has shown that persistent bitterness may result in anger and hostility that can affect someone's physical health. Forgiving someone doesn't mean that they will be free of the consequences of their actions. Forgiveness actually benefits the forgiver and not always the person in the wrong. God has said that he will judge the offender.

We have all sinned, and God in his mercy has offered each of us a full pardon for all we have done wrong. He also knows that without forgiving our enemies our lives will be anxious and agitated. He understands that bitterness will poison our lives, so he simply asks that we forgive others as he has forgiven us. It's not easy but with courage it can be done.

God, show me how to forgive those who have wronged me. Please help me to be slow to take offense. Help me with bitterness within my heart.

Are you holding onto resentments or wrongs against you? Do you easily take offense? What can you do to get rid of these feelings?

serenity

May the Lord of peace himself give you his peace at all times and in
every situation. The Lord be with you all.

2 THESSALONIANS 3:16 NLT

Who doesn't yearn for peace? There is violence in various parts of the world, a house fire takes the lives of children in our state, and the pressure over a work project is mounting. Arrgh! Stop the madness! What we yearn for is harmony, tranquility, and serenity. You may not be able to alter the circumstances or the people around you, but you can take a step back and ask the Lord for peace. Amidst the turmoil surrounding you he will create a place of refuge.

When the stress gets to be too much, it can be good to take a short walk, breathe deeply, listen to quiet music, delve into God's Word, and listen. God has promised to give you his peace in every situation and at all times. He wants to give you calm in the middle of the storms of life, serenity in the hectic schedule, and tranquility in your heart.

Lord, sometimes life is too chaotic for words. Help me remember that you want to give me peace. Let me ask for your help.

What are the biggest stresses in your life? How can God help? In time of need do you remember to ask him for peace?

doing good

"Love your enemies! Do good to them. Lend to them without expecting to be repaid. Then your reward from heaven will be very great, and you will truly be acting as children of the Most High, for he is kind to those who are unthankful and wicked."

LUKE 6:35 NLT

Charlotte owned a small retail store and had interactions with each of her customers. Grace was an especially persnickety regular customer. Everything was fair game for Grace's criticisms: the music played, the clothes they wore, the displays, and the merchandise. No one wanted to wait on Grace. One day Charlotte decided that the best way to manage this situation was to go overboard with kindness. She complimented Grace's outfit, hair, and shoes. She smiled at her and never showed impatience or hurt when Grace found fault. She did this time and again. After a while, Charlotte began to look forward to seeing Grace in the store. And then Charlotte realized that she had actually grown to like Grace. She began to see her as a loyal customer.

By taking the courage to change the way she saw Grace and extending kindness, Charlotte benefited from the relationship. Look for the best in others. Show kindness and offer grace. It's not always easy to do, but it's well worth the effort. Follow the Lord's example of loving your enemies.

God, help me to respond in love to those who are hard to deal with. I want to show them your love in my dealings with them. Thank you for these opportunities.

Is there someone in your life you can "kill with kindness"?

ask away

This is the confidence we have in approaching God:
that if we ask anything according to his will, he hears us.
1 JOHN 5:14 NIV

It's all too easy to think of God as Santa Claus. In the Gospels we hear Jesus say to ask whatever we want, and it will be done. So, does this mean to just ask away? How about a million dollars, a vacation home, to win that race, or make the person of our dreams love us? If we had been there listening to Jesus, it would have been obvious what he was actually saying. This wasn't a flippant offer of a lifetime. This was Jesus, the Son of God, telling us that the God of the Universe wanted an intimate relationship with each of us. He wants us to share with him what we are thinking about.

Just as much as he wants to lavish his generosity upon us, God knows that not all things are beneficial. He knows the future. He desires the very best for us. It takes courage to pray "If it be your will." Don't let fear keep you from asking the Lord for the desires of your heart. Being willing to abide by his will means that he will change our hearts to accept the answer he gives.

Lord Jesus, I long for a deeper relationship with you. Help me to pray more and to be willing to accept any answer you may give me. I know you have my best at heart.

Have you asked God for something and been disappointed? Can you see his wisdom in past prayers that were not answered? Do you see answered prayer in your life?

wisdom

Whoever walks with the wise becomes wise,
but the companion of fools suffers harm.
PROVERBS 13:20 NRSV

Studies have shown that what our parents told us was true, "we are the company we keep." By surrounding ourselves with a circle of friends who are heavily into partying, we become partiers. If our closest companions are believers, our faith is strengthened. When we let Google be our guide we can go off on a tangent. In the Bible we find direction and encouragement.

Proverbs is full of instruction for living a blessed and godly life. Many people make a habit to read one chapter of Proverbs every day. There's a chapter for every day in the month and they are packed with a wondrous road map to life, containing both advice and cautions perfectly suited to the present. Living as the Lord would have us means going against flow of today's culture. You need to be brave to live as a Christ follower. This doesn't mean you need to wear a linen robe and eat grasshoppers! It doesn't mean you need to give up TV or going to the amusement park. It means we need to be grounded. God tells us to seek wisdom. Find a person older in the faith who can counsel you, join a Bible study, or memorize Scripture that will help you. All of these can keep you on the road to becoming wise.

Dear Lord, it seems I can never know enough of your Word. Help me to look for ways to become wiser in you. Thank you for those you have put in my path to help me.

Do you go to a regular Bible study? Do you have a go-to friend when you need godly advice? Do you regularly read God's Word?

loving yourself

Love patiently accepts all things.
It always trusts, always hopes, and always endures.
1 CORINTHIANS 13:7 NCV

Are you a glass half-empty type of person or is your glass half-full? God wants you to have a glass overflowing! How God loves you is pure and constant. Does your mind turn to the negative when hearing what others say? If someone gives you a compliment, "You did great today!" Do you hear "Yesterday you really messed up?" Do you let the opinions of others determine your own self-image?

It's easy to let this spill over into our relationship with God. It's easy to only see the ominous warnings and condemnations in God's Word and miss the blessings and messages of hope and love. Christ died for our imperfections. We are a new creation. It takes courage to change the way we think about ourselves. The Lord patiently accepts and loves everything about you. Embrace God's love for you which always (every single time) trusts, always (yes, every single time) hopes for the best for you, and always (forever) continues.

God, thank you for loving me even when I find it hard to love myself. Help me to see myself through your eyes.

Do you have problems of self-worth? Does this affect your relationships with others? Can you accept God's love?

always faithful

"Know therefore that the LORD your God is God; he is the faithful God, keeping his covenant of love to a thousand generations of those who love him and keep his commandments."

DEUTERONOMY 7:9 NIV

Do you have days when everything seems to go wrong and you feel hopeless? It might be that you feel worthless and unloved. This is when we especially need to remember that God loves us. That he chose us individually and has promised to be faithful. God made a covenant, a promise, a contract with his people that he would always love us, always care for, and always be merciful to us. God has assured us that he has us in his care. Each day, each moment is a new start.

Scripture promises "If anyone is in Christ, he is a new creation. The old has passed away; behold, the new has come" (2 Corinthians 5:17). Whatever has caused your distress is in the past and as of this moment you can choose to change your circumstances. Take courage to lean on God and trust him to handle the stresses and disappointments you encounter.

Lord God, sometimes I am discouraged and afraid. Help me to trust in your love and mercy. I want to lean on you.

What is your biggest fear? Can you trust God to handle it for you? Do you believe he has your best interests at heart?

words matter

Do not let any unwholesome talk come out of your mouths, but only what is helpful for building others up according to their needs, that it may benefit those who listen.

EPHESIANS 4:29 NIV

"Sticks and stones will break my bones, but words will never harm me." This often-quoted childhood rhyme isn't true at all. Words do hurt. Words do matter. Taunts, rants, and criticisms hurt the hearers, and God has called us to build up one another. Old habits die hard, but you can break those habits. How you speak with others will define you. Do your friends consider you trustworthy or incapable of keeping a secret? Are you a gossip? Do you use your words as a weapon, or are your conversations encouraging and helpful? Just as a compliment that comes your way can improve your own self-esteem, giving one to others can improve your relationship.

We are reminded in Scripture that keeping our conversations wholesome and heartwarming can be gratifying and cheering for both speakers and hearers. Choose your words and conversations carefully. Take a moment to gather your thoughts before speaking and especially before responding to someone else. Don't return one mean statement with another. Being kind in thought, word, and deed are qualities to aim for.

God, I want to speak better to others. Help my speech to be encouraging, kind, and beneficial to my hearers. Remind me before I speak to choose my words carefully.

Are you critical in your speech? Can you think of one or two changes you would like to make in the way you speak to others?

salvation

With joy you will drink deeply from the fountain of salvation!
ISAIAH 12:3 NLT

As Christ-followers we strive to become like Jesus. We put aside those habits and pastimes we know are unbecoming. We pray for ourselves and the people we hold near and dear. We pray for those in the world around us and for circumstances beyond our control. We regularly read and apply the Scriptures. We attend a church and surround ourselves with like-minded believers. There is much in our lives that we have turned over to God—we have given him the reins of our life and much of what we think and do models Christian morals. Living the Christian life is amazing. It is fulfilling and wonderful, but it is not all God has for us. He wants us to have joy!

Coming to Christ involves acknowledging that we are sinners and asking his forgiveness. At that moment we are granted salvation. What a joy to know we are no longer condemned but granted a wondrous life with God after we die. In our sophisticated world, we enjoy many creature comforts and more than enough to eat, even to excess. Our real treasure, our paradise will be our eternal life in heaven with God. Such joy we cannot even imagine.

Lord, I am grateful for the life you give me now. Keep me ever mindful of the joy of heaven to come. I want to rejoice with you for eternity.

Do you think of your salvation as a joy in your life? Do you put your salvation second to a life in the here and now? Are you thankful for the gift of eternal life with God?

bickering

Remind everyone about these things, and command them in God's presence to stop fighting over words. Such arguments are useless, and they can ruin those who hear them.

2 TIMOTHY 2:14 NLT

Bickering can be exhausting for everyone. Endless arguments over words can get you nowhere. There is no winner of contemptuous arguments. Both parties feel wronged. The wise and courageous know when to stop fighting. In the Church it can be destructive. Many churches have split over somewhat minor differences or interpretations of minor doctrine. When you face a disagreement over a small thing, it is best to ask for a cooling off period.

Paul reminds us what is important: "If we have died with him, we will also live with him; if we endure, we will also reign with him; if we deny him, he also will deny us; if we are faithless, he remains faithful" (2 Timothy 11-13). Quibbling over small things minimizes the good news of the Gospel. This is especially lethal when there are non-Christians or new Christians present as it can discourage them in their faith. It can be intimidating in a group to be the peacemaker, but we are called by God to speak up.

Dear Lord, help me to be the peacemaker when arguments arise. Give me the courage to speak up. Help me to stop disagreements when I am able.

Do you like to argue? Have you felt uncomfortable speaking up in a group situation? Can you think of a way to calmly call for a time out?

give me joy

*"Until now you have asked nothing in my name.
Ask, and you will receive, that your joy may be full."*
JOHN 16:24 ESV

Birthday parties are so much fun. Imagine all the hoopla of games, party hats, songs, and cake. Oh, and the most exciting part: the presents! The highlight of every birthday party is when it is time to open the presents. The look of sheer joy on the birthday girl as she receives each gift is memorable. Who doesn't love getting gifts?

The definition of a gift is something given without the expectation of return. God wants to give you a wonderful gift—joy. The catch? He doesn't want you to strike a bargain. He doesn't want you to sacrifice anything. He just wants you to ask for it. It is so simple. When you don't feel you are worthy of joy, be brave and ask God for it anyway.

God, I need a blessing in my life. I need joy. I want to ask you to fill my heart. Help me to take the step of asking you for what I need.

Are there things in your life you don't dare ask God for? Can you take a step of faith and ask him for joy?

priorities

Make every effort to keep yourselves united in the Spirit,
binding yourselves together with peace.
EPHESIANS 4:3 NLT

Olivia grew up in church, attending Sunday services, giving her life to Christ at age fourteen and enjoying youth group events all through high school. She enrolled at a Christian university 300 miles from home, eventually graduating and forging a life in her new home town. She now had church friends, friends from the gym, work friends, and neighbors. Now there were more options for her on Sundays other than just going to church. She ran a 5K one week and several weeks later had a work trip over the weekend. A neighbor wanted her to go to a show on Sunday and her nephew had a ball game playoff the following week. It seemed she made it to worship service less and less.

The story ends well, though. Olivia's absence was noticed by a friend who commented that she was missed at church and Olivia took stock of her priorities. She knew that meeting together with her brothers and sisters to seek God was the most important thing she could do. She made fellowshipping together a priority.

Lord, help me to unite in the Spirit with your body a priority in my life. Show me ways of improving my participation in my church. Thank you for giving me a group of like-minded believers to meet with.

Do you often skip church? Are you connected with people within your church? Can you think of more ways to become a part of the local body?

eternal perspective

"As the heavens are higher than the earth, so are My ways higher than your ways, and My thoughts than your thoughts."

ISAIAH 55:9 NKJV

There are days when your activities and thoughts are concerned with the mundane. Will the traffic light stay green? What should we have for dinner? Is there anything in the refrigerator to make dinner? Is my green shirt clean? How is there time to get that report done for work? You throw up a quick, "Help me God!" and rush to the next task on your never-ending list of things to do. Busy days rush into tiring weeks, turning into bustling months of preoccupation. It can feel as if we are on an ever-faster spinning carousel, clinging to a brightly painted steed, hoping against hope that we can just hold on. Sound familiar?

God knows your thoughts. He knows the peace your spirit yearns for. He is concerned with eternity while you struggle with this moment. Spending quiet time with the Lord will help you find a perspective that transcends the confines of today's world. He knows the pressures you feel and wants to give you peace. A heart in sync with God will help you to be joyful and serene in chaos. Take time to seek the Lord every day.

God, my life is full of responsibilities and work I must accomplish on a daily basis. Help me to see my priorities. I want to meet you every day and seek your peace in the center of my being.

Do you struggle with too much to accomplish in the time you have? Are there ways you can prioritize what you need to do and weed out some things for time with the Lord?

august

Say to those with fearful hearts, "Be strong, and do not fear, for your God is coming to destroy your enemies. He is coming to save you."

ISAIAH 35:4 NLT

a love story

The Lord appeared to us in the past, saying:
"I have loved you with an everlasting love;
I have drawn you with unfailing kindness."
JEREMIAH 31:3 NIV

Who doesn't love a great love story? A good and kindhearted man gets to know a lovely and brave woman. He brings her gifts of candy and flowers and silly little remembrances. They do fun things together. He sings love songs and her heart melts. There may be a few rocky moments but those only help to solidify the relationship. He asks for her hand in marriage and she accepts as birds sing and the sun shines and all is well. Forever and ever. Curtain down.

This experience may be yours or perhaps not, but do not despair. You have had your very own everlasting and heavenly love story. God has loved you from the beginning of time. He knew all about you before you were born. Each step of your life he was there, gently wooing you. Giving you every chance to get to know him. His love for you is unending and eternal. He wasn't discouraged when you didn't see him. He waited. And then you became his bride. He isn't disappointed in you. His face of love shines for you. Tell him your hopes and dreams. Listen to his still, small voice. Read the love letters he's written to you in the Scriptures. You are his beloved!

Lord, help me to see myself as your bride. I want to keep our love story fresh and new. Show me ways to love you more.

Do you have a problem seeing yourself as God's very special bride?

success

"Keep this Book of the Law always on your lips; meditate on it day and night, so that you may be careful to do everything written in it. Then you will be prosperous and successful."

JOSHUA 1:8 NIV

In any city today, there are thousands of laws, perhaps hundreds of thousands. How can anyone know them all? Many of them are common sense while others are learned through careful study, but no one seems to know them all. "But I didn't know that it was against the law!" offenders claim all the time. To this a judge will reply "It doesn't matter. The law must be enforced. Ignorance is no excuse."

How can we know God's laws? The Bible is a gift. It contains history, instructions, and warnings for successful living and best of all, the way of salvation. When you read a passage, slow down and think about it. Think about it again. Memorizing verses is a useful way to keep the Word of God in your heart. Singing Scripture songs is particularly meaningful. Encouragement and insight from other Christ-followers can also be favorable. When we understand the Word of God, we can live confidently, choosing to do what is right and good. And that will bring us joy, peace, and mercy.

God, I want to know you and your Word better. Help me to understand what I read in the Bible and make it part of my life.

Do you read your Bible with regularity? Is it easy to understand? Have you ever memorized Scripture passages?

mercy and grace

God is so rich in mercy, and he loved us so much, that even though we were dead because of our sins, he gave us life when he raised Christ from the dead. (It is only by God's grace that you have been saved!
EPHESIANS 2:4-5 NLT

Imagine a courtroom; directly in front of you sits a stern judge in a black robe. You stand, knees knocking and anxious. You can hardly breathe. You know you are guilty. There is a roaring in your ears. It is just a matter of how much time you will serve in prison. Your life as you know it is effectively over. BANG! The gavel comes down and the judge says, "Pardoned." Oh, the joy that fills your heart. The heartfelt elation enters your whole being. It is hard to take in.

When we realize that even in the middle of our sins God showered us with unfathomable mercy and grace by sending Jesus to die in our place, it should be apparent to us that we should extend both grace and mercy to those who offend us. The grievance may be small or immense. It may even seem insurmountable. By offering forgiveness we help ourselves more than the offender. We can move on without bitterness and the pain it causes us. It isn't easy, but when we look to God's example of love, we can trust that it is to our benefit to model him.

Dear God, thank you for the grace you extended to me, so I might live eternally with you. You showed me mercy. Help me to be merciful to those who wrong me.

Have you thought about what your life would be like without God? How has his model of mercy and grace made a difference? Do you find it easy to forgive others?

in the whisper

"Call to me and I will answer you and tell you great and unsearchable things you do not know."
JEREMIAH 33:3 NIV

A surprising study on parenting styles revealed that one of the best ways to get the attention of a child is to whisper. When instructing an important lesson, imparting it in a whisper helps the child to focus, to remember, and to act upon the information. Yelling or pontificating doesn't work as well. Taking the child onto your lap or sitting closely and softly speaking causes both memory and comprehension to improve. This is true with your heavenly Father. He wants to share so very much with you. He wants to gather you up in his arms and give you strength.

God longs to tell you of his unfathomable love for you. He wants to lighten your burdens and help you grow. Are you willing to listen to his still, small voice? Let him whisper in your ear. Our lives are noisy, and we need to slow down, be quiet, and listen to God. Take a deep breath, sink back into his arms, and allow God to feed your soul.

Father, I want to learn from you. Help me to slow down and listen. Fill my soul with joy and understanding.

Have you listened quietly to God? Have you heard him? What do you think God wants to tell you?

aware of needs

When he saw the crowds, he had compassion on them, because they were harassed and helpless, like sheep without a shepherd.
MATTHEW 9:36 NIV

Every day in the news we hear of a new disaster. Famines, floods, fires, plane crashes, and the like happen every day. Children need parents, girls cannot attend school because they don't have uniforms, communities look for help and appeal for money. It's easy to tune them all out. After all, what can one person do to alleviate world hunger? How could you even try to clothe a nation's children? A single person can't do much.

Jesus was aware of the needs of those he encountered. When he fed five thousand people gathered on the hillside near Bethesda he did what he could. He took up a collection of five small loaves of bread and two fish, began to break them, and instructed his disciples to distribute them to the crowd. Jesus knew they were hungry, and he fed them. He didn't feed all the people in Bethesda. He fulfilled the need as he saw it. We can't feel all the starving, but we could support one child. We could volunteer at the library's literacy program. We could give money to our church's fund for meeting the needs of the community. Keep your heart open to see opportunities in which you can help make lives better.

God, allow my heart to be opened to the needs of those around me. Help me to find ways to show compassion. Make me grateful for what you have given to me.

What ways do you show compassion? Can you pray for needs too?

simplicity

The LORD has told you what is good, and this is what he requires of you: to do what is right, to love mercy, and to walk humbly with your God.

MICAH 6:8 NLT

Book upon book has been written on how to live the Christian life. There are some by giants in the faith like Martin Luther, St. Augustine, John Wesley, Florence Nightingale, C.S. Lewis, and Billy Graham, just to name a few. We can find hundreds of thousands of books all on following God. There are so many thoughts and so much information to sift through, how can we know it all? It must take a lifetime to find out what God wants us to do. It must be complicated. In fact, it is simple. Jesus said, "I am the way, the truth and the life. No one comes to the Father, except through me" (John 14:6 ESV).

To be a Christ-follower you don't have to wear your hair a certain way or sport a particular style. You don't have to be married or have children. You aren't expected to be a certain age when you come to Christ. Too often a group or church will set up guidelines for those who are Christians. You must pray one way, or only play a specific kind of music, or read these books, or associate with certain kinds of people. Beware! Micah has told us what is required: do what is right, love mercy, and walk humbly with God. It is a simple challenge. Are you up for it?

God, I want to get back to the heart of the Gospel. Help me to live the simplicity of your Word. Thank you for the courage not to be swayed by extraneous doctrines.

Have you ever been led astray by the latest and greatest fad of doctrine? Does your church preach the Bible? Do you put unnecessary rules on your faith?

a gentle answer

"Blessed are the gentle, for they shall inherit the earth."
MATTHEW 5:5 NASB

Proverbs tells us a gentle answer turns away anger. Jesus tells us that we will be blessed and inherit the earth if we are among the gentle. This makes perfect sense! Happy people are kind, gentle, slow to anger, and show compassion to the needs of those around them. They are well-liked and admired. Their relationships flourish.

Bitterness and hostility breed discord and dissatisfaction with life. Jesus knew we needed a gentle spirit to be blessed and happy with this life on earth. Can a boisterous, active, jubilant person be gentle in spirit? Of course! Gentle doesn't mean wimpy. Gentle means thoughtful, kindhearted, hospitable, polite, respectful, and gracious. Gentle spirits are benevolent, selfless, diplomatic, and courteous. All allow us to live at peace with those around us.

God, make me gentle and kind. Remind me when I am at odds with life that it is time to look within. Help me to see your blessings and pass them along to others.

Are you kind and respectful? When was the last time you blew it? What can you learn from that incident to be better prepared next time?

a gentleman

The LORD must wait for you to come to him, so he can show you his love and compassion. For the LORD is a faithful God. Blessed are those who wait for his help.

ISAIAH 30:18 NLT

It's been said that God is a gentleman. He doesn't insist that we love him. He doesn't force us to love him. He woos us patiently. His desire is for a relationship with us. Christians can look back to the time before they accepted Christ and see how God was there all along. He was persistently waiting for us to return his love and accept the sacrifice of his Son, who died for our wrongdoings. He designed a path for us to follow to the cross, and when we deviated from that path he made a new way.

He made another path and another, until we stood at the cross and asked him for forgiveness. God is always faithful. He keeps his promises. A wise person will trust the Lord. A brave person will ensure successful living by waiting for God's help. Relying on the Lord instead of our own intellect takes courage. Giving up our will and wanting God's will isn't easy, but the reward is great.

God, I want to wait for your help. Too often I rely on myself. I want that to change. Make me willing to wait for your answers. Help me to hear your voice.

Do you remember a time when God was patiently waiting for you to come to him? Do you rely on his will or your own? How can you identify his will for you?

obedience

"Blessed rather are those who hear the word of God and obey it."
LUKE 11:28 NIV

Do you follow the rules or act as if they don't apply to you? How about coloring within the lines? Is your philosophy that all rules are made to be broken? No one is hurt when someone wears a plaid shirt with striped pants, and mixing sweet and savory suits some palates just fine. Many of our day-to-day experiences are left to our own choice. Eat meat or not. Pursue an advanced degree or not. Choose a dog or cat or hamster or not.

When Jesus gave us the lessons in the Beatitudes, he was telling us how to be happy or blessed and that hearing and knowing God's Word and not obeying it would make us unhappy. He knew that actions have consequences. Knowing how to treat others, what activities to avoid, what spiritual qualities to aim for, will make us blessed. Obedience shouldn't be a negatively charged word. It should be a pleasurable experience knowing that when we do what the Lord has set for us in Scripture it gives us an abundant, delightful life. Make it a habit to regularly read your Bible to hear the Word of God for you.

Lord, I know you want only the best for me. Help me to listen to you and be obedient. Lead me on your paths.

Do you find it hard to obey God? Do you feel guilty when you know you are off track? How do you get back on God's path?

speech

*"By your words you will be justified,
and by your words you will be condemned."*

MATTHEW 12:37 ESV

Would anyone listening to you talk suspect that you are a believer? If you were accused in court of being a Christian would there be enough evidence to convict you? These queries have been put out there before, and they are worth thinking about. Are you truthful? Are you reliable and dependable? Is your speech kind and uplifting? Using crude or rude language is a learned habit that can also be unlearned.

Do you lift up the name of Christ or deny him? It may be scary but evaluating what you say and how you say it is an important step in determining how deep your commitment to the ways of God are grounded in your life. Be bold and take a chance at proclaiming your faith the next time an inappropriate conversation begins. Change the subject; speak truth and light and life and love. When you hear complaining, speak hope and compassion. Be known as someone who is kind, speaks wisely, and walks uprightly. A good reputation is priceless.

God, help me to speak righteousness. Alert me to bad habits and let me offer truth. May others see you in me.

Do others see God at work in your life? What one thing could you change in your conversations? Are you willing to work at ending bad habits?

enough to share

"Anyone who has two shirts should share with the one who has none, and anyone who has food should do the same."

LUKE 3:11 NIV

Brianna was in the car on her way to the park with her four children. Together they had packed a lunch before going. Each child had chosen a special item: Olivia wanted donuts, so she put five donuts in the basket. Ava's favorite were the peaches. One, two, three, four, five peaches were carefully tucked in the corner. Noah wanted ham sandwiches and proudly made all five sandwiches himself. Brianna helped bag them up. All little Grayson wanted was string cheese and he got the sticks from the refrigerator. After the car was parked, the children raced to climb and swing and play on the new equipment the city had installed the week before.

As Brianna called them for lunch, along came Jessica, a woman they knew from church with her three small children. Brianna invited them to share lunch. Noah leaned toward his mother and protested, "But Mom! We don't have enough. We only brought five of everything." Brianna smiled and said gently to her son, "Noah, no matter how much or how little we have, we always have enough to share." Wise words from a wise mama. We always have enough to share.

God, give me a generous heart. Alert me to how I can share what I have with others. Make me ever-grateful for what you have given to me.

Have you missed an opportunity to share? Do you feel what you have isn't good enough to share? How do you feel when someone shares generously with you?

just believe

Jesus paid no attention to what they said.
He told the synagogue leader, "Don't be afraid; just believe."

MARK 5:36 NCV

Can faith move mountains? Most certainly! The question is, can your faith move mountains? Can you trust God to handle momentous things in your life? When the doctor says, "Cancer," when the call comes to tell you of your father's heart attack, when you open the envelope and the note inside says "Terminated," or when the fish tank breaks and spills ten gallons of fishy water all over your cream-colored rug, the right thing to do is turn it over to God. You may wrestle for a long time or you may send up a quick prayer, but give it to him. Jesus says, "Don't be afraid; just believe." Believe that he will give you the support you need, the wisdom to make the right decisions, and the strength to carry it out.

The world has it all backwards. Following God is not a hard and arduous journey along a bomb-strewn path. Rather the answers are simple: believe. Believe that Jesus is the Son of God, that he died to save you from your sins, that he wants to give you life abundantly, and that he has a very special place for you in heaven. Simply believe. The mountains will move, or God will help you go around them. It's that easy.

God, when things get crazy, help me to believe. Grow my faith to trust you to handle the hard times. I want to have faith to believe in moving mountains.

Can you look back to a time when Jesus helped you in a time of need? Do you ask him for help in the big things and the little things?

agape

Be on guard. Stand firm in the faith. Be courageous. Be strong.
And do everything with love.
1 CORINTHIANS 16:13-14 NLT

In the Bible we are instructed to do everything with love. Ah, love! That mushy, marshmallowy, song birds, hearts and flowers, romantic love! Well, obviously that's one kind of love but not the love that Paul talks about in 1 Corinthians. Agape love is kind, compassionate, enthusiastic, full of faith and truth. It is sympathetic, merciful, trustworthy, and honest. Agape love always puts others first, is helpful and hopeful, forgiving, and it continues even when not reciprocated. This love is never ending, unrelenting. It is how God loves us.

God has called you to be a brave and courageous Christian. You should be on guard at all times from attacks by the enemy. You need to stand firm in your faith especially when the world is against you. Rely on the Lord and walk in his will. How can this be done? Seek God's agape love in your heart to withstand all that you may encounter. Live your life in love. Show the love God has given you to those around you.

Jesus, thank you for loving me. Help me to understand courage and strength in the light of agape love. Please let others know your love through me.

Can you remember a time when you were strong and courageous? Did you also mirror love?

keep the faith

Do not throw away this confident trust in the Lord.
Remember the great reward it brings you!
HEBREWS 10:35 NLT

Have you ever waivered in your faith? Was there a time when you felt that living for God was just too hard? Perhaps he seemed distant and unhearing. Many Christians across the ages have felt just like that. Even giants in Christian history have had their doubts. C.S. Lewis concluded there was no God in his early adulthood, finally coming back full circle to not just believing but spending the rest of his life writing and lecturing about Jesus. Millions have read his books and seen the movies about them.

God loves you. He understands what you are going through. He knows you have doubts. He wants to remind you that this time is fleeting. He recognizes how you feel. Put your trust in him and get through this hard situation. God is always there listening to you. There is great treasure awaiting you. Be brave, be fearless, have courage, and continue to trust the Lord who guards your heart.

God, sometimes it seems as if you are far away and I wonder if you are really there. Help me with my unbelief! Let me hear your voice. Help me to renew my devotion to you.

Do you sometimes wonder if God is there? When you are low is there someone you can go to for encouragement? Do you ask the Lord for help?

heaven

Those the LORD has rescued will return. They will enter Zion with singing; everlasting joy will crown their heads. Gladness and joy will overtake them, and sorrow and sighing will flee away.
ISAIAH 51:11 NIV

Ashley had been helping her mom, Ginger, for the past three years, ever since the Alzheimer's disease had made it difficult for Mom to live on her own. In the beginning, Ashley had just taken over writing the bills and later arranged for a cleaning lady once a week. After a few months, she had Meals-on-Wheels come five days a week. It was hard for the grandkids as Nana began to forget how to do simple tasks. The family was supportive and loving as Ginger had good days and bad. All too soon the day came when Nana had to leave her home. She couldn't dress herself or cope on her own anymore.

Ginger was admitted to a care facility and Ashley and her family visited as often as they could. It pained Ashley so to see her mom go downhill so quickly. Her general health began to decline, and she suffered a stroke. One night the home called, and Ashley raced to her mother's side. As Ginger breathed her last, Ashley could thank the Lord for heaven. Mom was out of pain, out of sorrow, and gone was the confusion that had held her for so long. God is faithful. We can look forward to an eternity with him in heaven with no pain, no sorrow, and no regrets.

Lord, help me to look towards the promise of eternal life with you in Heaven. Help me when I grieve and miss those who have gone on before me. Let me long for life with you.

Do you grieve for a loved one? Does heaven seem real to you?

firm foundation

This is what the Sovereign Lord says: "Look! I am placing a foundation stone in Jerusalem, a firm and tested stone. It is a precious cornerstone that is safe to build on. Whoever believes need never be shaken."

ISAIAH 28:16 NLT

Architects know that for a building to stand it must first have a good foundation. This means digging down to the bedrock and supporting the weight by laying strong footings. Only then can a successful structure be built. Your Christian life is like that tower. God laid the foundation when you gave your life to him. It is a strong foundation. Since that time, each bit of knowledge, every prayer, every verse has laid down the walls. When you obeyed the Word of God and showed his love to others the walls took shape. Slowly they rise, strong on the cornerstone of your faith and held together by God. Those walls keep the enemy away; they cannot be broken down or shaken.

You can take a brave stand in your relationships with others. Share what you know about the Lord and what he has done in your life. Don't be afraid of standing strong when the world mocks you. God stands with you. He is the firm foundation, ever mighty and carrying you through the perils of life. Don't be afraid. Stand strong.

Lord God, thank you for the foundational truths you have shared with me. Help me to be strong and remember that you are always supporting me. I want to learn to share my faith better.

Do you feel God's strength when you are afraid? Do you remember a time when you know that it was his power that was working through you?

slow to anger

Those with good sense are slow to anger,
and it is their glory to overlook an offense.
PROVERBS 19:11 NRSV

Everyone seems to be taking offense these days. With the rise of social media, civility is a thing of the past. It used to be simple to have a conversation with a friend of differing political or religious views. Everyone treated others with respect and didn't expect to be confronted in an escalating battle of wills; not any more. There is still time to change this disturbing trend. A wise are slow to anger, slow to take offense. Arguments can easily turn to verbal battles and anger can turn even the most thoughtful individual into a monster.

Proverbs 16:24 tells us that gracious words are sweet and healing. If we can keep our discussions calm, we can dispense hope instead of discouragement. When we purpose to be peacemakers, we can show compassion and mercy. It is not a sign of weakness but of good sense to keep check on our temper, and gloriously rewarding to nurture our relationships with others.

God, help me keep my temper. I want to bless those around me and be known as a person of peace, not of discord. Help me to think before I speak and to be slow to anger.

Do you have a quick temper? Do you have broken relationships because of it? Are you brave enough to seek out those you may have hurt?

be brave

"Have I not commanded you? Be strong and courageous. Do not be afraid; do not be discouraged, for the Lord your God will be with you wherever you go."

Joshua 1:9 NIV

Courage! As a Christian you can be strong, secure in who you are as God's child. You show compassion to those in need, love to those around you, and think pure thoughts. You are kind and generous; you speak truth and don't compare yourself to other people. When the enemy sends his darts your way, you stand firm, you are persistently seeking your heavenly Father's help. You read the Word regularly and remember God's promises and obey him. You look forward to heaven and are grateful for your salvation.

Worry and anxiety flee as you give over your troubles to the Lord. You have the courage to be bold in proclaiming your faith. Blessed are you that in time of fear and discouragement you have the Lord to help and guide you through all your days. You are a child of the King of the universe!

Lord, your words are a comfort to my soul. I want to take that stand and enjoy all the benefits of being your child. I want to be brave and courageous.

Do you see yourself in these descriptions? Which are you confident about? Are there areas you need to work on?

compassionate step

Be kind and compassionate to one another,
forgiving each other, just as in Christ God forgave you.
EPHESIANS 4:32 NIV

Have you hurt someone? Perhaps you shared their secret, misled them, or purposely caused them great pain. It takes a brave person to acknowledge wrongdoing and ask for forgiveness, not just with family and friends but enemies as well. Your heavenly Father has forgiven you for so much and it is his will that you offer forgiveness as well.

Relationships can be difficult. A careless word or action can be misunderstood, a "joke" can get out of hand or sometimes we just plain mess up. There are times we say or do something that seems unforgiveable. Feelings get hurt, plans and reputations are ruined, or physical injuries may result. God has called us to take the compassionate step of forgiveness. He wants our heart to be soft, kind, thoughtful, and sympathetic. A heart filled with bitterness and hostility eats at your spirit. Show compassion, offer mercy, and free yourself from the hold of unforgiveness in your life. Remember all God has done for you.

Lord, help me be quick to seek forgiveness when I wrong others. Help me soften my own heart and forgive the people in my life who have hurt me. Make me more like you.

Is there someone in your life you can't seem to forgive. Do you think it affects your joy? Can you forgive them even if they don't ask for it?

love deeply

Above all, love each other deeply,
because love covers over a multitude of sins.

1 PETER 4:8 NIV

When we love a person the way Christ loves, we open the door for mercy and grace to flow into that life in a way that only God can create. We open our hearts to a truth that is bigger than our own understanding, and we give ourselves to actions and resolutions that are beyond our own abilities.

One of the transcendent qualities of love is forgiveness. When we forgive, we give a clean slate that we promise not to take back. This does not mean the problem has vanished. It does not mean trust has been rebuilt. It certainly does not mean that we have thrown away wisdom to give someone warm fuzzies or a get out of jail free card. Rather, the rubble has cleared away to a foundation of love and forgiveness. The forgiven person can rebuild in greater wisdom. On the foundation of love, we each wisely build our lives. In forgiving, we say, "Come, now. Let us start over, better."

God, people are aching for forgiveness. Where do you want me to help someone have a fresh start?

Go forgive someone. Do not announce it to others, but protect the person's good name in quiet love.

builders of humans

Encourage one another and build one another up,
just as you are doing.
1 THESSALONIANS 5:11 NASB

Each of us is a builder when we walk through growth with another believer. We are a house for God as well as for ourselves. We are a temple and one of the Holy Spirit's places of habitation. When we are encouraged, we take on greater faith that God is constructing us according to his will. When we invest time and energy into learning from others we grow and create a better house in which the Holy Spirit dwells.

All we do is for the glory of God. When we encourage others, and share our testimonies, insights, and lessons learned, we become construction workers who build humans. What a wonderful joy it is to create a glorious habitation for Christ's Spirit. What a wonderful honor it is to help others do the same.

Thank you, Holy Spirit, for living inside me. Help me to give and receive timely encouragement and instruction from others so we can all build one another up.

When you consider your inner life, what do you want to offer to Christ for an upgrade? Be bold.

grateful always

*Be thankful in all circumstances, for this is God's will
for you who belong to Christ Jesus.*

1 THESSALONIANS 5:18 NLT

We seek out God's will in so many ways: reading the Bible, attending church, listening to friends and other counsel. We pray, we fast, we jump to get seats at the next conference. Sometimes, it is easy to see what God's will is. Today's verse falls into that category.

In everything you do, wherever you are, or whatever happens to you or around you, be grateful. Why? Because God rolls you into his presence on the wheels of your gratitude, and he loves to spend time with you. You belong with Christ, and whenever you are in his presence, his face lights up. He seeks to comfort you and bless you. That's why there is a fullness of joy in his presence.

Father, thank you for your clear directive to be grateful. I am so glad you want me to know your will, and you reward me for doing it.

What are you grateful for? Write that gratitude on a slip of paper, and then place it in a jar. Add to your jar daily so you can review its contents whenever you need a pick-me-up. Thank God for all that makes you grateful.

over the top

All of God's promises have been fulfilled in Christ with a resounding "Yes!" And through Christ, our "Amen" ascends to God for his glory.
2 CORINTHIANS 1:20 NLT

In the sixth chapter of Judges, we read about a man named Gideon. He was the least revered man of the lowest clan of Manasseh at a time when the Jews were lowest on the pecking order in their land. Everyone in Israel was desperate for relief from their assailants. The angel of the Lord spoke to Gideon and assured him that he was with him. He called him a mighty man of valor! Gideon did not agree. He did not understand how he could lead the Jews to be saved and the enemies obliterated.

God had not taken advice from earthly counsel, and he surely did not need Gideon's permission to fulfill his promises through the knee-knocking protestor. The promises of the Lord are "Yes," and "Amen!" He does not need your permission, he only requires your obedience. God did not ask more of Gideon than he could give. He told him to go in his own strength and promised that his presence on Gideon's life was enough. Gideon pushed through his fear and became the champion God saw. You, too, are a champion.

Lord, you were with everyone who ever did something remarkable for you. Be with me, and I will do your remarkable work, as well.

What is God's "Yes, and Amen," for you to accomplish in your own strength as he goes with you?

on your heart

"These commandments that I give you today are to be on your hearts. Impress them on your children. Talk about them when you sit at home and when you walk along the road, when you lie down and when you get up."

DEUTERONOMY 6:6-7 NIV

God's Word will strengthen you to faith. Faith makes you brave. Nothing gets God's Word into your soul like reading the Bible. If you study it, it will hone your heart to be sharp and discerning of what is good and what is bad. You will not be in question when you come to a decision, because you will have already understood the nature of God.

It is much easier to study God's Word and incorporate it into your life if you meditate upon it all day long. That doesn't mean you keep a Bible open and neglect your work. It means you tuck God's Word into your heart, so you won't be sinful. You talk about God's Word when you can, so you get a depth of understanding and can pick out misguided beliefs before they are woven into your thought patterns and actions. Then, you know you please God, and you become brave.

Lord, help me to plant your Word deeply in my heart so it dwells richly within me. Help me live out of the wellspring of truth, and of the knowledge that you are with me.

How can you incorporate God's Word more meaningfully into your lifestyle?

precious child

I praise you because I am fearfully and wonderfully made;
your works are wonderful, I know that full well.

PSALM 139:14 NIV

She drew a piece of artwork from a box of rumpled news. It was a bowl she had made in school; she recognized it immediately. Hadn't she thrown that away? Ah, but it had been precious to her mother, and so it was kept and cherished. Now, it might make a nice jewelry bowl for her own dressing table. She held the bowl up to the light and analyzed it with care. Under the veneer of fired gloss and green paint, she saw her own fingerprints! As sunlight washed over them, she considered how faithfully each line still represented the molds of her fingertips.

Oh, the thoughts of God toward us! The divine wonder that we could be so fearfully and wonderfully made. We are all cherished by our Father, far beyond our own regard. God has made us each as he has intended, and his intentions do not change. His fingerprints are upon us. And though we will always strive to be useful, Jesus will always see us as precious.

God, thank you for loving me beyond my own understanding. Let me rest in your hands and understand you how you understand me.

How are you precious to God? List the ways. Let him update your list. Take him at his word.

eternal motivation

We are fully confident, and we would rather be away from these earthly bodies, for then we will be at home with the Lord. So whether we are here in this body or away from this body, our goal is to please him.

2 CORINTHIANS 5:8-9 NLT

When we pass from this realm, we will still be present with Christ. This changes our earthly demands. Success will never look the same to a believer as an unbeliever. We live for the long game of eternity. Consider those who doesn't know there is an afterlife. They focus on what they can do to make the world better right now. They maximize their comfort, stability, and power in various aspects. They may become philanthropists and reach the highest echelons of their field or expertise. Regardless, the endgame falls within this realm, and this is shortsighted.

Consider now, Christians who are rooted and grounded in Jesus. On the outside, they may look no different than the unbelieving counterpart. They may have good 401Ks, may be philanthropists, may rise to the height of their fields. They will, however, be doing it all as a prayer to God. They will be in righteous obedience, led by peace to create rewards for Jesus. In all we do, we focus our hearts on Christ, and we daily train our conduct to follow. Wherever we are, we please him, and this is why we choose the long game.

Father, help me focus my affections and attentions upon you. What shall I do, today, that pleases you?

Daily attention to God's pleasure builds a pleasant life that will glorify God. What can you give him of yourself today?

character

We also glory in our sufferings, because we know that suffering
produces perseverance; perseverance, character; and character, hope.
And hope does not put us to shame, because God's love has been
poured out into our hearts through the Holy Spirit,
who has been given to us.

ROMANS 5:3-5 NIV

It is hard to square off in the face of suffering; put on
a smile and walk directly into that storm. Nobody looks at
suffering every time and says, "I would really like more of
that!" Suffering is painful. It chips away at our resolve. It can
rock our faith. Ironically, it is the very tool that can strengthen
our faith as well.

One of the things that predominantly sets apart those
who thrive is the ability to stay in righteous intimacy with God
throughout the duration of the test. This is when the hearts
of the believers are steeled. They become patient, grow
in character, and embody hope in the face of trial. When
suffering takes place, the weight of the burden becomes too
great for the believer to bear while juggling other unnecessary
baggage. The process of refining sloughs off those weights,
and the believer becomes renewed in a way that no other
event—other than suffering—can ever trigger. Suffering
becomes a joy and a gratefully accepted gift allowed by God.

God, help me to see the opportunities in suffering that will
bring me closer to you and the destiny you have for me.
Thank you.

Where have you experienced adversity, and what would
the Lord like to redeem in that to bring you closer to him?

the proper time

There is a time to cry and a time to laugh.
There is a time to be sad and a time to dance.
ECCLESIASTES 3:4 NCV

Think of the unusual few instances when you have witnessed a person crying during a happy occasion or laughing during a misfortune. It seems oddly absurd, and it tends to derail the momentum of whatever is happening. Sometimes this is good, like using humor to disarm a stressful situation. Other times, it can be detrimental.

In Ecclesiastes 3, the man of wisdom underscored the importance of not only doing the right thing, but doing it at the right time. Would you send in your taxes at the end of the year instead of the beginning? Probably not. Would you wait three years before apologizing for a wrong done or thanking a person for a gracious gift? Not likely. In the same way, we must all use wisdom in doing the right thing at the proper time. It may not always be fun, and it may require ample doses of bravery. This is why God, in his love, encourages us toward righteous behavior through his Word.

Heavenly Father, thank you for caring that my actions are appropriate and well-timed. Please help me to be brave and see things your way so I will step out of my limitations and into your perfect grace.

Follow up with God in completing tasks that you should do today. Eliminate two tasks that you never needed to do, but that were fillers for your day.

grow your gift

Do not neglect the gift that is in you, which was given to you by prophecy with the laying on of the hands of the eldership. Meditate on these things; give yourself entirely to them, that your progress may be evident to all.

1 Timothy 4:14-15 NKJV

Jesus gave you special gifts and talents. It is as though he has a garden full of the most beautiful flowers, and if you do not rise and bloom, nothing will take your place.

This is exactly what is happening in the spiritual realm. If God had two of you, one would be redundant. Enjoy your life, your uniqueness, and your opportunities to bloom where you are planted, or be transplanted into a new pot to be enjoyed elsewhere. God has good things for you. Bloom!

Lord, thank you for making me your flower. I love you and am glad to be your cherished blossom.

Where are you planted right now? How might you bloom?

each important

From him the whole body, joined and held together by every
supporting ligament, grows and builds itself up in love,
as each part does its work.

EPHESIANS 4:16 NIV

You are important to the body. What good is a hand without a wrist? It has nothing: no way to support it. It doesn't matter if the fingers can articulate massive symphonies on the piano if the wrists cannot hover them above the keyboard.

You are God's treasure, a special organ in the system of God's body. You make a difference. Let no one despise you for your differences with them. You are important.

Lord, thank you for giving honor to every member of the body. Help me to enjoy myself as you have made me and be at peace with that.

How are you different than everyone else? How are you alike?

consider

"I tell you, do not be anxious about your life, what you will eat or what you will drink, nor about your body, what you will put on. Is not life more than food and the body more than clothing? Consider the birds of the air; they neither sow nor reap nor gather into barns, and yet your heavenly father feeds them. Are you not of more value than they?"

MATTHEW 6: 25-26 NIV

You are cared for today, child of God. Not being anxious is not just a cute suggestion. It is something that is never called for in the life of a believer because as a child of God, you are assured of his continual care. Jesus gave this word knowing our temptation would be to worry mightily.

So, don't condemn yourself when you catch yourself doing it. Rather, use this verse as a directive on what to instead do with your mind—consider.

Lord, when I am anxious, remind me to consider the birds of the air.

Do you give allowance for anxiety in your life or do you resist it like Jesus calls you to?

september

God gave us a spirit not of fear but of

power and love and self-control.

2 Timothy 1:7 ESV

partnering

*The Lord has looked down from heaven upon the sons of men
to see if there are any who understand, who seek after God.*

PSALM 14:2 NASB

Earlier in Scripture we see Abraham looking down toward Sodom, over the valleys into the infamous city. A city guilty of pride, injustice, and lust. The Lord is contemplating destroying it. And in this moment, he asks a question, "Should I tell Abraham what I am about to do?"

If you read the rest of the account in Genesis 18, the answer is yes, and Abraham intercedes and is instrumental in saving the life of his nephew. The key here is that Abraham was found as one who understands. It is Abraham's heart of submission before the Lord that brings him to this moment where he is asked to partner with God. We see Abraham boldly bargain with God for the life of his nephew. He asks the God of justice to act justly, and God hears him, sparing Lot. God is looking for those who seek him. Are you one who is waiting and willing to be a part of his plan?

God, I want to be in on what you are doing in this world. I'm listening; I'm seeking after you. Where are you moving? Give me a heart of understanding.

Are there lives that you need to boldly bring before the throne of God?

avoiding traps

The LORD is your security.
He will keep your foot from being caught in a trap.
PROVERBS 3:26 NLT

One phone call can be it. One news story that flashes before our eyes. One post on social media. One comment from a doctor. Sudden terror crosses our lives in so many forms. Will we always live on the defensive, trying to prevent these instances from crossing our path, or will we remember this promise? Don't let the spiral of worry take you down into a trap of paralyzed days.

Consider what is meant by this word trap. When setting a trap for an animal, what makes it successful is its hidden nature; the animal falls into it because it is unaware. The Lord is your security guard, the Holy Spirit your radar. Avoid the trap of fear and despair in the face of uncertainty by constantly putting your need before God to fill these roles. How you view Jesus will largely play into how you conquer sudden fear. Do you trust that God is good no matter what? That he has your very best interests in mind? That he holds every situation in this world in his most capable and loving hands?

Lord, keep my heart from being paralyzed by fear, keep my feet from the traps laid out. I trust you! Help me to trust.

How can you use Scripture to keep Jesus in your vision and avoid traps?

not abandoned

"No, I will not abandon you as orphans—I will come to you."
JOHN 14:18 NLT

The life of an orphan is vulnerable, lonely, isolated, and overrun with the feeling that one is only able to rely on self for the basic resources of life. The disciples at this point in John had spent three years alongside Jesus, and now he tells them he's leaving! Surely a deep feeling of abandonment rose up within them. But Jesus' promise is as much for us today as it was for them. You are not a spiritual orphan.

As a believer you have the confidence that you can depend on God. You are defended by him, he is always near you, and you have access to all the Father's resources for your life. Jesus sent us the Holy Spirit to comfort, guide, correct, and instruct us. Sometimes we still act like orphans, not like heirs of the King.

Jesus, I rest in the promise that I am your child and you have abundant love for me—all that I need. Thank you for that promise.

Can you identify areas in your life that you still walk like an orphan, dependent only on yourself instead of in communion with the Father?

brave work

If your gift is serving others, serve them well. If you are a teacher, teach well. If your gift is to encourage others, be encouraging. If it is giving, give generously. If God has given you leadership ability, take the responsibility seriously. And if you have a gift for showing kindness to others, do it gladly.

ROMANS 12:7-8 NLT

Have you ever read a memoir about a woman who went on a great adventure traveling the world, and thought to yourself how brave she must be? We often take the glamourous acts like travel and project onto them courage and destiny. It is probably true, that whatever woman you are looking at did have to find great courage to do whatever it is you are admiring. But perhaps being brave is more about being exactly where you are, doing exactly what you are doing right now.

Courage often feels like a doing and a going, like an action verb ready to take off across the page. But to be brave is more often in the daily breathing in and out of working in our giftings right where we are. Here Paul is telling us to do the work, and by doing the work, you are being brave. Being where Jesus wants you doing his work is bravery of its own accord. Don't fall snare to the lie that one's life must be striking to be a display of bravery. Do the work in front of you.

Jesus, help me to be content in what you have called me to here, and to use my giftings now for your glory.

In what areas do you need to stop looking at what others are doing and move forward in what God has called you to?

a gift

LORD, every morning you hear my voice.
Every morning, I tell you what I need,
and I wait for your answer.
PSALM 5:3 NCV

Christmas morning with children is unparalleled. What exalts it into this status is the anticipation and joy that kids seep out to all those around them at the possibility of one thing: a gift. In the same manner, every single time our sun has moved its way over the horizon line into our skies can be defined as one thing: a gift.

It doesn't matter what season it is, or if those skies are cloudy, full of storms, crystal clear, or speckled with fluffy white marshmallows. When our eyes flutter upon that first light, God himself is there holding the gift for you. Anticipation is full. Not only is he waiting with a gift, but he's waiting to hear your response to the gift. And be honest with him, because it is your voice he wants to hear, not your polite, religious, etiquette. Let the beauty of this sink into your heart for a moment. The God of the universe is presenting you with extraordinary gifts. What do you need?

Father, thank you for the gift of breath in my lungs and a new day around me. Speak; I'm listening.

Greet God this morning, with your praise, and be unabashed in telling him your need. What do you need? Write, speak, or sing out some honest prayers right now.

mouthguard

Set a guard, O LORD, over my mouth;
keep watch over the door of my lips!
PSALM 141:3 ESV

The coming of fall brings many of us to bleachers or in front of television sets for a favorite American pastime: football. As we watch our favorite teams and players begin a new season, we see them outfit themselves in all the appropriate protective gear. One small piece will be our focus here, and that can be found dangling from most of the player's helmets: the mouthguard. It might not be listed in the armor of God, but a holy mouthguard is vital to the daily clothing of a Christian.

As you step out in courage toward God's calling on your life, you will find yourself in situations that you feel the need for a strong defense. Personal attack and false accusations will come toward even a righteous person. It is here that we must ask the Lord to put our holy mouthguard in place. Instead of jumping to speak or rushing to self-justify, set yourself before the Lord. With your mouthguard in place, ask him to be the defender of your life. Often, things are best left unsaid, and God will protect you and bring justice in his way, with you geared up and mouthguard in place.

Jesus you are my defender. Keep my mouth from evil and bring glory to your name through all situations in my life.

Are you tempted to self-guard instead of letting God defend you? Pray about the situation that you are tempted with today.

laying down dreams

I know that you can do all things;
no purpose of yours can be thwarted.
JOB 42:2 NIV

What a beautiful thing it is to be living in step with the purposes of God. And not just a god, but the Alpha and the Omega, the all-knowing, all-powerful, only true God of the universe. How can we know though, that our dreams and plans align with his purposes? When they seem to be thwarted at every turn, how can we know that we are aligned with our God who can do all things?

First, be in the Word. Learn to study it, don't depend only on what others tell you about it. Next, pray for wisdom, and take direction. If you want to be able to hear God's voice you must obey in the little things. Lastly, be willing to lay your dreams down if he asks you to. Labor over your dreams and goals in prayer, constantly laying them at his feet. When you've done these things and feel the peace of being aligned to his purposes, then you will see areas that he is asking you to take steps of faith in to complete these purposes.

Jesus, I'm full of dreams and desires, but I submit them all to you; I lay them at your feet.

Do any of these steps resonate with you as one you might need to take in a current dream or life choice?

be-loved

Put on then, as God's chosen ones, holy and beloved, compassionate hearts, kindness, humility, meekness, and patience.
COLOSSIANS 3:12 ESV

This Scripture comes to us after a list of things Paul asks the believers in Colossians to put off or stop doing. When reading this verse, did you fly right past the beginning to the list of things we needed to do? Put on compassion, kindness, humility, and so on? I think most of us rush right past these three little with big meaning found at the beginning of the verse. Read this next part slowly: you are God's chosen one.

You are found Holy in Christ. You are beloved. What does this even mean? It means esteemed. Favorite. Worthy of love. The love we receive from God is not the "scratch my back and I'll scratch yours" kind of love. It's not a love you earn. It's the God who paints sunsets and brings forth life asking you to be-loved. You want to know what might be the bravest thing you do today? Stop working, achieving, and racing, and allow yourself to be-loved by God.

You call me favorite, worthy of love, esteemed, God. Thank you for your devoted love toward me. Let me walk in the confidence of that truth today.

How can you slow down today to focus on the truth of being loved by God?

patient decision

"Be strong and courageous! Do not be afraid and do not panic before them. For the LORD your God will personally go ahead of you. He will neither fail you nor abandon you."

DEUTERONOMY 31:6 NLT

Emergency situations demand emergency responses. EMTs are skilled in remaining calm in the face of decisions that need to be made in a split second. Often life decisions arise that feel like we need to do the same. Should we take this job or not? Should we move? Should we grasp whatever opportunity lies before us, or should we run to find another open door? With the choice placed in front of us, we often suffer unknowingly from fear of missing out. Panic then rises. This is the rule of thumb: God leads, Satan pushes.

When you are making decisions out of panic and rush, it's apparent you're trusting your own wisdom and judgement. Decisions made in haste are not decisions made with godly wisdom. What if you paused and prayed about the decision? Give it even a quick five minutes, or better yet, a day, a week, to see how God has already gone before you? To release control in this manner is no easy task. Let God lead; don't be pushed around in the little, medium, or big decisions that come across your path today.

Lord, you take the lead. I give you control, and I ask for your direction in my decisions today.

How can you wait on the Lord in all decisions today?

loyal love

Hold on to loyal love and don't let go and be faithful to all that you've been taught. Let your life be shaped by integrity, with truth written upon your heart.

PROVERBS 3:3 TPT

A person with a large, loving personality is called magnanimous. Perhaps you know someone like this. Typically, it's someone others always want to be around. It seems that joy and laughter are part of who they are. "Steadfast love" is a term we see often in the Bible. It's used here, and it's translated many different ways like faithful love, gracious love, mercy, or here, loyal love. It's used over 250 times in the Bible, so I would say it is clear that God is trying to communicate something to us about his character. His love is who he is; it is a part of his character.

It's a promise made that cannot be broken because it is based on God's very character. God wants you to know that you can rely on his love. He overcommunicates this fact. So, when you are holding on to loyal love, you are holding on to God himself.

God, I trust in your loyal love—my most faithful friend. Thank you for always sticking by me.

In what part of your life do you need to rely on God's loyalty today?

spinning plates

Where there is no guidance the people fall,
But in abundance of counselors there is victory.

PROVERBS 11:14 NASB

Most of us lead in some capacity in our lives: at work, in our home with our children, at church, in our social groups. No matter what your circle of influence looks like, do not fall into the prideful trap of going it alone. God has placed us in a body of believers and in each of those believers is a gift. What an abundance of resources we have in relationship! It is easy to believe the lie that we must do it all ourselves.

We take on many plates and believe that it is God's will for us to keep them all spinning on our own. Eventually though, just like the leaves in autumn, some plates will fall to the ground and smash. More and more plates do not make you a wiser person, it makes you a person headed toward having broken dishes. Turning to those around us for godly wisdom, prayer, or physical help brings us into a victorious life.

Thank you, Jesus, for the gift of community and friendship. Help me to see those around me that I can turn to for help.

What areas of your life do you need to ask for help and fellowship in?

applause

Better to be patient than powerful;
better to have self-control than conquer a city.
PROVERBS 16:32 NLT

Social media gives us the ability to look over the sea of humanity and see highlight reels from people's lives. We fall into the trap of comparing ourselves to others. We look out and see our friends building empires and conquering dreams. To help fight the comparison trap, which murders our courage and seizes us with fear, a key principle needs to be remembered. In God's kingdom, he is looking at your heart. That means it is better to be unseen and growing the fruit of the Spirit than to be applauded by the masses.

No reward you could gain through the applause of many as you conquer mountains can compare to the smallest reward handed out in heaven. If you want to truly conquer, to live a powerful life, then pay attention to the laws of the kingdom of God. Man looks at and applauds your outward achievements and gains, but God examines your heart. Submit every day to the Holy Spirit's desire to grow fruit like patience, self-control, and peace in you, and then you will be able to conquer.

Jesus, forgive me for areas I sought power before character. Do the work inside of me that needs to be done.

Are you working harder for man's praise and outward power or growing your character?

association

Live in harmony with one another. Do not be proud but be willing to associate with people of low position. Do not be conceited.
ROMANS 12:16 NIV

Who are those in low position? Often our minds immediately fixate on matters of economic status. The homeless, the poor, children in faraway countries. It doesn't feel hard to associate with them, if by associate you mean give from a distance at our leisure. Perhaps this low position has not as much to do with economic standing, but that person at church you just don't like. That person you subconsciously lift yourself above because frankly you just don't agree with their political standings. Or maybe their theology isn't like yours.

Are we willing to carry on with people we don't agree with? It doesn't mean compromising a standard of integrity or throwing yourself into the path of temptation. Paul is talking about relationship between believers. Are you willing to carry on with, to bear the burdens of, to lift up in prayer, to humbly learn from, those you don't agree with?

Jesus, bring me into humility today. I know you are calling me to carry on with those around me I have ignored.

How can you follow the example of Christ and lay down your rights, your opinions, your life, to associate with others?

humble gift

The LORD grants wisdom!
From his mouth come knowledge and understanding.
PROVERBS 2:6 NLT

Do you like surprises? Some people love the buildup and anticipation surrounding surprise gifts. God has a gift for us today, but we must be willing to let him surprise us. This is the gift of humility. Humility is when we come to God confessing we don't know the answer; we don't have it all figured out. Where there is pride, there is no room for surprise. We feel the pressure to have all the answers, but God is asking us to let go of that. When we unwrap humility, we are positioned to receive this wisdom, knowledge, and understanding that Proverbs is talking about. Gifts upon gifts! God cannot be manipulated, bossed around, or controlled.

Humility is us posturing ourselves small before him. Maybe the things you continue to struggle with and try to figure out alone, you now submit to him. Or believe God when the odds are stacked against the promise. Open your hands in areas you typically want to grasp tightly. The wonder, delight, and surprise at the glory of God that might be missing from your relationship can be found when you unwrap your gift of humility.

God, you are almighty, and I am not. You know everything; I do not. I give you control today. Humbly I open my hands before you and release my control.

What area do you need wisdom in right now?

weight of worry

Worry weighs a person down;
an encouraging word cheers a person up.
PROVERBS 12:25 NLT

Have you ever worn ankle weights at the gym? Suddenly even a task like walking takes extra effort. When considering your worries, picture yourself as a person with ankle weights who has never worked out. Worry does nothing but add heaviness to your life. When you take into consideration that we are called to run a race, it is significantly more difficult to run with our ankles carrying weights. The solution seems to be right in this verse, but sometimes we find ourselves in seasons where an encouraging word from the outside seems scarce.

The Psalmist had many of these lonely seasons, and he turned his worries into praise. He never ignored the problem at hand but used the problem as an opportunity to pray. After his problem is laid out, and sometimes even before, he turns into a time of praise that encourages his soul and sets him free from the weights. The Psalmist did not have minor struggles. He was betrayed by friends, chased by enemies, and lost his infant son. Just like the Psalmist, free yourself today from weight of worry and transform it into praise.

Jesus, I release all my worry to you. All the things crowding my mind, I give them to you, Author of my life.

How can you turn your worries into prayer and praises today?

waiting spaces

If we hope for what we do not see, we wait for it with patience.
ROMANS 8:25 ESV

The waiting spaces of life can feel like dead air. We sit in these seasons of interim, feeling impatient and abandoned. Consider a different perspective. When you are waiting, you could choose to stall out in life. Or perhaps in waiting you could be growing. If you chose patience, a needed character trait, you are growing fruit. God is using the waiting to carefully cultivate your character. In the broad scheme of things, we should all be living in a season of waiting—for the future hope of glory. Waiting for restoration of creation and reunification with our Savior.

We should not allow our souls to grow too attached to earthly things but always wait for Christ's return. In the smaller seasons of waiting, don't be dormant. Move toward the light and the nourishing water, and root yourself into good soil. God is working in you to produce good fruit, lasting fruit, and what looks to the outside world as nothing but a hold up or time wasted is truly a most beautiful time of growth.

Jesus, I want to be more like you! Use my seasons of waiting, when it doesn't feel like much is happening, for me to grow closer to you.

Are you using this time of waiting to grow?

by your walk

You make known to me the path of life;
you will fill me with joy in your presence,
with eternal pleasures at your right hand.
PSALM 16:11 NIV

If you are fortunate enough to live near an ocean, you've seen people walking up and down the jagged line of wave meeting sand. Some walk alone, but often in pairs. Imagine sitting on the shore, when you spy a couple walking a pole's length apart, frowning, and casting dirty glances at each other. Or maybe one is stomping ahead and the other is yelling, trying to catch up. Deep down those two might be in love, but you sure wouldn't guess it by their walk, would you? Then you see another couple, older in age perhaps, her hand gently wrapped around his forearm, their pace in perfect tune. These always make us imagine fifty years of relationship. You judge their relationship by their walk.

What does your walk with Christ say about your relationship with him? Does it speak of years of perseverance, of walking the path of life with him and being filled with joy in his presence? Or are you stomping your feet and scowling every step of the way, with more of a duty than love? Stop today, beloved and ask yourself, where is the joy?

Jesus, I want others to know your joy by my walk with you. Show me areas that I have lost joy in and restore to me the joy of salvation.

Is your Christian walk filled with joy? Ask God how to reclaim some of it.

the right fear

His pleasure is not in the strength of the horse,
nor his delight in the legs of the warrior;
the Lord delights in those who fear him,
who put their hope in his unfailing love.

PSALM 147: 10-11 NIV

Do you ever feel like your dreams may be big, but you are small? Looking around, you see others conquering their careers, flexing their muscles of influence, slaying projects, galloping by as they accomplish all on the to-do list? She got the promotion, or the baby, or the marriage, or the house, or the leadership role, or the talent. In our ladder-climbing world, it often feels like our rungs are breaking off in our hands. And when our source of worth comes from climbing up, what happens when you just feel stuck at the bottom?

Remember, all those outward signs of power are not what brings delight to the Lord. It is your heart. His delight is in finding you seeking after him to be the fulfiller of your dreams, your source of strength, your only hope for power. More than the praise of any man or woman, wouldn't you like to know that the God who created the universe is delighted in you, specifically? You who fear and hope in God, he takes great pleasure in you.

God, I want to be counted amongst those who fear you and follow your voice. I hope in you and you alone. Thank you for delighting in me.

Are you found as one who fears God? Search your heart for ways you need to return to the fear of the Lord today.

wild freedom

"If you abide in my word, you are truly my disciples,
and you will know the truth, and the truth will set you free."
JOHN 8:31-32 ESV

Before we knew Christ, we lived in slavery. We dwelt in sin, shackled to its power, back bent and broken by its weight. Sullen eyes, malnourished, stripped of dignity. This is not how we view people without Christ though is it? Often Christians look in envy at the non-believers around them. And to the outward eye, they seem to be doing just fine. But sin is decay, and all those under its authority are rotting in bondage. Let's stop observing the wicked with envy and put on the glasses of true sight! We are free. We have abundant life!

There is wild freedom found in life with Christ. Freedom that is so expansive we haven't even begun to explore it. All those years of slavery to sin have left you in a broken state. But your redeemer has come and wants to bring freedom into every crevice of your life that you didn't even know was in bondage. Dwell in the truth of Scripture today, let it be like the antidote to the poison you've been swallowing all these years. Let it swim through the veins of your heart and bring freedom to a new area of your life.

Jesus, thank you for the wild freedom I have in you! Give me clear sight to see that your ways are higher and better.

How can you walk in more freedom today by not focusing on what the world has that you do not?

wisdom to please

If any of you lacks wisdom, you should ask God, who gives generously to all without finding fault, and it will be given to you.

JAMES 1:5 NIV

There are two types of wisdom. Wisdom that is godly, and the wisdom of man. Think about the writer of Proverbs, King Solomon. As a young king, he asked God not for riches or fame or wider borders, but for wisdom to lead his kingdom. Wisdom meant knowing how to live a life that pleased God. Does this describe the kind of wisdom we seek in our lives? Decisions can feel like a rainstorm, with one after another pelting us relentlessly throughout the day.

We release the power of God into our lives and into even the smallest decision when we have the humility to ask for wisdom. Without the Holy Spirit, we do not know how to please God. But a humble heart in the hands of God is the beginning of wisdom. All you have to do is ask.

God, I need wisdom! Hear my cry and richly pour out your wisdom today. I want to honor you with my life.

Is the wisdom you seek leading you to lead a life that is pleasing to God?

tethered

Be joyful because you have hope.
Be patient when trouble comes and pray at all times.
ROMANS 12:12 NCV

Your to-do list is a mile long. Daily, you wake up and stare it in the face. Often, you find yourself mumbling about there not being enough hours in the day. Nightly, you fall into bed, feeling unfulfilled. You feel detached from God, underwhelmed by hope, overwhelmed by the undone. Be Joyful? You don't even know where to start with that.

Have you ever played tetherball? There are two players. A ball is attached to a rope that is tethered to a pole. The point of the game is to wrap the rope up tight against the pole in the direction you hit the ball while your opponent tries to stop it and hit it the other way. Imagine if that rope became unattached after a hit—it would go soaring! Be tethered to God by prayer, not to your list. It might feel crazy, but it is vital to tackle life first with prayer. It is the rope that will keep you holding onto the life source. Are you void of hope? Neglect the list and pray.

Lord, I feel overwhelmed by all I need to do. I bring to you this list: help! Let me be tethered to you.

What do you need to move around today to make more room to pray?

carrying the weight

Cast your cares on the LORD and he will sustain you;
he will never let the righteous be shaken.

PSALM 55:22 NIV

If you've ever cared for small children, you know they require a monumental amount of stuff whenever you leave the house. Since they are small, they cannot carry all this stuff, making it your responsibility. Or maybe you've been to the mall and seen couples after a shopping spree, with the women still shopping and the men surrounded by all the bags. This is the picture that comes to mind for this verse. It is the picture of us giving our baggage to God for his shoulders to bear. He lovingly serves in this manner, leaving our shoulders free from the weight of what previously bore down on us.

There is no load too heavy for God. If you continue to carry it all yourself, the weight of it will topple you over. How do we let go of the load? Through prayer and meditation on truth. List out what is weighing you down right now. Then tell him the truth about them, one by one. Find verses that apply to your worries, write them down, and keep them close by.

Jesus, I admit I often carry all my cares alone. Help me to cast these burdens on you, like you ask me to.

What worries do you need to lay down before the Lord?

external confidence

*Let us then approach God's throne of grace with confidence,
so that we may receive mercy and find grace to help us
in our time of need.*
HEBREWS 4:16 NIV

Confidence can be defined in two ways. One is from within—we feel self-assured by our ability. The other is external—we believe we can rely on someone to do what they said they would. We cannot be brave without confidence, but the confidence we need does not come from the first definition. It is not wise to conjure up feelings of bravery through self-assurance of our own abilities, for they inevitability will fail us.

To succeed in life, our confidence must come from a firm trust in Jesus Christ, what he did for us on the cross, and how he continues to intercede for us. Our confidence does not come from our own power, but from Christ-given power. Walk into every situation today knowing that you have immediate, VIP access to throne of God, and there is an abundant warehouse of grace and mercy waiting for you.

Jesus, let my confidence arise from you and from your strength today.

What self-assurance do you need to trade for God's assurance today?

where to fight

When hard pressed, I cried to the LORD;
he brought me into a spacious place.
The LORD is with me;
I will not be afraid.
What can mere mortals do to me?
PSALM 118:5-6 NIV

We must remember who our enemy is. It is not people who choose lifestyles different from ours, other nations, religions, neighbors, children, or even a spouse who is our enemy. Our enemy is spiritual. When we remember this, we cannot help but then remember where to fight our battles—in prayer.

Being brought to a spacious place by the Lord can paint a lovely picture in our mind. Green fields, wide skies, marshmallow clouds. But the psalmist is in battle. For those of us who feel like we have a target on our backs for constant attack, a wide-open field feels sounds like the perfect place to be shot! Why would God want to bring you there? Because he is with you. He won't leave. He fights for you. Take courage. Be filled with hope by remembering that God is with you.

God, I know you are for me and with me every step of the way. Teach me to fight this battle with the true enemy and by your strength.

How can you direct your fighting at the spiritual today instead of toward the physical?

awe inspiring

When I consider Your heavens, the work of Your fingers,
the moon and the stars, which you have ordained,
what is man that You are mindful of him,
and the son of man that You visit him?
PSALM 8:3-4 NKJV

If it is possible right now, go outside. They say there are 100 billion stars in our galaxy alone. In the observable universe, there are about 10 billion galaxies, each containing these stars. He has named and remembers each one. Our planet is set in perfect fashion on its axis, spinning in such a way that seasons and days are maintained. When it snows, there are thousands of snowflakes swirling down into even just one tiny city, and each of those snowflakes is uniquely crafted. Sunsets and sunrises are painted across the sky with a mastery that cannot be likened to any man's hands. God's fingers held the brush that stroked that sky, and his fingers embraced the clay that he formed into man. We could go on all day considering his natural works. The examples that inspire awe are boundless.

But what was his focus? The one thing he chose to breath his very life into, to make in his image? You. You reflect the likeness and the image of God. He is consciously aware of everything about you. He wants to dwell with you today.

Father, thank you for your creative hand in making me. Thank you that you dwell with me. Thank you for making me in your image.

How have you considered God's handiwork in your existence lately?

battling envy

Every good gift and every perfect gift is from above,
coming down from the Father of lights with whom -
there is no variation or shadow due to change.

JAMES 1:17 ESV

The easy road is to glance around at others and, upon seeing what they have, be full of envy. The courageous road is to be full of joy for them. What good gifts have been bestowed on you? Quickly think of three.

Christians have unity no matter their race, economic status, marital status, or child-bearing status. No matter what classifications we define ourselves as, Christians should have unity in the Word of God. It is our common ground, and standing upon it means we can shout for joy when we see others receiving gifts. Think back to three gifts you identified. To battle envy, cultivate thankfulness towards the giver and acknowledge the truth of his goodness. Don't believe that he prefers others over you. Keep in mind his character today.

Father, thank you for these gifts you've given me! Help me to be happy for others when they also receive gifts.

What other gifts can you be thankful to God for today?

get back up

The LORD directs the steps of the godly.
He delights in every detail of their lives.
Though they stumble, they will never fall,
for the LORD holds them by the hand.
PSALM 37:23-24 NLT

We cling to all the verses in the Bible about God being with us, prospering our ways, lifting us up. This verse is one of them. But a little section we often pass by: Though they stumble. It doesn't say if, or maybe. It says that they will.

Too often we think we should never fail. If we have failed, or stumbled, things must not be going right. We maybe even think that because we fail at something God is not with us. Here, the Psalmist almost guarantees us that we will fail. But failure is not the end. Steps of faith and acts of bravery are often paired with failure. It is a trap for us to believe that we shouldn't fail. That trap makes us not want to get back up, try again, or step out in faith. Read the rest of the passage. Who is holding your hand? Who is directing your steps? Who is taking pleasure in the details of your life? Jesus. Though you fail, he is with you. Get up and take another leap of faith today.

Thank you, Lord, that you grab me by the hand and lift me up, that you are with me through success and failure.

What failures do you need to acknowledge and get up from today?

in a name

Let all who take refuge in you rejoice;
let them ever sing for joy;
and spread your protection over them,
that those who love your name may exult in you.
PSALM 5:11 ESV

Many people do not place a lot of significance on naming. They use names that sound good with last names, re-use family names, mimic characters in a story. Names don't reflect character in our culture. That's why it is easy to think of God as just "God." One name. But he has many names in the Bible—names that reflect his awesome character. When you dive into the names of God, it's like looking into a multi-faceted diamond, with each new angle reflecting even more light. We can become personally acquainted with his character.

As you fight your battle today, no matter what you are going through, find refuge in the names of God. Call them out loud as a praise offering, acknowledging who you are loved by. And take joy in the fact that as you step out today, you have safety in God.

There is so much to you, God, you are never ending! Reveal more of your character to me through all your glorious names.

Look up some names of God today. How can you acknowledge more of who he is through these names?

sharing wisdom

Get all the advice and instruction you can,
so you will be wise the rest of your life.
PROVERBS 19:20 NLT

If you are part of the human race, you need community. Humans are made to be in relationship with one another. Part of being in relationship means getting advice from each other—it's a good thing! Inevitably, we will come face to face with situations that we haven't dealt with before. If we surround ourselves with people, chances are one of them might have already faced a similar situation and they have some wisdom to share. We can learn from their success and failure and become wiser ourselves.

Wisdom means knowing how to please God. This should direct us to what kind of people we should gather advice from—students of the Word of God, people who seek after his will. But this is not just a one-way street: you have wisdom to offer as well. How are you pouring out your wisdom to those around you? Are you willing to bravely share your story, your mistakes, victories, trials, and triumphs for the good of those around you?

Thank you, God, that you are the author of my story. Let me use this story for your glory and grow more united with your body through it.

Who can you share your testimony or wisdom with today?

number your words

Wise words bring many benefits,
and hard work brings rewards.
PROVERBS 12:14 NLT

Do you want to be powerful? Learn to number your words. James talks about the tongue as an uncontrollable fire: a small instrument impossible to tame. In Matthew, Jesus warns us that we will give an account for every word spoken. There is much said in the Bible about what comes out of our mouths. It takes hard work to make sure it is God-honoring.

Think of your words as seeds you are planting. Are you sowing a harvest of good fruit, or will your baskets be full of nothing but weeds? Do you carefully select the seeds, or are you just throwing out handfuls, hoping something will take? Do you consider the timing of your planting? All this hard work cannot be done on your own. It is out of your heart that your mouth speaks, and Christ is the one who changes hearts. Find your strength to change how you plant in him. Allow him to cleanse your heart through daily repentance.

God, it is so easy to say everything that pops into my head without giving it a second thought. I know this does not produce good fruit. Forgive me for the harsh, thoughtless, or flippant words that I have spoken, and help me to work harder at taming my tongue with your help.

Review the questions presented above. Which one hits closest to home?

october

"Be courageous! Let us fight bravely
for our people
and the cities of our God.
May the LORD's will be done."

1 CHRONICLES 19:13 NLT

righteous roads

Cleanse my heart God and let out of it flow
pure words and life abundant.
Follow the steps of the good
and stay on the paths of the righteous.
For only the godly will live in the land,
and those with integrity will remain in it.
PROVERBS 2:20-21 NLT

Anyone who runs regularly knows it is good to stick the well-lit path. If you are running at night and decide to take a different, unknown way down a dark road, it is more likely not to go well for you. Wisdom says to stay on the well-lit, pleasant paths of the righteous. God has prepared this path for us. He knows every turn and hill along the way. The way becomes familiar through the reading of his Word and asking him for guidance. He has also given us the gift of others who have walked these righteous roads before.

Who do you imitate? Is it the latest influencer, movie star, or your non-Christian friends? Look for the gift of other believers who passionately follow Christ and imitate them. They have walked these roads already, and you would be wise to follow.

God, guide me in the well-lit path; lead me in the way of righteousness. Show me others I can fellowship with who have hearts burning for you.

Who do you imitate most? Are they godly examples?

bravely waiting

Wait patiently for the LORD.
Be brave and courageous.
Yes, wait patiently for the LORD.
PSALM 27:14 NLT

No one likes to wait. At the core of waiting is the reminder that we are not in control. There is a reason we find the phrase telling us to wait right next to the command reminding us to be brave and courageous. It takes a lot of courage to admit you are not in control of your life. With fists clenched tight, you run ragged, attempting to control all the details. Planning and calendars are the sweet spot because in those neat little squares you can achieve while you go.

What audacious dream might God have for you right now that you are missing because you can't unclench your fists? Maybe he is asking you to stop planning every moment and detail, look up from your calendar, and see where he is moving. Slow down on the achievement and see how he is at work in the world around you. His wild, courageous, dreams for you might be found when you surrender control and partner with his movement.

I'm listening, Lord. I've opened my hands and surrendered to you. Lead me in dreams that are bigger than I can imagine.

What dream does God have for you that maybe you can't see or hear right now?

mountain mover

What then shall we say to these things?
If God is for us, who can be against us?
ROMANS 8:31 ESV

Mountains in creation are awe inspiring, beautiful and majestic. Mountains in our lives are a different story. We often liken our troubles to mountains because of their looming nature, their size, and even the treacherous manner it takes to cross them. Faith allows us to see how much larger God is than our mountains. We stand at the base in disbelief. But faith zooms us out to a view that shows us that though there might be ranges of mountains in our future, God is more expansive than even the atmosphere that surrounds them.

Our focus has to be on how big God is. A lack of faith has an awful tendency to glue our feet to the ground, so we are unable to see anything but negativity. Those who walk in faith are people who admit they might not know how the mountain will be moved, but that God will supply no matter what. He is the mountain mover. Pray for faith to arise, to see how big God is.

God, you are almighty! You are larger than any mountain that looms in my way. Help me to have faith that you can move the mountain or help me climb it.

How can you apply faith to your mountains today?

sanctification celebration

Then our mouth was filled with laughter,
and our tongue with shouts of joy;
then they said among the nations,
"The LORD has done great things for them."

PSALM 126:2 ESV

Deep belly laughter, joyous shouting, the picture painted here is one of celebration! Imagine people dancing, singing, rejoicing at news that bubbles up through them and cannot be contained. What creates such a scene? Restoration. If you are a Christian, you have already been restored to God. Through the work of Christ on the cross you have peace with God. As you continue to walk in faith with him, you are being sanctified daily.

Sanctification is the process of making all the areas of our lives and hearts holy. Often, we focus on the painful aspects of sanctification, but today let us rejoice. God is restoring things the enemy has stolen, things sin has marred, freeing us from our chains. Spend time today in worship of the one who is making all things new. Tell someone what God has done for you, so that they may say, "The Lord has done great things!"

I rejoice in you, oh God! You are mighty to save. Thank you for the work you are continuing to do in my life.

When was the last time you celebrated the work God does in your life? Find a tangible way to celebrate today.

spelunking

Your love is so extravagant it reaches to the heavens!
Your faithfulness so astonishing it stretches to the sky!
PSALM 57:10 TPT

Spelunking is the exploration of cave requiring crawling through tight spaces or standing miles underneath the earth. Dark is a word that probably comes to mind when you think of caves. Tight spaces, lack of air, though some people call spelunking fun, many couldn't be paid enough money to do it. It's from this type of scenario—hiding in a cave, running for his life—that David wrote Psalm 57, longing for a glimpse of the radiant sky, pining for a delicious gulp of fresh air. In this tight spot, he penned words of praise that speak of longing and familiarity as well.

Maybe you can relate. You feel very much stuck in a dark, tight spot. Focus your prayers on God's faithfulness, his never-ending love. Just because you are in this situation does not mean that his character has changed. He has not forgotten you. And you will not be stuck in the cave forever.

Jesus, you do not abandon me. Thank you. I feel stuck in this spot, and it's tight and uncomfortable. Please be near to me and help me breathe. I need you.

How can you find God when you are in a dark, tight spot?

inheritance

Do not forget this one thing, dear friends:
With the Lord a day is like a thousand years,
and a thousand years are like a day.
2 PETER 3:8 NIV

Inheritance. When you hear this word, does your mind autopilot to financial gain? Jokingly think about hopes of a rich uncle that you forgot about leaving you a large sum? Inheritance is so much more than money. An inheritance is something handed down to the next generation. As Christians, called by God and filled with purpose for the future, it can be easy to slip into nearsightedness. We dive full speed ahead into pursuing a vision or dream. But we must also be brave enough to let it go for a moment if that is God's will.

It takes courage to dive into what you believe God has for you and to also hold it in an open palm. God does not work on our timetables. That calling that you have might be a grand vision, but all God wants you to do is plant seeds and hand it off to the next generation. Plant well. Learn to stay away from nearsightedness, and let God expand your eyesight to see his grand work throughout the ages.

Jesus thank you for my inheritance! Thank you that you are faithful from generation to generation. Show me how you want to use me to lead the next generation into relationship with you.

Do you suffer from nearsightedness? Examine your spiritual eyesight today.

no comparison

It is better to take refuge in the LORD
than to trust in people.
PSALM 118:8 NLT

There are so many promises of God wrapped up in this one verse. No matter how good people may be, they are no comparison to our holy God. If you need more evidence to back this fact up, read on.

First there is the promise that God cannot change, but man can. We see his character matching up again and again throughout history. Second, man lies, but God does not. Every word written in the Bible is true. Third, God cannot forget his promises, but man often breaks his. Fourth, God is all-knowing, and man has only a small fraction of knowledge. Fifth, God cannot fail; we fail ourselves and others often. Lastly, God is always faithful. He is unchanging, without falsehood, promise-keeping, all-knowing, and unfailing. That makes him the best place to take refuge.

Lord, you are the only one worth taking refuge in. I will abandon all other shelters to dwell in safety with you.

Which part of the promises stand out most to you, and why?

darkness

The unfolding of your words gives light;
it gives understanding to the simple.
PSALM 119:130 NASB

The number one fear of most children is darkness. Darkness has an interesting way of making things larger and scarier than they are. It distorts the truth, turning dressers into monsters and curtains into ghosts. It robs you of your ability to see danger, like a Lego looming on the floor in your path. To be people of courage, we need light.

Psalms clearly tells us how to let such light enter our lives— through God's Word. Remove any roadblocks like pride and apathy. Without his Word there is no illumination, and we remain in darkness. Let light expose what seems scary and see that they are never too big for God. Let light show you danger that is lurking—like unconfessed sin—so you can alter your course. There is no end to the wondrous work that happens in us when we allow light to penetrate every nook of our heart. Keep his Word ever close and walk as children of light.

Jesus, you are glorious light! Bring illumination into the dark parts of my heart today by your Word. Let it become more alive to me today.

Ask God to show you areas of your heart that are dark. Let him lead you to Scriptures that will help illuminate the path.

right and left

Be still before the LORD and wait patiently for him;
do not fret when people succeed in their ways,
when they carry out their wicked schemes.
PSALM 37:7 NIV

It doesn't make sense, when you look to the right and to the left and see those not following God doing well. Your co-worker who acts in unethical manners gets the promotion you wanted, and that girl at the gym who has been with many men gets engaged while you remain single. Should not success be reserved for those who follow God? It is in these times we need to find the courage to trust God's justice and let him be our defender.

When you fret, it shows you are relying on yourself to make everything right in your time, instead of letting God take care of it in his. He knows every desire of your heart, and he sees the big picture of your life. While our justice is often short sighted, God has the eternal game plan in mind. Cast aside your self-sufficient ways and acknowledge that he is in control, and he is perfectly able to take care of you.

God, help me keep my eyes focused on you and the plans you have for my life.

Are you envious of those who do evil? Are you spending too much time looking to the right and the left?

encouraging bravery

When I am afraid, I will trust you.
I praise God for his word.
I trust God, so I am not afraid.
What can human beings do to me?
PSALM 56:3-4 NCV

We hear parents admonish their children not to be afraid. The older we get, the more there seems to be afraid of. Who can you encourage today, not by telling them to not be afraid, but by asking them to be brave? Asking people to mask their fear will only work temporarily at best. Asking them to make a choice for bravery gives them confidence in God's character and care.

Don't stuff down what you are feeling and move on by your own strength. Be brave in the situations that strike fear in you, knowing that God is fighting for you. Who do you know that needs to hear this today? Let God use you as his vessel to bring freedom. Help others remove their masks and hand them the bravery banner.

Jesus thank you for freedom from fear. Please help my friends to walk in freedom today. Use me as a vessel for your chain-breaking power in their life.

Who can you help to walk in bravery today?

a steady heart

They won't be afraid of bad news;
their hearts are steady because they trust the LORD.
PSALM 112:7 NCV

God has asked you a specific thing. As you begin to put the legwork behind the calling he has given you, you cannot expect the road to be without opposition. Maybe God has asked you to take a step and adopt a child, start a business, plant a church, put your kids in public school, move, or lead a small group. The possibilities are endless, but the end is the same—all for the glory of God. In moving toward what God wants you to do, the forces of darkness will move back.

Can you steady your heart when people whisper behind your back or criticize your actions? Can you steady your heart when you fail along the way? Can you steady your heart when others fail you? Our hearts can be firm as a rock when we trust that God is working and moving on our behalf. If he has placed something on your heart today, don't let fear of what could happen get in your way. Step out in faith and anchor your heart in the Lord.

Jesus, please steady my heart. Free me from fear. Be my anchor in this choppy sea.

What "what-if" scenarios do you need to silence and bring before God today?

spiritual gifts

As each has received a gift, use it to serve one another,
as good stewards of God's varied grace.
1 PETER 4:10 ESV

When you see an orchestra perform, you will notice there are a variety of instruments. Violins strumming softly. Horn instruments all ready to explode with triumph. Flutes and clarinets that steadily lead you along, percussion that can be as subtle as a triangle or as monumental as the cymbals crashing. In the same way, we have each been given various gifts. Your gifting will not be the same or play out in the same way as others'. Just as the instruments are all varied, so can be the music they play.

You can't be ashamed of the boldness your cymbal crashing may entail, or the quiet significance your steady rhythm drum brings. Each of us have a gift to use that we cannot waste our time wondering if those around us think our gift is worthy, fitting, or significant. Use your gift to join in harmony with the music being played to the glory of God by the body of Christ. Every crash, every soft verse, every rise and fall of a string has its place. Serve God boldly in your gifts today.

Thank you, Father, for giving me gifts. Thank you for the way you made me. May I not be ashamed of what you have called me to.

In what way do you need to uncover your gift and use it to its fullest?

accomplishing holiness

"My grace is all you need. My power works best in weakness." So now I am glad to boast about my weaknesses, so that the power of Christ can work through me. That's why I take pleasure in my weaknesses, and in the insults, hardships, persecutions, and troubles that I suffer for Christ. For when I am weak, then I am strong.

2 CORINTHIANS 12:9-10 NLT

God does not delight in your suffering. Many may read through the Bible and think God takes pleasure in our suffering. Nothing could be further from the truth. What God does want to accomplish in your life is holiness. Often it takes insults, hardships, persecutions, and troubles to humble us before God. Our best life is not one free of suffering, but one totally reliant on God's grace.

If you look back a couple of verses, it speaks of how Paul was being harassed. This was directly from Satan—and what Satan intended to harm and discourage him with was used to bring Paul to his knees before God in humility. If whatever is thrown our way is constantly keeping us from becoming puffed up with self-reliant pride and on our knees before God, let it come! God is not delighting in your pain. Though relief may not come, God is at work in you through it.

There are situations in life right now I don't understand, Jesus. Remove pride from me and help me to bravely use only your strength.

How does this passage change your view of suffering?

harvest time

No discipline seems pleasant at the time, but painful. Later on, however, it produces a harvest of righteousness and peace for those who have been trained by it.
HEBREW 12:11 NIV

Harvest time in America is marked by the return of kids to school, bonfires, the crisp smell and satisfying crunch of fallen leaves, pumpkins and apples, trees exploding in warm hues all around. We celebrate harvest with the holiday of thanksgiving, gathering with friends and family, cooking all day and feasting all night. In our life, there are seasons. We are all rather quick to point out our seasons of discipline. They stick out more to us because of the presence of the pain. What season does this verse say always follows? Harvest!

Feast today on the harvest of righteousness and peace. Be quick to celebrate the peace God has brought into your life. Shout for joy, praise him, throw a party. Let us not major on the pain and minor on what it reaps. Let us speak of the work of God in our lives and join in creation with the celebration of harvest.

We praise you, Lord! You are good and full of righteousness and peace.

How can you celebrate God's goodness, tangibly, today?

your part

God is working in you, giving you the desire
and the power to do what pleases him.
PHILIPPIANS 2:13 NLT

Jesus did the most loving work for you on the cross. His perfect life, sinless death, and holy resurrection is all the work that needs to be done regarding salvation. However, if you have been a Christian for any length of time, you've realized you are still in a struggle with sin. You are not alone in this battle. God is working in you. This is the process of sanctification that takes place after our salvation during life on earth. This is the part of the story where you get to live in cooperation with what the Holy Spirit is already doing inside you.

Take heart in this battle. Your part in this work is submission to what God is already doing. Your part is those active steps of obedience that are given power by God. Every step of obedience, every prayer of surrender, is more open doors for the Holy Spirit to work more in you, molding you into his image. Pray courageously today, giving the Holy Spirit more freedom to work the construction zone he is already working at in your heart.

Jesus, your Word calls me to lay down my life and follow you. Show me how I can be more obedient to that call.

What area do you need to take a new step of obedience in?

acts of service

"Just as the Son of Man did not come to be served, but to serve, and to give His life a ransom for many."
MATTHEW 20:28 NASB

When we see the word serve we often think of physical tasks like cleaning, cooking, and yard work. Though it is true that these are acts of service, a person can serve physically their whole life and miss the mark on deeper levels of servanthood. Jesus washed feet and ended his life in the ultimate act of servanthood, laying down his life for each one of us. Jesus opened himself up to people and was betrayed. He was lied to, his name was dragged through the mud, his friends turned their backs on him, and still he laid down his life.

Sometimes servanthood looks like submitting yourself to others, which can feel as vulnerable as lying naked on an operating table. Why be exposed before people when you know they could rip you apart like wolves? Because that's exactly what Jesus did. Our human tendency is to armor up when someone hurts us. But sharing your story, reaching out to that women who has gossiped about you, seeking restoration with a friend who betrayed you, though painful, is a brave act of servanthood.

Jesus, you dwelled with us, washed feet, and served by giving up your life. Teach me how to serve others to the magnitude that you served us.

Have you gone to great lengths to restore a relationship?

the prize awaits

Forgetting what is behind and straining toward what is ahead,
I press on toward the goal to win the prize for which God has called me
heavenward in Christ Jesus.

PHILIPPIANS 3:13-14 NIV

Paul's earthly past was a resume of accomplishment worth looking over, a "person of the year" by TIME magazine standards. Paul's life as he wrote this Scripture was sitting in a dank, dark prison with a future of execution. Which life of Paul's would we say would be devastating? Which life of Paul's would we stand up and applaud for? The answer might surprise you.

Paul let go of all the accolades and accomplishments that made him the influencer he was and said that every one of them were garbage. He finds himself in prison with a singular focus of continuing to take steps in his race to know God. One of the most important decisions you will make in your lifetime is this: can you courageously forsake your reputation, social status, material possession, and passionately press into knowing God? The prize that awaits you is eternal communion with God.

God, show me the good and the bad that keep me from you.

What past weight holds you back from pressing in hard toward Christ?

pilgrimage

How blessed is the man whose strength is in You,
in whose heart are the highways to Zion!
PSALM 84:5 NASB

We are a go, go, go culture. We keep it running 24/7 as fast as we can. Do you have the courage to slow down? Too many of us are plagued by fear of missing out. This fear grips us to take life more at the speed of a motocross race and less the way it was intended to be: a pilgrimage. An exodus out of bondage and into freedom. Out of darkness, into light. Out of death, into resurrection. A pilgrimage is a slower journey, not a race run at remarkable speed.

We run quickly for two reasons: either we don't want to miss out, or we want to hurry up and get past all the hard stuff. You won't be rewarded for how fast you obtain the prize, or how much you accomplished along the way. On this exodus, quality matters. Miss out. Say no. Go slower. Don't give in to the temptation to run. Walk with Christ, allowing him to mature you as you move.

You have set us on a pilgrimage, Lord, and this world is not my home. Help me to live this day as a sojourner.

Are you going at a speed that is too fast? Pray about what a slower pace could look like.

sharing truth

Since we are surrounded by such a huge crowd of witnesses to the life of faith, let us strip off every weight that slows us down, especially the sin that so easily trips us up. And let us run with endurance the race God has set before us.

HEBREWS 12:1 NLT

Crowds at sporting events are generally similar: boisterous, full of opinion, and somewhat disorderly. This may be the picture that comes to mind when you read this verse: a whole crowd of them, from Noah to Rahab, peering down from the bleachers of heaven giving their two cents about how our sporting event of life is going.

But this verse communicates a very different picture. The cloud of witnesses are not your heavenly critics; they have forged a path before you. The imperfect people listed in Hebrews 11 have stories of failure and triumph mingled. They had the courage to press on in their journey. They walked the path, and they made it to the other side. Their stories testify of abounding grace. Their monuments are not of sinless living or pain-free lives. But they encourage us that this faith journey is one worth continuing.

Jesus, you have brought me out of darkness and into life. Thank you for your grace and mercy. Give me courage to share this truth with someone else today.

How can you share your brave faith story with someone else as a testimony to grace?

musical expression

Be filled with the Spirit, speaking to one another with psalms, hymns, and songs from the Spirit. Sing and make music from your heart to the Lord.
EPHESIANS 5:18-19 NIV

Memory is a fascinating part of our brains. We have memories triggered by specific smells, like freshly washed laundry, or tastes, like an ice cream cone. Many memories are activated by music. Songs can make or break a moment and stick in your head with relentless tenacity. As powerful as music is, we often shy away from using it as a tool. God wants us to participate in musical expression. Maybe he is nudging you to spend your commute time listening to worship instead of talk radio.

The beautiful thing is the song can hold the words of encouragement that you need. A worship song can also cause you to remember a friend in need and draw you into prayer for them. Don't shy away from expressing yourself in music from your heart. Fill your life with songs that point your eyes upward, and let music lead you to fight for others in prayer.

Every moment of my life is for you, God. Thank you for giving me the gift of song. Help me see how I can encourage others with it.

What songs have been on your heart and mind lately?

intertwined

Always be humble and gentle. Be patient with each other,
making allowance for each other's faults because of your love.
EPHESIANS 4:2 NLT

People travel from all around to see the mighty sequoia trees in California that sometimes reach heights of 300 feet. Surprisingly, these mighty beasts have shallow root systems that shoot out in all directions attempting to gain the surface moisture. Their roots intertwine with the trees around them. This interlocking of roots helps the trees stand in the face of storms despite their shallow roots. Sequoia trees grow best in clusters. High winds would quickly take out any tree that attempted to grow alone.

This is a picture of Christian unity. The recipe Paul gives us for walking with others is humility, gentleness, patience, and the ability to bear with people. Often our first reaction to hurt is to withdraw. If someone in church offends you, find another church. A friend misunderstands you, so you don't speak to her for a while. But we are called to help carry other people's loads. There will be stress and pressure, but because of love, we should continue. Relationships take courage. Don't be quick to walk away, leaving yourself open for storms. Intertwine yourself with other believers and shoulder the storms together.

Jesus, thank you for other believers around me who I can encourage and who do likewise for me. Bring unity to your body and to my circles of relationship.

What relationship have you given up on that just needs some courage and bearing with?

crown of creation

We are God's handiwork, created in Christ Jesus to do good works,
which God prepared in advance for us to do.
EPHESIANS 2:10 NIV

Do you ever think of God as an artist? If we do, we often ascribe him the beauty of creation around us. The towering, majestic mountains. Cool, crisp lakes. Vibrant sunrises and sunsets. There is a piece of creation, that Psalm 8:5 calls the crown—humanity! How quick we are to notice his hand in the world around us but not in ourselves and others; yet, we are his most prized creation.

God is an artist. He doesn't go around the earth with a rubber stamp, making everyone the same. In art, there are a myriad of expressions. God is working in you, fully aware of your personality, ethnicity, race, and talents. He is the potter, and he is molding and shaping you for his glory. Take heart that God is in control of your life. He is weaving together a tapestry more beautiful than your human hands could muster.

God, you are creative, and all you create is lovely and good. Help me to view myself the way you view me.

How do you feel about God being the artist and you being the canvas?

peaceful truth

The God of peace will soon crush Satan under your feet.
The grace of our Lord Jesus be with you.

ROMANS 16:20 NIV

Have you ever met someone who is afraid that God is out to crush them? Their view of God is that the almighty is waiting to destroy them. Maybe you struggle with this fear. In this verse, there are two interesting descriptive words. Peace and crush. Which is directed at whom? It says, "the God of peace." We are at peace with God by faith in Christ's work on the cross. Who is being crushed? Satan!

This is a fulfillment of the promise all the way back in Genesis 3:15. We are not to live in fear that God is out to get us. We can be confident of the peace we have found with God in Christ. With this in mind, we want to keep ourselves innocent of evil. We don't want to hang out with the one who is going to be crushed. Do not let the one who will be crushed accuse you any longer. You are at peace with God, and he desires to draw near to you.

Peace is what I long for, Lord. Thank you that I am at peace with you. I want to walk in peace. Help me avoid the path of evil and walk on in righteousness.

How can you apply this peaceful truth to your life to silence the accusations of the enemy?

endurance

When troubles of any kind come your way, consider it an opportunity for great joy. For you know that when your faith is tested, your endurance has a chance to grow.

JAMES 1:2-3 NLT

We have devised many ways to alleviate troubles. We have aisles of cards dedicated to get-well wishes, communicating a hope to escape trouble as fast as possible. We have flip-flopped James' advice, considering better to escape suffering and misery when we have to endure it. The struggle you are going through has not been sent to trip you up or have you laying in the mud. It has come to lift you on wings, so you soar above greater heights. It's not there to weaken your faith and leave you desolate, it should strengthen you while building your spiritual muscles.

Endurance is a quality in the kingdom of God that is prized. When we workout, we don't get stronger by lifting two-pound dumbbells forever. The weight must increase for the muscle to grow. Don't hide today from whatever trial you are facing. Use it as a springboard to spiritual growth.

God, you are the giver of joy! Fill me with your joy and peace, no matter what circumstances are around me. Help me to endure hardship with grace and to lean into you so I learn from it.

How can you change your perspective to see trouble as an opportunity for joy?

true hospitality

Don't be selfish; don't try to impress others.
Be humble, thinking of others as better than yourselves.
PHILIPPIANS 2:3 NLT

There is bravery in hospitality. Hospitality is a lost art that perhaps draws our minds to tablecloths and elaborate, five-course meals. But we've got the thinking all wrong. True hospitality is not a competition to see how we can out Martha Stewart each other. When our heart motivation behind cooking and cleaning into the wee hours of the morning is to impress our guests and find that Pinterest-worthy groove, we've missed the point. (And how unnecessary the burden we place on ourselves.) So, we camp out on that crazy side of hospitality, or we swing the pendulum all the way to the other extreme and never host people at all.

True hospitality is letting people in, paper plates and all—laundry on the couch and mud in the entryway. It's letting the dishes pile in the sink, so you can sit a little longer and hear the heart of the visitor. Hospitality takes courage. You let people peek into the intimacy of your home and your heart.

Lord, free me of the burden of pride in hospitality. Help me to see those around me that need welcoming, and to also receive hospitality from others with graciousness.

When was the last time you practiced hospitality or received it?

people of courage

The fruit of the Spirit is love, joy, peace, forbearance, kindness,
goodness, faithfulness, gentleness and self-control.
Against such things there is no law.
GALATIANS 5:22-23 NIV

These aren't just quaint words found on decorative plaques. They are the character traits of a courageous Christian. Courage loves with perseverance through the years. Courage is full of joy, smiling without fear because joy is set on eternal hope. Courage is at peace: the kind of peace that builds bridges for reconciliation. Courage is patient, waiting on the Lord and trusting in his timing. Courage shows kindness, acknowledging that God's kindness leads to repentance.

Courage is faithful, allowing bravery to shine through thousands of small moments. Courage is gentle, meeting slanderous, unjust words with the wisdom and grace of Christ. And courage practices self-control, implementing the discipline needed to glorify God. You have the courage you need to produce the fruit of the Spirit. All you have to do is ask for it.

Jesus, I want to be a woman of courage. I want to grow fruit that is lasting and good. Thank you for the work you have already started in me.

What fruit is God working on in your life right now? What fruit do you feel has grown the most? Thank him for it.

hypocrisy

Do everything without complaining and arguing, so that no one can criticize you. Live clean, innocent lives as children of God, shining like bright lights in a world full of crooked and perverse people.

PHILIPPIANS 2: 14-15 NLT

A common complaint against Christians is hypocrisy. People don't see a desired level of perfection in Christians and claim that they are hypocrites. This causes Christians to either stop trying or hide their faith. The world we are living in is a dark place, and it could use some bright light. A pitch-black room is illuminated when even the smallest match is lit. Don't be discouraged in your witness; let your light shine bright. If people claim hypocrisy over you, point them to the beauty of the cross.

When you sin, demonstrating repentance, forgiveness, and grace to a world that isn't fluent in that language speaks a powerful message of light. God is not calling you to live a perfect life. He is asking you to live boldly as a model of forgiveness in a world that is dark. At work, at school, with your family and your friends, let those whose eyes are so adjusted to the dark see the beauty of light.

Jesus, let me live a life of repentance and dependence on you. Help my witness to be one of grace and truth.

Do you tend to shy away from proclaiming Christ for fear of being labelled a hypocrite?

living in wisdom

Be very careful, then, how you live—not as unwise but as wise, making the most of every opportunity, because the days are evil.
EPHESIANS 5:15-16 NIV

The older we get, the quicker life seems to pass. Those who have lived into their nineties often comment on how short life has been. How do we spend our short time here living as people who are wise? One application would be to filter the world through the Word of God. God's Word becomes our caution for everything from moral issues to entertainment. To live wisely means everything is filtered through the perfect, holy lens of God's Word.

The current state of the world is just as the verse says, full of unwise people who do not realize the darkness they are living in. The more we read and acquaint ourselves with God's Word, the more bravery we will have to exercise as we implement the backwards kingdom principles of God.

God, thank you for giving me your Word. Help me use it as a measuring tool for everything I hear and see in the world. I want to be guided by your light.

God's Word is the best tool you have for becoming wise. How will you use it today?

audience of one

Work with enthusiasm, as though you were working for the Lord rather than for people.
EPHESIANS 6:7 NLT

Have you ever heard the phrase audience of one? Christ is the only one who needs to be in our audience while we work. What freedom! When your audience is just God, you are not bound by the criticism of co-workers, strangers, or even your children. You do not rise and fall on their opinion of you. With Christ, you have a perfect defender who will uphold you if injustice strikes. He sees every mundane task you accomplish and adds them up for reward. When you work for just Christ, small things done faithfully are seen by the Father.

Your identity doesn't rest in your title on your desk, your webpage, or whatever those you serve and work with may call you. Your identity is the child of the only one in the stands. And when your Dad is watching, don't you tend to do your best? His eyes full of love are focused on you. When you work, do it for him.

Help me today, Father, to work only for you.

How can you change your work attitude to perform for an audience of one?

provision promised

*"Give, and it will be given to you. A good measure, pressed down,
shaken together and running over, will be poured into your lap.
For with the measure you use, it will be measured to you."*
LUKE 6:38 NIV

In a world that firmly proclaims every self-centered pursuit is worthwhile, grasp on to this kingdom principle. Generosity is the way. A generous person is marked by bravery. Most of us rank in the top 10 percent of wealth in the world. We have been given much. To be marked up by the tattoos of brave generosity is life changing. We can hold our hands open, finding ways to give abundantly.

God has promised to provide for us. Perhaps he also wants to you use you and the resources he has blessed you with as a means of providing for someone else. Generosity isn't restricted to wealth. Can you generously forgive? Offer mercy? Encourage others? Find a way to breed generosity in your life, so you can be used to bless those around you.

God, your people are people of generosity. Help me to give freely of all you have blessed me with.

Generosity spreads through all aspects of life. What area do you need a boost of it in today?

seeking affirmation

"If anyone would be first, he must be last of all and servant of all."
MARK 9:35 ESV

You can't measure the success of your Christian experience by the results you see in this age. This includes results that are seemingly good or bad. God judges differently than the world. He rewards meekness and humility. He rewards servanthood and obedience. The world often rewards the antithesis of those.

It's important to simply commit your way to the Lord. Faithfully follow him in the path you sense him leading you. And then leave the results up to him. He will honor your obedience.

Father, help me look to you for affirmation and not to depend on the world for my results.

Do you gauge how well you are doing based on how the world praises and rewards you or based on how God does?

november

On the day I called to you,
you answered me.
You made me strong and brave.

PSALM 138:3 NCV

light

The LORD is my light and my salvation;
Whom shall I fear?
The LORD is the defense of my life;
Whom shall I dread?
PSALM 27:1 NASB

Darkness can intrude on our inner peace. If left unchecked, our healthy concern for safety may turn into fear. This fear can sift through the thoughts in our minds. Where we might begin a trek through the darkness feeling for the switch plate or dodging furniture, our minds can wander beyond the realistic. We consider the potential of open windows or unlocked doors. We try to remember if everything was picked up off the floor, and we revisit the pain of losing to the coffee table in our last midnight skirmish.

We can tie our minds in knots when we respond to fear in the guise of safety. Fear does not protect anyone. It does not have that ability. In the Scripture verse above, the Psalmist proclaims that the Lord is his light. Where there is light, doubt cannot creep in, and fear flees. Jesus is our eternal light, and he will protect us from danger.

God, thank you for being my light and salvation. I choose to fear no one and to trust you.

What dreadful fears can you lay at the cross? What action step cements that choice?

faulty thinking

"Be strong and courageous and do the work. Don't be afraid
or discouraged, for the Lord God, my God, is with you.
He will not fail you or forsake you."

1 CHRONICLES 28:20 NLT

When the work before us is daunting, we may rush through it or stall out in the process. Jesus has an answer for that. He says he will not fail you or forsake you. To fail you would be to give you an answer or technique that does not work for what you are supposed to be doing. To forsake you would be to walk away from you in your time of need.

If you truly believe God has done either of these to you, you really need to sit in the quiet with your Bible and an open heart toward God. He promises that if you seek him fully, you will find him. In doing this, you will eradicate faulty thinking and get back on your feet with the strength and courage to do what had once seemed daunting. Jesus is with you!

Heavenly Father, what fear has displaced the truth of who you are for me? What truth do you want me to carry in my heart, so I will strongly go forward into the work you have for me? Thank you for caring for me and for guiding me in your ways.

How can you apply today's principles in an area where you hesitate?

the point

If I had the gift of prophecy, and if I understood all of God's secret plans and possessed all knowledge, and if I had such faith that I could move mountains, but didn't love others, I would be nothing. If I gave everything I have to the poor and even sacrificed my body, I could boast about it; but if I didn't love others, I would have gained nothing.

1 CORINTHIANS 13:2-4 NLT

"Be a success," they said. So, she tried. She made a plan and worked at it, she jumped through the right hoops. She succeeded in work, she succeeded in finance, she considered her body her temple and she made the right social connections and personal choices. She ticked items off her bucket list. She filled herself emotionally, intellectually, and spiritually. Then she passed to the other realm.

"Love is success," the Bible said. So, she received Christ's love. She let Christ's love spill into her finances, her relationships, her work, her play, and her bucket list. Everything she did was motivated by his great love. And, when she passed, the fingerprints of God were all over her life and her legacy. Which "she" will you be?

Jesus, I want to be the grateful recipient of your love. Let this great, vast love of yours spill into every area of my life so I am a walking vessel of the truth of who you are. I love you very much.

If love motivated a new area of your life, what would it be, and how would it be expressed?

before a wreck

Yes, there are many parts, but only one body. The eye can never say to the hand, "I don't need you." The head can't say to the feet, "I don't need you." In fact, some parts of the body that seem weakest and least important are actually the most necessary. So, God has put the body together such that extra honor and care are given to those parts that have less dignity. This makes for harmony among the members, so that all the members care for each other.

1 CORINTHIANS 12:20-21, 24-25 NLT

No role is more important than another. It is hard to remember that sometimes, isn't it? This is especially true if you are excited about your own religious, social, or industrial role. It is easy to become puffed up. But we are all part of a whole, and each of us is uniquely and wonderfully constructed for God's glorious redemption of the earth.

If God recognizes each job as equally important, then they truly are; his mind will not change. It follows that you are to recognize every person's position as very important and to honor the less dignified positions beyond the dignified ones. This proves you honor God and love others, rather than strive to garner love and honor for yourself.

Lord, I see you love and revere each person, equally. Please help me to do so, and to encourage others, likewise. Thank you for the grace and clarity that I need to be mindful of this truth.

Where may you emphatically undergird, with honor, those in less dignified positions? Where might you give a break to someone who already bears up the ungodly expectations of others?

mature choices

When I was a child, I used to speak like a child,
think like a child, reason like a child;
when I became a man, I did away with childish things.
1 CORINTHIANS 13:11 NIV

Maturity is not a stodgy disposition or an inability to be flexible. Maturity is the fullness of God, rightly fitted in a person, and walked out over time to create patterns of habit that are helpful, wise, and loving. Markers of maturity are kindness, self-control, and goodness. Do these sound familiar to you?

It is hard to let go of childish behaviors because they are usually protective and self-centered. They seem, to the person exhibiting the behavior, to preserve and promote where other methods fail. But the truth is that preservation and promotion are not our main concerns. Jesus and his will are. Jesus has an easy yoke and a light burden for you. Preserving and promoting you are his job. Praise him, draw near, and accept what he has for you: fruit and comfort.

God, show me where my childish ways have clung to my personality and my actions. Help me shed them and restore maturity to my whole person.

How can you exercise maturity today?

lighted path

*If we claim to have fellowship with him
and yet walk in the darkness, we lie and do not live out the truth.*

1 JOHN 1:6 NIV

When you expect friends to visit your home at night, you probably turn on an outside light to guide them down your drive or to your front doorstep. What if you were to issue an invitation to a friend for a visit, but you did not bother taking that one step when the time came? At best, they might assume the oversight. At worst, they might miss a long driveway, assume they came over on the wrong night, or attempt to reach your door and be injured on the way.

Jesus is a good friend, and he never forgets to leave the light on for you. If you want to have fellowship with him, day or night, just go to his Word. It will bring you safely to his heart every time.

Lord, thank you for your Word that guides me to abide in you and to live in your truth. Please help me to read your Word often so I will be faithful in assuming your image and living a full and holy life.

How can you find time to read and study the Bible frequently?

anchor and sail

Stand firm. Let nothing move you. Always give yourselves fully to the work of the Lord, because you know that your labor in the Lord is not in vain.

1 CORINTHIANS 15:58 NIV

An anchor keeps a sailboat locked into position, regardless of the tide or any weather that beats against the vessel. A sail grabs the wind and pulls the boat in the direction it chooses. The sail determines how much the boat will interact with the wind.

Every sailboat needs both an anchor and a sail. You, too, need the anchor of conviction to ground you to the rock of faithful obedience to Christ. You need the sail of living, moving, and having your being in Christ. You follow the direction of the Holy Spirit, moving with him as he lives and moves in you. Stay grounded and fully given to the desires of God, just like Jesus did.

God, bless my life to be anchored to and grounded in you while following you, without reservation, wherever you may carry me.

In what truths do you ground yourself? Where do you see God leading you into further obedience?

love indeed

Whoever has the world's goods, and sees his brother in need and closes his heart against him, how does the love of God abide in him? Little children let us not love with word or with tongue, but indeed and truth.

1 John 3:17-18 NASB

Have you ever noticed what a delight it is to give gifts to a friend? You watch the loved face light up after peering into your wrapping with focus and expectation. What a nice thing it is to be the benefactor for a grateful recipient. The dearer the friend, the more the gift exchange means to you.

Whenever you give to the poor, you lend to the Lord. Is he your favorite friend? Of course. And the Lord returns the favor by gifting you with eternal rewards for your supernatural love expressed in earthly gifts for the poor and needy. He wants you to be willing to give to anyone—even those who have wronged you. God understands the needs of others. It is in putting them first that we become selfless like him.

God, show me where to send my goods. I know if I balk, I have found an opportunity to grow inside. I relish this opportunity to join you in giving.

Think of where you might best give. Let the thought take action.

otherworldly

*All that is in the world—the desires of the flesh and the desires
of the eyes and pride in possessions—is not from the Father
but is from the world.*
1 John 2:16 esv

Have you ever avoided a sale because you knew you would just come home with something you did not need? It is okay to turn off those impulses. Every one of us needs to decide where our time, money, and energies are best spent. This is a way we can focus our love and attention on Christ.

Two thousand years ago, Jesus made a sacrifice for us. It was not something that his flesh or his eyes or his pride desired. It was the joy of his heart—you and me—that brought him to the cross. Every day, we relish in and benefit from that joyful sacrifice. Never be fooled by what your flesh, eyes, or pride would have you do. Those things will rot, they will burn, and they will pass away. But the things of God are eternal and otherworldly. They should be treasured by you as you would treasure jewels in the very crown of Christ.

Heavenly Father, set in my heart the jewels you would have me place in the crown of Chris. Let it be in helping a neighbor, driving kids to a game, or helping people in need that I draw toward you in my affections.

How can you relinquish a worldly attitude to make way for a godly perspective on this very day?

never quelled

We have come to know and have believed the love which God has for us. God is love, and the one who abides in love abides in God, and God abides in him.

1 JOHN 4:16 NASB

God's love for you is never quelled. He has loved you before you were born, through your first steps, through your coming of age, and he will love you beyond your years here on earth. What if his eternal love is something you can share with others?

Just being loved changes the circumstances of a situation. Knowing that you are wholly loved and accepted by your Father in heaven gives you the latitude to make wise decisions and to love others as freely as you know yourself to be loved.

Holy Spirit, you abide in me. Fill me with your love so its overflow will permeate my world.

God abides in you. Take a moment, now, to renew your intimacy with him.

heart truth

"Do not look on his appearance or on the height of his stature, because I have rejected him. For the LORD sees not as man sees: man looks on the outward appearance, but the LORD looks on the heart."

1 SAMUEL 16:7 ESV

Every now and then, we are all surprised by the outcome of a situation. We think the dark horse will not win the race, or we underestimate the quiet contender vying for the workplace promotion. It is time to rest in the Lord and let him speak to us in his considerable wisdom.

God knows what he is doing. Perhaps your life has not turned out as you thought it should, and perhaps this has seemed for the better or for the worse. In either case, God sets in place those he wishes to use for his purposes. It is best to be a clean, yielded vessel and to chase after what drives you toward your best offering to Jesus. Let him look at your heart and judge you beyond what your peers may see. He is always pleased with the humble heart that is rendering the fruit he desires.

Lord, help me see who you have molded me to be in my heart. Help me make my outward actions reflect this honestly and unapologetically. I choose to be your obedient and brave vessel, and I turn from the ideas of the world, so I may freely serve you in my life.

Where have you followed earthly direction instead of acting upon the truth of your identity or calling?

fearless love

There is no fear in love; but perfect love casts out fear, because fear involves torment. But he who fears has not been made perfect in love.
1 JOHN 4:18 NKJV

Where are your fears, today? Take a moment to think about it. Probably, the first thing that popped into your mind is your biggest fear. We try to think that we are bigger than our fears. We try to sound strong and do the right thing by being fearless. The truth is, there are often things we fear right before us, and if we do not address our fears, our responses to them will color our worlds a very dingy shade of grey.

When Jesus walks into a situation, we trust him. We place our trust in Jesus instead of continuing to trust our fears. God is love, and perfect love casts out all fears. God with us is Emmanuel—Jesus. Jesus asks us to cast out our fears by placing our trust in him. It is an ongoing project to be sure we are trusting Jesus and not our fears, but it is well worth it.

Heavenly Father, please give me your perfect love. Abolish fear wherever it has hindered me by stepping into the situation. I step forward, too, in love, and reject the fear that has bound me.

Love is issued forth in the face of fear. Where can you use your love from God as an unstoppable weapon against fear?

living hope

Blessed be the God and Father of our Lord Jesus Christ! By his great mercy he has given us a new birth into a living hope through the resurrection of Jesus Christ from the dead.

1 PETER 1:3 NRSV

Think about gifts. The gifts of a living hope and the resurrection of our Lord, Jesus, through whom it is given are great and mighty in our lives. We have a reason to hope, to live. Our love for Jesus is a response to his goodness. We are very blessed and loved. Mercy flows to us, daily, and we rejoice in it.

Today is a new birth of hope and goodness from the Lord, just as the new life he has given us through his death and resurrection. For how much can we be thankful? Certainly, it is not enough. God is good. In all things, God has his eye on you, and his love is spilled out on you because of his great affection for you.

God, I bless you! This is a very special day for me, because I know you love me and care for my life.

Relish your living hope, today. Spend the day reveling in him and in his great goodness.

faith before sight

*Though you have not seen him, you love him. Though you do not now
see him, you believe in him and rejoice with joy that is inexpressible
and filled with glory, obtaining the outcome of your faith,
the salvation of your souls.*

1 PETER 1:8-9 ESV

The longer we walk with the Lord, the more we appreciate and enjoy his salvation and his unending companionship. Jesus' faithfulness is a cornerstone for our own faith in him. We know we can trust him because he has proven himself trustworthy.

One day, you will reach a point where you need to know God is real in your own situation. You won't be able to look at him physically. You won't be able to call and hear his audible voice, perhaps. But you will know, from past experience, that he knows you intimately and is there for you. There is not a thing you face, not a thought that crosses your mind, that God hasn't dealt with yet. He is there for you. You can trust him.

Lord, thank you for reminding me that you are always there for me. Your faith in me brings me salvation. What joy fills my soul when I ponder this!

The unseen is more tangible, eternally, than the visible. Can you place your faith in Jesus to become eternally tangible?

chosen ones

You are a chosen race, a royal priesthood, a holy nation, God's own people, in order that you may proclaim the mighty acts of him who called you out of darkness into his marvelous light.

1 PETER 2:9 NRSV

On occasion, we need a little nudge for all the pieces of our disposition to fall into alignment with God's. Today's nudge is a grand reminder of our identity as a Christian body. We are each holy priests serving the Living God! He is risen, and we are singly and corporately his. Because of this, we each walk in his light, and we shepherd others into the light as well.

Sometimes, it is difficult to get rid of the grumpy feelings of the day. It seems okay to have a lower opinion of ourselves and our circumstances (and maybe other people). But the truth is that God's opinion is our opinion, and we are to shout that in everything we do. Priests carry a message to the people. What message are you carrying today?

Lord, move me into your marvelous light. I need to see better, and the darkness of my understanding is halting me. Thank you for your love, your insight, and your great wisdom.

How will you share the good news of God's attitude toward others?

respect for all

Show respect for all people: Love the brothers and sisters
of God's family, respect God, honor the king.
1 PETER 2:17 NCV

Treat people the way you want to be treated. Give the fellow believer extra favor and love. Defer to God when you consider your actions. Respect your earthly ruler and esteem him or her highly. Sounds straightforward, doesn't it? Then, why did Peter bother to pen these instructions?

Sometimes, the correct choice is straightforward but seemingly impossible. "Fly to the moon," for example, is an instruction we might not execute. "Love one another," seems easier, but is it so? Sometimes, we need a simple reminder to tell us we are not exempt from the obvious wisdom of proper conduct, regardless of how we may be pushed or pulled. Godly respect is something we train and nurture within ourselves under the watchful care of our Creator and Redeemer.

God, thank you for creating me in a respectful and honoring society and recreating me in your Body. Help me to show others love and you and my earthly leadership suitable respect.

In what way are you interested in pursuing God in the context of greater respect?

joyful suffering

Rejoice inasmuch as you participate in the sufferings of Christ,
so that you may be overjoyed when his glory is revealed.
1 PETER 4:13 NIV

"Everyone who wants to live a godly life in Christ Jesus will be persecuted" (2 Timothy 3:12 NIV). This less than heartwarming message was written to Timothy by his mentor, Paul. It is true that we are ridiculed and demeaned at times, whether in media or in person. We are slighted because of our faith at work and in social circles. In certain places, Christians can be tortured, displaced, shunned, or even killed because they profess Jesus is Lord.

It would be easy to cower, to ignore, to place our faith under cover. But Jesus strongly admonishes us to not only let our light shine, but to expect rebuff and rejoice in the pain we will undoubtedly endure as his faithful followers. To shine is to share life. Would we cower in fear when perfect love casts out all fear? Of course not! Instead, we rejoice in Christ's glory revealed.

Lord, I receive your joy as my strength and your love in displacement of my fear. Thank you for being my constant companion and for joyfully suffering for me.

How might you encourage a person who is suffering for Christ today?

goal of likeness

This is how love is made complete among us so that we will have confidence on the day of judgment: In this world we are like Jesus.
1 JOHN 4:17 NIV

"Dad, why are you mad at me?"

"Well, I am not mad. I am disappointed, because you represent me, and you were not nice to the Seekers' boy."

"I don't understand."

"The Seekers are new, here. They don't know anybody. They need a helping hand and good friends. We Christianson's try to be friendly and love those around us."

"But he took my ball!"

"I understand, and we can work that out. But for now, I want you to make amends. Reach out for the sake of friendship. Treat him how you want to be treated. Then, the Seekers will know they can come to us when they need a friend or need some help."

"I can see it your way, Dad. Nobody is perfect. I just need to be a friend and have compassion."

"That's it, child. I love you."

"I love you too, Dad!"

This is how it is when we treat our neighbors with love instead of as the world does. Everyone needs Jesus, and we are his face to the world.

Jesus, make my love complete in you. I wish to be you to my neighbor, to my friend, and to those who oppose me.

How are we to be like Jesus in this world?

put it to bed

In your anger do not sin. Do not let the sun go down
while you are still angry, and do not give the devil a foothold.
EPHESIANS 4:26-27 ESV

Are you ever bumping heads with someone who just gets under your skin? Probably not. That is just a concern for the rest of the world! In case you fall into the realm of fallibility, sometimes, let this be your gentle grace to let go of a grudge before it harms you.

It is easy to be angry when we have been wronged. It is hard to hide in Christ when our eyes are on our problems and we are not sure the pain will let up anytime soon. We could hear it in Gideon's voice as he responded to the angel of the Lord: he was fed up with being oppressed. But Gideon, who got over his grudge and trusted Christ, found he was far more powerful going with God's wisdom than he was relying on outward appearances and his own strength. You are too.

Lord, help me sift through my feelings about people who hurt me. Help me to see your perspective and forgive them from the heart fully.

What goes to bed as anger may awaken a prideful grudge. Is there someone you are angry at right now? Can you let it go?

no island

Let the peace that Christ gives control your thinking,
because you were all called together in one body to have peace.
Always be thankful.
COLOSSIANS 3:15 NCV

It seems to be that just the right person may come along and alter our point of view to the better. The whispers of a friend to soothe our hearts, the inspiration of a message, the encouragement of a teammate: these all are building blocks of unity and opportunities to grow and share peace.

In Psalm 133, David rejoices in how good it is to experience unity within the church. The Israeli church is a family, so their unity was more pronounced. But make no mistake: we are both grafted into the eternal faith and enjoying the adoption of that family as believers. How great is our peace when we come forward, as called, into the unity of Christ with God?

Father let me be united with the Body. Let there be no faction. Let there be no strife. Let us live in gratitude and joyful peace.

Has someone helped you change your perspective recently? Can you open yourself up to receive that more often?

penetrating word

The word of God is alive and active. Sharper than any double-edged sword, it penetrates even to dividing soul and spirit, joints and marrow; it judges the thoughts and attitudes of the heart.

HEBREWS 4:12 NIV

If we were to look at our lives today, would we say we live up to the standard of what the Bible says believers possess and do? Chances are good that we fall short here and there. The phrase, "joints and marrow" refers to the difference between what we are doing and what gives us life.

Where do you go through the motions because society says you must do something different than your heart tells you? Your marrow gives your heart life-giving blood; your God-given desires feed God's will in your life, and he has gifted you toward this end. Move in that direction so your joints will not ache. It is better for man to be dissatisfied with you than for you to miss those good things God has. Get into the Bible and discover them.

God, you will cut asunder, with your Word, whatever does not give life. I am excited to pursue this journey with you.

Where can you submit to the Lord in choosing the actions that maximize your vitality and your dependence on him?

quiet and free

Let it be the hidden person of the heart, with the imperishable quality of a gentle and quiet spirit, which is precious in the sight of God.
1 PETER 3:4 NASB

No jewels shine brighter than your eyes as they light up in his presence. No song is as pretty as the waver in your voice when you share your testimony. Nothing about you is as beautiful as your holiness. God desires a quiet and gentle spirit because he is quiet and gentle within you. Only those who have quieted themselves enough to be stilled by his voice know the nuances of his whisper, his hidden treasures of wit, tenderness, and compassion that are abundant to those who seek.

If you can hear his whisper, and a little less, you will know him more and more. It is not that he is hiding himself from you; he hides himself for you. The Prince of Peace has the treasure of peace for you. As you wait upon him in his presence, you become peaceful and gentle, and your spirit becomes a quiet and free one.

Jesus, thank you that your beauty rests in your holiness. Help me to reflect your beauty as I walk more closely with you.

How do you see the beauty of the Lord reflected in your life?

humble people

Humble yourselves under the mighty power of God, and at the right time he will lift you up in honor. Give all your worries and cares to God, for he cares about you.

1 PETER 5:6-7 NLT

If you stay under the power of God, you walk in that power. If you humble yourself under God, you will not topple as he tries to lift you up in honor. Are you worried about anything? Give it to God. Nothing you do can change who you are, your status, or his love and care.

People who will trust in their own righteousness have no footing, or strength, or freedom from worry at all. When they are moved by circumstance, they will fall. When you are humble, you are abased. Your whole life becomes a foundation for God's glory. Nothing is wasted or left out. When God lifts you up, your foundation can be solid enough to handle it. People will see Jesus instead of a Christian trying to gain glory.

Lord, I humble myself before you. Remove from me anything that does not give you glory. I understand this invitation to change.

What response does this invitation to humility and full dependence upon God cause to rise up within you?

heaping

Because you have these blessings, do your best to add these things to your lives: to your faith, add goodness; and to your goodness, add knowledge.

2 PETER 1:5 NCV

The Word brings hearing, and hearing brings faith. Faith in motion is good works, or goodness. Goodness draws us in to God, to know him better. It all starts with God, but he heaps on the blessings when we join him in life and act out our roles as his beloved.

As Jesus completes his good work in us, time and time again, we come to know him better, and he promises us that one day we will know him as well as he has always known us. How good it is to be known by God!

God, I want this heaping. Please help me to act faithfully and create good in the world. As I do, I will identify with you and become your close, close friend.

What good works has God planned for you today?

content

There is great gain in godliness with contentment, for we brought nothing into the world, and we cannot take anything out of the world. But if we have food and clothing, with these we will be content.
1 TIMOTHY 6:6-8 ESV

We chase after so many things: the newest fashions, hip music, fun cars, and pretty dwellings. But when it all comes down to it, we do not take anything with us to heaven, and all that has consumed us has wasted our time for Christ.

Will we be happy with food and clothing? Paul's admonition to Timothy requires just that. Because it is in the Bible and is directed to a disciple of Paul's we know this is a general directive, good for all who read it. If God puts this before you, you can be sure he is going to walk you through it, and your journey will be joyful. Every good and perfect gift comes from him, and godliness with contentment is quite a gift!

God, I hand my desires over to you, so I will be weaned. I will walk with you in this joyfully.

What earthly possessions are getting in the way of your godliness with contentment?

obedient hearing

"What pleases the LORD more: burnt offerings and sacrifices or obedience to his voice? It is better to obey than to sacrifice. It is better to listen to God than to offer the fat of sheep."

1 SAMUEL 15:22 NCV

Have you ever tried to make up with someone by bringing him or her a gift with your apology? The gift goes a very long way, especially if it fixes whatever issue you have created. In most cases, though, a simple avoidance of the initial problem would have better served your relationship. Jesus is all in regarding his relationship with you. Although he has the right to do as he pleases, he puts you first, and he puts the good of all the family of God first. He does not trespass upon our needs, so he does not ever have to apologize or bring a gift to reconcile.

Jesus took his regard for our relationship one step further by becoming the gift of reconciliation between us and our Heavenly Father. To obey is better than sacrifice, but not a single one of us has successfully pulled that off. Jesus loves you and was crucified to fulfill that law, not to abolish it. He stepped in to become your sin, so you could become his righteousness. He wants you to experience the fullness of life you have never known.

Thank you, Father, for sending Jesus to die for me. This is the greatest gift for which I can show gratitude. I accept this gift and gladly exchange my sin for his righteousness.

If you have not made this your prayer, what are you waiting for? If you have, how can you now share with others your new life in Christ?

peaceful holiness

Strive for peace with all men, and for the holiness without which no one will see the Lord.

HEBREWS 12:14 ESV

Jesus is the Prince of Peace; peace abounds where he abides. In a world of strife where the majority of the population do not know Jesus, you are the key to redemption.

How do you say that Jesus is the Prince of Peace if you are trying to argue a person into the kingdom of God? It is not very likely that this person will accept Christianity from the heart. Yet, our holiness and our peaceful dispositions brew up a curiosity among non-Christians that render the questions, "What is so different about you," or "How do you stay so calm?" Live in peace with others and holiness before God who watches.

God, let me be the peace people see in the storm. When someone looks at me, let them see holy behavior, and reflect on you. Forgive me where I have failed, and give me wisdom and strength to start, again.

What does holiness look like to God?

pray with gratitude

Devote yourselves to prayer, keeping alert in it
with an attitude of thanksgiving.

COLOSSIANS 4:2 NASB

To enter God's presence we start praising him, worshiping him, and thanking him for who he is and what he has done. These offerings from our hearts show we understand who he is, and we honor him with all we know to give. Generally, in prayer, we continue to make our requests known to God. Then we end our praying with worship, adoration, and thanksgiving once more. Wait a minute: is this a constructive criticism sandwich?

All too often, what we are really doing is making a shopping list for holy people, and we are sandwiching our complaints in between the bookends of praise we were taught to use even as children. Jesus said we have perfected praise in children. When we complain, we are expressing faith that God did not follow through for us. This could not be further from the truth. We live in a fallen world marked with the effects of free will, poorly used. God is faithful. If your prayers are ebbing in the middle, consider God's solutions for the problems at hand, and pray those instead of the complaints you may have been tempted to express.

Lord, thank you for showing me your praise is crucial, and you are unfailing. I look forward to greater intimacy with you.

Make a list of prayer concerns and then write out the opposite crossing off every concern as you go. Pray with God about that prayer list.

made whole

The Lord is close to the brokenhearted
and saves those who are crushed in spirit.

PSALM 34:18 NIV

Two promises comprise this verse: your Master will be near when you are hopelessly discouraged, and he will rescue you when you are broken.

When have you experienced this? It is proof that Jesus truly will never leave you or forsake you, and that he is, indeed, a constant help in time of need.

Jesus, please help me overcome my discouragement. You do not just have the answer, you are the answer. Let me feel your support and see your salvation as I rest fully in you and give you the cares of the world. Thank you.

Who might be grateful for some godly encouragement? Can you find a way to bless someone else even when you feel discouraged?

training for steak

Solid food is for the mature, who by constant use have trained themselves to distinguish good from evil.
HEBREWS 5:14 NIV

Have you ever noticed that the more you read the Bible, the more you want to learn about it? The watering of the Word creates its own thirst, and when you are drinking regularly from the fountain of life, you begin to take on a healthy thirst for it. When you do this, the Word applies itself readily to your life, and you become sensitive to God and his tender heart.

A tender-hearted Christian does not want to hurt God in any way. We do the things we think will please him. Over time, we begin to understand what is truly good, and we are so trained in doing it that our obedience and aptitude for discernment becomes a necessary foundation for greater learning and discernment.

God, I want to eat solid food each day, and grow in that. I look forward to going further on this journey of discipleship with you as my guide.

How can you set a routine of deeper reflection on each verse you read in his Word?

december

Be strong in the Lord
and in his mighty power.

EPHESIANS 6:10 NLT

move forward

*Leaving the elementary teaching about the Christ, let us press
on to maturity, not laying again a foundation of repentance from dead
works and of faith toward God, of instruction about washings and
laying on of hands, and the resurrection of the dead and
eternal judgment.*

HEBREWS 6:1-2 NASB

Sometimes, we are so wrapped up in rehashing what we have already heard under the guise of "rightly dividing the truth" that we waylay ourselves out of our purpose and goals. We do not need another Bible study or support group to move forward in our walk. We need to get real with Jesus and let him get real with us.

What do you know you should be doing, instead of looking for an enlightened viewpoint on a well-covered topic? Where are you in need of growth for maturity? Where did you stop obeying a command of God in order to placate a person or take a detour? These are hard questions, but they are fruitful if we pursue them to gain maturity and responsibility in our walks. We are not held back by what is outside of us. We are released to progress by our convictions set in motion.

God, I want to become mature in the way you have intended. What would you like me to do?

What has freed up in your life as a result of renewing your focus on the Lord and your personal progress?

unswerving

*Let us hold unswervingly to the hope we profess,
for he who promised is faithful.*

HEBREWS 10:23 NIV

Jesus has placed an eternal hope in your heart. No discouragement changes the intentions of God in your life. No act of free will can erase it. Nobody and nothing can change his mind about you. In reminding you of his faithfulness, God extends you an invitation to respond by reflecting that faithfulness back to him.

Hope is a life-producing force. It sifts through the rumble of our discouragement, and it reconnects us to God's promises, our standards of belief, and our appropriate action choices. As a result, we do not bend in our ethics, our love, or our walk with Jesus. We remember he is faithful, so we remain in him and grow in faith.

Lord, please strengthen me in your faithfulness and remind me of your promises. Transform my wavering heart into a steadfast one that is a glory to you.

How might you recognize a situation that needs God's help, then introduce Jesus' eternal hope?

forgetful

> "Forget the former things;
> do not dwell on the past."
> ISAIAH 43:18 NIV

The reason we forget the past is so we can focus on the future. Each person has 24 hours in a day, seven days in a week, and 365 days in a year. If we spend each day looking back at what could have or should have been, we will never embrace the future and its opportunity. Instead, we wash our personal canvases blue with harbored pain and brokenness. Is that where we want to spend our precious time?

Ecclesiastes 7:10 says, "Do not say, 'Why were the old days better than these?' For it is not wise to ask such questions." Even in the case of good memories, the past steals our future when we dwell upon it too much. God expressly states that his own plans for each of us focus on hope and a good future. This is where we find our strength. Let us exchange our past for Christ's future which cost him much and is ours to pursue. There are better things to do than sit in your past. Look forward to Christ.

Father, I am sorry for holding on to the past. Show me where I have focused on what has been, and exchange within my heart a desire for what you want me to do now.

What do you need to do right now?

weightlifting

Carry each other's burdens,
and in this way you will fulfill the law of Christ.
GALATIANS 6:2 NIV

Americans enjoy freedom in a way that others do not. We celebrate it as we celebrate our independence itself. But independence and freedom are two completely different concepts. As Christians worldwide, we recognize that we are both very free and very interdependent upon one another. Although we have the freedom to do many things without guilt or moral repercussion, we rein in our freedom to fulfill the law of Christ by loving each other through various difficulties in life.

Are you in financial crisis? Ask for prayer and guidance. Are you feeling guilty for something? Contact a friend in Christ who will forgive you and help you be accountable. Do you have work that requires more skill or power than you possess? Look for resources within the body of Christ. When we work together, we strengthen ourselves in unity. When we are united in our holy lives, we become like Christ. A burden is an opportunity for Christian fellowship.

Show me where I can pursue unity in the Body by loving others through their burdens, Lord. Show me where you want me to get help for my own burdens, and I will gladly pursue it.

Where are you destined to make the biggest impact for the truths in Galatians 6:2? What will you do to pursue the law of Christ?

faith is proof

Faith shows the reality of what we hope for;
it is the evidence of things we cannot see.
HEBREWS 11:1 NLT

Faith is seeing. If you look at something by faith, you will see it clearly, and you will have a goal that you can reach through God. The dreams God has for you will line up with Scripture and God's personality. They will make sense to you in a supernatural way because you are made in God's supernatural image. They may not be accomplished in your lifetime, but that is not a litmus test for the truth of the vision or plan. If Abraham would have backed down when he saw he could not create children greater in multitude than the stars of the sky, he would have aborted the plan, and all the Christians in the world would not have become his children.

Abraham was faithful to see that faith is evidence and reality for what God has promised. He was faithful to pursue his leg of the journey in history, then to pass the baton to others for completion. God asks that you do the same with the gift and faith he has given you. Will you be brave and live out the proof of your hope?

Stir my heart to follow you in faith, God. Let my leg of the journey be completed according to the plans you have for me.

How will you fulfill the promises of hope in your walk with Jesus, today?

heavenly hiding place

Set your mind on the things above, not on the things that are on earth. For you have died and your life is hidden with Christ in God. When Christ, who is our life, is revealed, then you also will be revealed with Him in glory.

COLOSSIANS 3:2-4 NASB

Jesus told his disciples it was God's will for him to be treated poorly by the religious leaders and then go to his death. It was a hard thing for Peter to hear, and he protested. Jesus sharply rebuked him. A step in the wrong direction, even for the expression of fondness, is not godly.

Not everything we will ever do makes sense or feels good at the time. We trust in Christ. It takes bravery. We remain hidden in him and are not exposed to the spiritual devastation of the enemy. Do we need our own glory? Do we need thoughts and reasonings independent to the morals and will of Christ? Of course not. It takes bravery to not overthink things, but to instead trust Christ over earthly logic. It takes bravery to remain hidden in him instead of expressing what we assume is our own power, strength, or individuality. This greatly pleases our heavenly Father, who waits with anticipation to reward us for our godliness.

Lord, thank you for hiding me in Christ as I obediently await your reward.

How can you surrender an earthly thought for a heavenly one?

hold on

Stand firm and hold to the traditions that you were taught by us, either by our spoken word or by our letter.
2 THESSALONIANS 2:15 ESV

We are taught to remember grudges. Team loyalties inspire them. Political events, social faux pas, historic atrocities and more vie to fill our brains with reasons we should be cross or judgmental. It is as though we are preserving an element of who we are—of tradition and identity—by strong arming those who have blocked our joy.

Our truest identity, however, is hidden in Christ. Likewise, our crucial traditions are faith, hope, and love. Hold on to what matters. Let Christ sift through the rest.

Jesus, I have things to get rid of—baggage to unload. Will you please help me declutter my heart of earthly traditions and choose to reaffirm and live out your heavenly ones? I choose to hold on to these because your words are life.

Restore one of God's teachings, within you, that has been displaced or needs strengthening. Read the Bible to gain new insight on it.

every good thing

May our Lord Jesus Christ himself and God our Father, who loved us and by his grace gave us eternal comfort and a wonderful hope, comfort you and strengthen you in every good thing you do and say.

2 THESSALONIANS 2:16-17 NLT

It is comforting to know that anyone can do something for someone. You do not have to be especially strong or knowledgeable, or even have most of your life straight. It is much better to be available for God than it is to be ready and waiting for the right opportunity.

Everyone has something to give, and there is no better time than now to do it. Do not wait until tomorrow, because most opportunities do not come around twice. God promises to comfort, strengthen, and give you hope in every good thing you do. Go ahead and step forward, not waiting for an invitation or opportune moment. Jesus will meet you within your good actions because they are the vessel of his comfort, hope, and strength.

Lord, today is a good day for good words and good deeds. Help me to be present in my opportunities.

How does this perspective on stepping out change your mindset regarding God's will?

stimulating relationships

*Let us consider how to stimulate one another to love and good deeds,
not forsaking our own assembling together, as is the habit of some,
but encouraging one another; and all the more as you
see the day drawing near.*

HEBREWS 10:24-25 NASB

If we assemble ourselves together, it becomes much easier to network and find close companions who will help us do the right thing. We see things more clearly when we bounce ideas off one another, and we usually work harder when we work as a unit. It is beautiful to see people working together under the Lord's hand. Conversely, it is difficult to do any of these things when we remain in isolation.

Note that the concept of forsaking church is juxtaposed with encouraging one another more. When runners are about to cross the finish line, the cheering crowd swells to a deafening roar. So, should we raise a growing cheer for our brothers and sisters in Christ. The end of the race is looming near, and Jesus wills that we all keep running to the best of our abilities.

Lord, thank you for the Church. Please help me to encourage others and to accept their encouragement as well.

How have you been encouraged by others, and what was its effect?

joyful captain

Looking to Jesus the pioneer and perfecter of our faith, who for the sake of the joy that was set before him endured the cross, disregarding its shame, and has taken his seat at the right hand of the throne of God.

HEBREWS 12:2 NRSV

"Do the seas look choppy right now? That's about right." You might hear a sentiment such as this from an encouraging older relative or neighbor who wishes to reassure you while you tackle a transformation or a problem. It is because they are loving, and they have the understanding to witness your chaos, see hope, and poke a hole in the tension through humor. It is comforting to know others have sailed rough seas before you and have reached the other shore.

The writer of Hebrews offers comfort to Christians in reminding us that our big brother joyfully weathered our perfecting storm. Jesus is brave, and so are you. We can rejoice in this! So much was set aside on that trek toward our perfection. We must finish our races, but the victory is secure in all who believe. We place our trust in Jesus, and we cast out for shore with Jesus trimming our sails.

Jesus, you know my messy is "about right." Thank you for your presence as my joyful captain and for your grace to finish this race well.

What looks difficult or unglamorous in your life? Ask Jesus for his take on it, and to give you the wisdom for excellence.

brave trust

"God did not send the Son into the world to judge the world,
but that the world might be saved through Him."
JOHN 3:17 NASB

Do you ever feel like God is waiting for you to appease him because of things you have done in your past? He is not! The purpose of Jesus' advent on earth was not to punish you, but to offer you clarity and forgiveness.

Part of becoming brave in Christ lies in trusting God to be who he says he is. He is your Redeemer, and he loves you. Trade in your fear for love right now. Put your bravery into motion by trusting in him for mercy and grace, by seeking his face throughout each day, and by walking in freedom and wisdom that stands the test of time.

Father, I accept your forgiveness for hesitating to fully rest in your forgiveness. I will trust you to teach me how to live freely every day, and I accept your clarity for doing it. I choose bravery in you.

You have accepted Christ's freedom, reverence, and gratitude. How will these be exposed or developed as expressions of bravery?

good food

Everything God created is good, and nothing is to be rejected if it is received with thanksgiving.

1 Timothy 4:4 NIV

What God provides is good. 1 Timothy instructs us that everything God created is good, including types of food we can eat. We are to receive food with gratitude and to consecrate it by God's Word and prayer.

Sometimes eating food that others condemn takes bravery. They may ostracize you for the freedom that you enjoy in Christ. God does not want you to succumb to guilt or shaming. He wants you to enjoy the food he has made, to receive it in joy, to bless it, and to recognize what he says about it in his Word. Part of standing on the rock is enjoying his good food!

Heavenly Father, thank you for all the food you offer. Please show me where I have not exercised the liberty you have bought with Christ's blood, and help me to receive all that should feed me.

What will you newly accept as holy and from the Lord?

guarded heart

Look after each other so that none of you fails to receive the grace of God. Watch out that no poisonous root of bitterness grows up to trouble you, corrupting many.

HEBREWS 12:15 NLT

When something offensive floods one of your senses, you close your eyes, plug your nose, cover your ears, or eject awful food from your mouth. You don't put up with it! Sensory offenses violate the limits of our natural boundaries, and spiritual offenses work the same way. Just as we do not offer people burned cake or play our music loudly at 2:00 am, we can protect others from taking on relational and spiritual offenses we encounter by dealing with them before God.

Although it is easy and convenient to vent your troubles to friends, they may become angry about your situation while they listen and sympathize with you. This is how offense is created, and it is a stumbling block for believers in their quest to be close to Christ. Rather than letting you risk your friends' tenderness, the Bible gives you this valuable directive: "Give all your worries and cares to God, for he cares about you" (1 Peter 5:7 NLT). We defuse the spark of hostility within each of us not by sharing it, but by surrendering it to Jesus.

God, I see the need to give my troubles to you. Please forgive me for going to people instead of to you.

What offense do you need to bring to Jesus instead of to your friends?

trustworthy intentions

"For I know the plans that I have for you," declares the LORD, "plans for welfare and not for calamity to give you a future and a hope."
JEREMIAH 29:11 NASB

Don't be afraid to take a leap. When you are faced with a challenge or a daunting task, your first reaction may be to doubt that your efforts will work. The truth is bigger than your fears. They are exactly the size of God's expectations and his great plans for your future.

Trust God to never leave you stranded in a situation you cannot escape or handle. God knows his intentions for you, and they are not for failure. You are not alone. God will not ask you to do something and then turn his back on you. He will be with you every step of the way. You are in good hands with Jesus.

Lord, remind me that I do not walk alone, and please give me the strength to fulfill your calling.

What do you need the Lord to give you courage in?

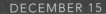

present

The Word became flesh, and dwelt among us, and we saw His glory, glory as of the only begotten from the Father, full of grace and truth.
JOHN 1:14 NASB

You can tell when people are present and engaged with you. They focus their attentions on you, ask questions, and respond with thoughtful answers. Relationships like that give life. When you read this passage, consider that God did not think it good enough to love you from heaven only. Jesus put on his best earthly robes and arrived as a baby. He fulfilled the whole earthly experience from birth to death. He was born without comforts, suffered indignation, and was treated cruelly by his family and strangers. Still, he loved everyone.

When we stay intimate with the Lord throughout the course of our day, we also become present with people. God intends this. We connect with others better, we love better. God's glory is present in our own lives, and this glory touches others. Then, these other people have a fresh understanding of God and an opportunity to meet him themselves.

Lord, help me to be present with you all day. Your presence creates my full, authentic joy.

Invite the Holy Spirit to share space with you, today. Foster deep intimacy with him all day and see how different your day becomes.

sowing and reaping

Sow righteousness for yourselves, reap the fruit of unfailing love, and break up your unplowed ground; for it is time to seek the Lord, until he comes and showers his righteousness on you.

HOSEA 10:12 NIV

Farmers know that much goes into readying ground for a fruitful harvest. Unfarmed soil is hard and lacks nutrients in almost every case. The farmer studies the land, tills it several times, removes rocks and weeds, and then amends the soil. When tilling and planting that seed, he must guard his investment by using proper seeding methods and by being diligent with any follow-up care that is required for optimal growth and production. He must think ahead to the harvest to plan and orchestrate labor teams, to move and store the grain, and to get a fair price at market or by other means.

When God tells you to break up the fallow ground of your heart, he is offering a promise of great returns. You must be diligent in reading his Word, obeying it, seeking his face and his wisdom. It is only God who can bring rain. He is asking you to be prepared and to seek him. Ask for wisdom and do what you have been told. Then you will reap the good seed that you have thoughtfully sown.

Heavenly Father, help me identify the fields and the seeds that you have set aside for my own harvest. Give me wisdom and help me walk in it. Let me be grounded in your Word. Let my heart become your very good soil.

To you, what does it look like to amend the soil of your heart?

examined

> "I the LORD search the heart and examine the mind, to reward each person according to their conduct, according to what their deeds deserve."
>
> JEREMIAH 17:10 NIV

It is easy to want to put our best foot forward at all times. We do it in public, in relationships, on social media, and in all areas of our lives where we have made a concerted effort to be our best. But it is true that there are moments we just plain fail. We would like to think that God is overlooking this foible-ridden area of our lives: our laughing at weaknesses, our indignation at scrutiny, our inability to take criticism from sources we do not respect. Even in our hearts, there are areas that do not respond to God very well. What will we do with ourselves? It seems utterly hopeless. Year after year we struggle, and it seems we are not yet those perfected Christians that we hoped we would be.

Jesus is the Lord, and he has come in the flesh. He has offered you salvation because he knows the weight of your immorality is too hard for you to bear. Instead of standing on your righteous behavior, stand on Christ. Let him transform your heart and mind and deeds to what he can reward. You cannot go it alone, and you were never supposed to try. Give up and let Jesus give you a reward. He knows what he is doing.

Jesus, remove from me the false basis upon which I believe you should reward me. Please deal with my heart, my mind, and my actions. I regret going it alone. Please make my life one that you can reward abundantly.

Where is God pointing for new, rewardable action?

hope sprung

To all who mourn in Israel,
he will give a crown of beauty for ashes,
a joyous blessing instead of mourning,
festive praise instead of despair.
In their righteousness, they will be like great oaks
that the LORD has planted for his own glory.

ISAIAH 61:3 NLT

This verse is commonly received to mean that when we are hurt, the Lord sees and will turn what has happened into a good thing. When our legacies are damaged, we will be restored. When we suffer personal loss, we will be rejuvenated in blessing and peace. Instead of losing hope, we will party in our hearts over the triumph of the Lord. Our good behaviors will ground us in Christ, and we will create solid foundations for others. This is true; everything that is promised by the Lord is sure. What if there is more, here, though? What if the promises are not just for the motivated believer?

It is not true in every case that harm befalls us because of our faults; that would be ridiculous. But let us not believe we have to be good enough for God's promises to come true in our lives. Let us take him at his Word, allow him to do his work in us, and retain the promise that we will, if we believe and follow him, become mighty oaks of righteousness.

Father, I come to you flawed and ask you to accept me and transform me so that I may receive your beauty.

Consider how this verse has implications in your past and how it can shape your future.

known before

"Before I formed you in the womb I knew you,
before you were born I set you apart."
JEREMIAH 1:4-5 NIV

His mother told him he was a mistake: a baby no one had intended, a gender discouraged, a timing unlikely. What was he to think? One day, he saw this verse. He knew God had planned him from the beginning of the ages. He was perfect in God's sight, respected and loved, and set apart for greatness. Had he not been—had he not become the exquisite person he is today—the world would be sadly different.

You are this man, in many, many ways. Upon your words, your actions, and your being, springs a world of possibilities only God is genius enough to imagine and ordain. You are very, very precious. Do not ever despise yourself in any way. You are good enough for God, and that is enough by far.

Thank you, Jesus, for making me. You say your children are not born of a person's desires but of your holy will. Thank you for accepting me for who I am. Please heal the breaches between my understanding of myself and your infallible truth about my identity, purpose, and worth.

How can you celebrate who you are today? Be brave if you must!

prayer starter

The end of all things is at hand; therefore, be self-controlled and sober-minded for the sake of your prayers.

1 PETER 4:7 ESV

When something big needs to happen, people take notice. They come together and pray. They lend a hand and do whatever it takes to produce a good result. If a person talks a big show but then does not pull through, it frustrates everyone, and the suffering of failure is more intensely felt. Your actions speak the weight of your words, so your actions must give you a platform to be heard.

This is not an earthly concept. As wrapped up as we are in God's grace and mercy, we must soberly remember that God speaks of right conduct constantly in the Bible. Your actions are important. Your life is a testament to who God is. Let your words to him be significant to that fact. Let your actions spring forth a well of life within you. Jesus created the world and then gave himself to save it. All his followers are imprinted with his love. Let our actions prove our words in salvation for the world.

Jesus, this life is yours. Direct my actions and tailor my obedience toward you. Make my words weighty and acceptable to you.

Where can you grow in self-control and sober-mindedness? How will this affect the way you pray?

an angle

The wisdom from above is first of all pure. It is also peace loving, gentle at all times, and willing to yield to others. It is full of mercy and the fruit of good deeds. It shows no favoritism and is always sincere. And those who are peacemakers will plant seeds of peace and reap a harvest of righteousness.

JAMES 3:17-18 NLT

Even the people we trust the most can sometimes have an angle. When we look at the reasons for a person's choices, we see motives of gain.

Wouldn't it be nice to live in a world where people did the right thing simply because it was right? Jesus is asking us to hold out hope and dismiss the temptation to do for ourselves. We are God's people. This means we are of a world where righteousness is love, and so God asks us to bring heaven to earth in the way we think and act. We are playing by a different rulebook, and we will gain the reward of heaven when we bring heaven to earth.

God, let your will be done on earth as it is in heaven.

God gives us wisdom whenever we ask. Can you expect him to be gentle and kind with you?

it will happen

"From the beginning I told you what would happen in the end. A long time ago I told you things that have not yet happened. When I plan something, it happens. What I want to do, I will do."

ISAIAH 46:10 NCV

God does not back down from what he says will happen. He does not exaggerate, he does not keep the secret from those he ordains to know. We know he is all-powerful, and we know he is just to declare his will and fulfill it. It is our duty and response to worship him and do his will.

The words of God are gracious to embolden us to response. We know Jesus loves us, and we know he is firm in his resolve to be Lord. It is not that we get a vote; he is Lord, and he will always remain in charge. We do have free will, though. It is our joy and privilege to offer and maintain that he is Lord of what we choose in our hearts to do. Let our responses be in line with what God chooses, says, and does. Jesus is our example in this.

Lord, what you say always happens. Help me gain boldness from that fact so I will fulfill your will.

What do you need to do to understand or fulfill God's will for you? What is your action step right now?

good intentions

*"If people want to brag, let them brag
that they understand and know me.
Let them brag that I am the Lord,
and that I am kind and fair,
and that I do things that are right on earth.
This kind of bragging pleases me," says the Lord.*
JEREMIAH 9:24 NCV

Jesus is the Lord. He came to take our infirmities. He knows what we need, and he knows what we want to do with our lives even better than we know ourselves. Why? Because he has planted wholesome desires in our hearts.

Jesus is also kind. He wants us to know that. He wants us to come to him. We should not hesitate to learn of him, to dwell in him and become one with his intentions. His intentions are always good. He is a kind, fair, and just master. Nobody has room to brag except to know that they should draw near to him and learn of him. That is a good thing to know and talk about to others. When you do, other people will come to know him as well.

Lord, please help me bring people to you. Let me change lives through your love.

What are you waiting for? Your invitation to serve God is as open as your invitations to receive him and rejoice in him.

with me

*"Do not fear, for I am with you; do not be dismayed, for I am your God.
I will strengthen you and help you; I will uphold you with my
righteous right hand."*

ISAIAH 41:10 NIV

It is comforting to know that an advisor you trust is helping you make decisions and walking you through an important process. God promises to do this with you in all your dealings and throughout all your days, even into eternity.

When was the last time you spent special time with the Lord, reveled in his attention, and exchanged your own issues for his resolutions? For your fears, Jesus has love. For your disappointments, he has hope. For your weakness, he has strength. For your labor, a helping hand. You are the righteousness of Christ, and by that truth you have been taken into his right-hand grasp. You are firmly planted in his nail-scarred palm. He will never relinquish you, and he will never regret pouring his love onto you. Make every exchange he offers.

Jesus, I am so grateful to have you with me. Help me to feel myself in the grasp of your nail-scarred hand. I love you.

How can you spend time with Jesus and revel in him?

great joy

The angel said to them, "Do not be afraid. I bring you good news that will cause great joy for all the people. To in the town of David a Savior has been born to you; he is the Messiah, the Lord."

LUKE 2:10 NIV

When heaven touches earth, something is going to change. Shepherds in the field witnessed angels descending, and they fell into great fear. Why? Because we are not holy and worthy, by our own accord, to witness or stand in the presence of the Holy One. We are not sinless, and something within us knows we have no right to stand before the perfectly holy.

The angels adjured the shepherds to be fearless. They had great news that would give joy to the whole world. Jesus, God and man, the only sinless one, would make us holy so we could stand before God and feel the utter joy of his presence. What a relief! We no longer have to stand in fear because Jesus has eradicated the need for shame.

Thank you, Jesus, for the great joy you brought to the earth. You make me brave, so I can live fully, not fearing my frailties or troubles. I choose to live in the strength of your joy!

How can you reach out to others with the favor, love, and grace that Jesus has given you?

enduring friendship

"Do you not know? Have you not heard? The LORD is the everlasting God, the Creator of the ends of the earth. He will not grow tired or weary, and his understanding no one can fathom."

ISAIAH 40:28 NIV

Christ is the Ancient of Days. He does not grow tired of helping us. Nothing escapes him: no detail of your life. He does not want to walk away from you or wait for you to have your act together. He is not embarrassed by you or repelled by your lack of understanding. He is waiting patiently for you, right now, to spend time with him. Even one minute is better than none, and each minute is life.

Perhaps you had a quiet Christmas. Jesus was in the room. He was there whether you had a noisy or quiet day. Jesus was with you wherever you were, however you celebrated. Jesus is kind. His day is made when you let him in. Let him into your heart today. Let him into your day, your thoughts, your compassions. Today is a good day for Jesus. He really does understand. Jesus is your everlasting companion, your friend for all times and seasons.

God, thank you for yesterday and for today. Today, I will celebrate you, with you, my everlasting friend.

How may I be more present with Jesus?

true judgments

Render true judgments, show kindness and mercy to one another, do not oppress the widow, the fatherless, the sojourner, or the poor, and let none of you devise evil against another in your heart.

ZECHARIAH 7:8-10 ESV

Do you see this verse? It says to be honest, kind, and merciful, to be careful about those who are marginalized, and to not even let our minds consider doing ill to another. Yet we do wonder, if we will be honest, why God lets people become orphans, widows, or otherwise marginalized group members. We wonder if God is really involved in our lives, and we wonder why God's mercy and kindness allow atrocities on the earth. Why are we experiencing evil when God is good?

Part of rendering true judgments is to spend time with God and let him help you rethink the world. Life is not perfect, and Jesus told us there will be many troubles. He told us the poor will always be with us. He told us a lot of things that would indicate that we will never be in a perfect world until this old one passes away and the new one is brought forth. Do good and love people. Be kind because God is kind. In all things, remember God is sovereign. This is enough.

God, I don't understand why bad things happen, but I hope, rest, and trust in you. Help me to reflect your kindness, mercy, and justice in truth and spirit.

How can you rise above your circumstances by drawing from Christ and his message?

a new future

"I will bring the blind by a way they did not know;
I will lead them in paths they have not known.
I will make darkness light before them,
And crooked places straight.
These things I will do for them,
And not forsake them."

ISAIAH 42:16 NKJV

God is capable of making your way straight. He can give you insights you never knew, restore health and relationships, and give you wisdom and understanding to manage all his blessings. He is capable of making this gift accessible to you and a way to draw you further into your relationship with him. How does this look?

When you give someone a gift, you make sure it is appropriate and will be something they will find useful and enjoyable. God is the one who came up with that idea. He does not say he will point the blind down a new path, but rather that he is going bring them along personally. Let us take one part of this verse for ourselves right now. Consider the question: what is a new path to the blind? Sight, of course. Take a bold leap and ask Jesus to give you new insight.

Lord, thank you for new insight. Please help me to apply it and make it a forever principle.

How can you apply the insights God gives you to create permanent change?

relent

"Even from eternity I am He,
and there is none who can deliver out of My hand;
I act and who can reverse it?"
ISAIAH 43:13 NASB

In this passage, God explains that he alone is God, and there is not going to be any other Savior except the Lord. That means Jesus, alone, is the way to God. God declares that we know him to be the Ancient of Days. It is established, it follows, that nothing supersedes him or displaces him or his Word.

When we try to be good for the sake of getting into heaven, we balk at the promise of Christ and his resurrection. We are trying to make a better way, one more suitable for us to enter eternity with God. But the fact is this: we want to be good because, deep down, we know this is the very reason we cannot stand before God. Do not let your attempts at good works be the reason you don't accept the fullness of Christ's grace through his blood and forgiveness. There is no other way, and the Ancient of Days has said it.

God, I relent. I will no longer plead with my good intentions and attempts to act well. I know good behavior is a product of forgiveness, and it is not a substitute for Jesus being my Lord. I accept him, now, and forego trying to prove to you my worthiness.

Can you see that the debt of perfection is not payable?

a reason

In your hearts revere Christ as Lord. Always be prepared to give an answer to everyone who asks you to give the reason for the hope that you have. But do this with gentleness and respect.

1 PETER 3:15 NIV

Eventually, each of us is asked why we are so different, or someone comments that they were changed because we said something that altered their perspective. Isn't it good to know you make change? But it is important that everything we do points to Christ, because he is our habitation and the hope of the world.

You are not made different because of a program or process. You are different because Jesus' Holy Spirit lit upon what you were doing and birthed new life in you when you asked. Now, others around you look at you because they recognize the touch of Jesus on your life. They need an explanation, so they too can receive the change God has for them. Have your testimony ready and be prepared to be used.

God, thank you for the change in my life. The world is hungry, and the fields are white. Send me into the fields.

How can you share Jesus with others?

unleash your love

*All of you, have unity of mind, sympathy, brotherly love,
a tender heart, and a humble mind.*

1 PETER 3:8 ESV

Unite with the rest of the body, and actively seek to harmonize within it. Walk in compassion for each other. Love in ways that affirms you recognize we are God's children and proves your loyalty regardless of differences. Be humble in the way you think about yourself. This is quite a list of directives! Here, Peter boiled down a whole lot of Old Testament rules into a simple five-point bullet list. This list guides us in how we treat our brothers and sisters regarding the second great commandment: love your neighbor as yourself.

Anyone who has ever been hurt by being kind to someone—and that probably includes everyone—knows that it takes bravery to get back in the arena and give fully with the sake of love in mind. Love protects. It is the best armor your heart can have. Why? Because when you love, the response will never dictate its value. A response can only reveal the heart of the recipient. When you love, victory takes place. That will always be a celebrated fact in heaven and at the very throne of God. Christ in you is the promise of a very strong love on the earth. Unleash it.

God, thank you for love. Show me where I need to love my brothers and sisters in you more fully. I humbly unleash my love for you.

Where can you soften your heart toward someone else?